Kat T. Masen

Chasing Him

A Forbidden Second Chance Romance
The Dark Love Series Book 4

Copyright 2020 Kat T. Masen
All Rights Reserved

This book is a work of fiction. Any references to real events, real people, and real places are used fictitiously. Other names, characters, places, and incidents are products of the author's imagination and any resemblance to persons, living or dead, actual events, organizations or places is entirely coincidental.

All rights are reserved. This book is intended for the purchaser of this book ONLY. No part of this book may be reproduced or transmitted in any form or by any means, graphic, electronic, or mechanical, including photocopying, recording, taping, or by any information storage retrieval system, without the express written permission of the author. All songs, song titles, and lyrics contained in this book are the property of the respective songwriters and copyright holders.

Disclaimer: The material in this book contains graphic language and sexual content and is intended for mature audiences, ages 18 and older.

ISBN: 979-8691794650
ISBN: 979-8782866440

Editing by Nicki at Swish Design & Editing
Proofing by Kay at Swish Design & Editing
Cover Image Copyright 2020
First Edition 2020
All Rights Reserved

PROLOGUE

There is a faint sound.
    A warning sound, it sends chills throughout me—I know it's all about to end.

Any ounce of hope, a miracle, is fading like the light in his eyes.

His eyes, they reflect death.

It's only a matter of hours, minutes, even seconds, and he'll be gone. Unable to be seen, touched, or heard, and being six feet under the ground, are his only destiny.

The man in the stark white coat gently places his hand on my arm. With a sympathetic glance, his calm voice speaks the inevitable. "Mrs. Evans, I think it's time you said goodbye to your husband."

My face is expressionless unlike everyone else in the corridor. My dad and brother have bloodshot eyes, their tears barely contained in a state of anguish. My mom is inconsolable, rocking our son back and forth in an attempt to shield him from the grief surrounding us.

If only someone could do that for me.

Soon, he will be only *my* son.

My brother is by my side, urging me forward, trying to encourage me to enter the room, pay my final respects to my husband. Following his lead, I enter the room, and immediately my eyes watch him for what could be the very last time. He is pale, gaunt, and sick. The remaining strands of his once-luscious locks are barely visible. Vibrant blue eyes have morphed into dull gray orbs shadowed by deep circles. His lips are a light shade of blue... *blue...*

I'm standing at his bedside.

With no strength to lift his hand, his ailing attempt to touch me one last time becomes too hard, and he gives up, defeated.

His own fault.

He should've fought. *For us, for life.*

Elijah chose this path. He refused any treatment which could've saved him. Instead, our love, our son, wasn't worth the fight.

With a strained voice, he mutters his final words, "I did this for us. You deserve a life with someone who will see it through with you till the very end. Don't hate me, Adriana... please..."

I want to scream, punch him in the face, but my emotions are brutally interrupted, the beep flat-lines followed by panic in the room. The voices echo as the scene before me becomes a blur—a frantic scramble to save him one last time.

Three... two... one... Clear!

His body jerks. Nothing.

Repeat... repeat... repeat.

Time is lost on me.

The doctor looks at the nurse, shaking his head slowly. At this moment, actions speak louder than words. The pity in their eyes, the removal of their masks, the impending glance at the clock.

"Time of death... 11:53 p.m."

The sobs are achingly loud, piercing the drum of my ear.

They don't belong to me.

I feel his arms wrap around me. My brother is trying to protect me. He pulls me in, smothering my face into his suit jacket. His warm tears fall freely onto my cold cheeks, blurring the vision of my husband being covered by a blanket.

Lost in his embrace, it starts to sinks in.

The reality has hit like a looming storm.

And just like a crack of thunder, I let out a startling scream which rushes straight to my heart, forcing my brother to embrace me tighter and shield me from the pain.

My husband is gone.

My son's father is dead.

I am alone.

ONE

There is chaos in the room, a madness which can only be tolerated for a few minutes before you're forced to sneak away and seek solace behind the glass doors.

It's called—daycare.

Today is no ordinary day. I've been dreading this event since a yellow note came home in Andy's backpack three weeks ago. A tiny piece of paper announcing 'Bring Daddy to Daycare Day.'

I mean, really, what the fuck? Who the hell thought this would be beneficial to young children?

It's bad enough Hallmark has staked their claim in the world, forcing consumers to celebrate an array of occasions, and if you didn't tick the box of being in a relationship or are short a parent, you're left to feel like the worst person in the world.

This is who I've become.

Not only that, preschool-age children have short attention spans. Asking them to sit on a rug while some lucky kid explains how awesome their dad is because he's a police officer who fights baddies, is asking a lot of the twenty-odd children inside the room.

The second I read the note, my cell goes into overdrive. My overprotective brother wants to make sure I'm okay, and he has to open his big fat mouth causing my parents to worry. You would think I'd be used to it by now, the constant fretting over my well-being.

I'm fucking fine.

Just like the song says, *Always look on the bright side of life.*

Well, the bright side is this ugly orange wall I stand against as I watch the room quickly fill up with parents. Dads every which way you turn. Several are happily playing with their children, some are dressed in suits like my brother, and others are dressed more casually—those are the stay-at-home daddies. You can spot them a mile away. They carry around a backpack like it's loaded with explosives only to know it's full of diapers, wipes, and other emergency items to keep the boo-boos away.

At least they aren't wearing overalls. Ugh.

It's no surprise police-officer dad is getting the most attention. When it comes to men in uniforms, the single mothers inside the room hover around them like leeches. Are we at daycare or a Tinder meet-up? It's amusing to watch, especially when you see them strategically try to adjust their blouse to show more cleavage.

I start to lose circulation in my leg as Andy clings to me for dear life, hiding his face in fear, aware of the unusual activity around him.

"Why isn't my grandbaby runnin' round like the other kids?"

Taking a deep breath to calm my annoyance, I turn to face Mary Jean, Andy's grandmother. She's borderline getting on my nerves. As far as mothers-in-law go, I guess I should count myself lucky, although she hovers over Andy like he's an abandoned baby bird. He has a mother, *me*.

"He's a little shy now, Mary Jean. Give him a moment."

"Don't know why ya put him in here. Told ya to move close to home, and I can take good care of him," she rattles on.

She waits for an answer, but I don't give one.

Geographically, the distance is welcoming. We mainly see her on holidays when she flies to LA or the one time we flew down south. Though, the death of her son impacted her so greatly, her knock on my door happens more often than I'd have liked.

And I mean way too often.

Mr. Lugo, a young male teacher, enters the room. Mary Jean adjusts her blouse, yanking it down to reveal her very full bust. Quickly pulling out her compact, she checks her face and teeth. For a fifty-something-year-old woman, she definitely doesn't show her age. Her bleach-blonde hair and bright blue eyes give her a youthful elegance. She is a firm believer in homeopathic remedies and weird-ass creams which take years off your life if you apply them every night.

Aging isn't in her vocabulary, and neither is the word 'privacy.' Every time she stays with us, I find her rummaging in my closet. At first, I was polite and gave her some items, even though she is slightly bigger than me, but that isn't an obstacle—it only means she flashed more skin than necessary. Then, she got on my nerves. My closet is my haven—nobody touches it. Charlie and Eric are the only exceptions.

"How do I look, darl?" She flattens her skirt waiting for my opinion.

"Like you're twenty-one, Mary Jean."

With a wide smile, she squeezes my arm and tails Mr. Lugo. God help me.

"Thank God, your mom is awesome. I really got lucky in the mother-in-law department." Charlie is standing on my right, carrying baby Ava who has vomited all over Charlie's chest.

I scrunch up my nose as the smell lingers my way. "Gross, cleavage puke?"

"Yep, the worse kind," Charlie complains.

"Oh, well, that's what you get for having knockout tatas," I point out.

She holds Ava out to Lex, then discretely tries to shove tissues down her blouse in an attempt to clean herself up. Lex, who's sulking as Amelia ran off, beams as Ava is resting in his arms. He rocks her gently as she stirs, and I smile watching my brother so at ease with his baby girl. Sometimes, I can't believe how much life has changed for him, for them.

This day is just as important to my brother. You see, Lex is such an important part of Andy's life. Aside from my dad, he is the only male figure in my son's life, and I know, at times, it confuses Andy. From an early age, I'd talk about Elijah and show pictures to Andy. It's important he knows who his father was, even if he never got the chance to know him.

Andy has several of Elijah's features, and many comment on how much he reminds them of him. It's the dirty-blond hair, the bright blue eyes, and the way his dimples set when he smiles. To add to that, Andy is smart. The daycare workers have mentioned to me his IQ surpasses the other children of the same age. They suggest some external programs to help further his knowledge and build on his strengths. It's a lot for me to take in considering he is just shy of three, and my understanding of being three is hanging out in the sandbox and stomping in mud puddles when it rains.

I want Andy to have a normal life as much as possible, not missing out on the important things just because Elijah isn't here. Quite often, he'll proudly tell everyone Daddy is working in heaven, though the reality of his words is too enormous for him to understand.

Today, he senses it's different. The toys and noise don't entice him. His lips tremble as the chaos overwhelms him, just about on the verge of tears. I'm trying to be strong, but that strength is turning into anger. I want to yell at the management for creating such a stupid event. I want to gouge the eyes out of everyone looking at Andy and me like we're circus freaks, and most of all, I want to scream at Elijah for leaving us in this mess.

Yet, I stand perfectly still, a fake smile plastered on my face.

"You okay?" Lex is annoying me again with his overbearing worry.

I nod, then smile. He doesn't buy it. After all, he's known me my entire life.

Lex leans down to talk to Andy, raising his voice above all the noise. "Switch. You take Ava, and I'll take Andy," he offers.

He hands me Ava, who has fallen asleep again. I lean down to smell her face. It smells like baby. I don't remember Andy smelling the same, but then again, I was suffering post-partum depression. I couldn't even get out of bed, let alone take care of my son.

Andy senses movement on my behalf and clings on tighter. Lex kneels to his level. I don't hear the words he is saying, I only see Andy wrap his little hands around Lex, burying his head into his neck to hide his face again. They walk outside to the sandbox to be with Amelia. I watch as Amelia tries to steal a shovel from a little boy, pulling it directly from his hands and causing the little boy to break out in tears.

"I swear that little shit is doing my head in," Charlie says, frustrated.

Lex leans down to Amelia's level, and from what we can see, he's trying to discipline her. It's laughable. Lex is the biggest softy, and Amelia has him wrapped around her little finger.

"Charlie! Don't call your angel a little shit." I laugh softly.

"Do you know what she did this morning? She took all of Lex's hair gel and smothered it on Ava's head. When I found her, I asked her why she did that. Do you know what she said? 'Eric says that you can never be too young to have fabulous hair, so work it, baby.'"

I place my arm around her shoulders in an attempt to comfort her. Struggling to hold in the laughter, I let out an involuntary snort. Charlie shakes her head in amusement. Amelia is like a sponge around Eric, and anyone who has met Eric knows he has no filter.

Apparently, we have that in common.

The head teacher announces it's time for the special presentation. The children assemble at the front, Amelia positioning herself right in the center, placing her hands on her hips as she waits impatiently for everyone to get their shit together. Andy reluctantly stands by the side. It's very out of character for him to be so withdrawn, and even though he's young, he knows well enough what everyone has in this room that he doesn't.

It doesn't last long, though. Amelia shoves other kids out of the way to pull Andy to the front with her.

One by one, the teacher calls the children to the front to present their dad with a handmade macaroni picture covered in paint and to say a few words. Amelia is called and no surprises, the mini diva walks to the front as Lex makes his way through the crowd and finally accepts his gift.

"This is my daddy. He is pretty and works in a big building with lots of people. When I grow up, I want to yell at people on the phone and be just like him." Her face smiles proudly at everyone in the crowd.

I let out a loose laugh. The hilarity is too much. Amelia is very in-your-face.

Charlie ignores her daughter's inappropriate speech, busily snapping away picture after picture.

Amelia poses perfectly, hand on hip, hair positioned behind her shoulder exactly like Eric taught her to pose.

"I'm gonna wring Eric's neck," Charlie mumbles under her breath.

"Oh, he tried to teach Andy the same pose, but it lasted two seconds. Attention spans of a toddler, you gotta love it."

Lex proudly shows off Amelia's artwork before moving to the side. We wait patiently until Andy's name is called, and thankfully, he has a wonderful teacher who's compassionate to his circumstances.

"Andy Evans," he calls gently.

I watch Andy as he stares at the crowd, his eyes wide with fear. Amelia makes her way back through the crowd to stand by Andy's side and hold his hand. Despite her overdramatic personality, she and Andy have a close bond. Amelia always has his back, and although they are cousins, their bond is tight like siblings.

I see Lex make his way through the crowd as well and watch as Amelia whispers something into Andy's ear. His eyes beam as Lex kneels and says something to Andy.

Proudly, he hands Lex his artwork and hugs him tight.

Andy doesn't say anything. His smile is worth a thousand words.

Charlie is trying her best not to cry, but her mascara is a hot mess.

Mary Jean's blue mascara looks like the artwork Andy brings home—a colorful display giving her terrible panda eyes.

Me, well, I'm all cried out.

Barely any fight left in me.

This is my life.

As the festivities wind down, Amelia and Andy busy themselves with some building blocks.

"Thank you, big brother." I bump his shoulder with mine.

He puts his arm around my shoulder and pulls me in, kissing the top of my hair. "Any time, short stuff."

I narrow my eyes at him. Sure, I'm short, but he is a man-giant.

"What are you up to today?" he asks.

"I have a meeting this afternoon with a buyer. Aside from that, not much."

It's a lie. I have plenty of things on my plate. Things Lex doesn't need to know.

"So, who's babysitting, Mama Evans?" Lex chuckles.

The three of us turn to look at Mary Jean. She's forgotten all about Mr. Lugo and is standing alongside another man much younger than her. He appears to enjoy the attention, her flirtatious smile and flicker of the hair more than a little cringe-worthy. It's like a car crash—you should turn away, but you want to see how it pans out.

"Definitely not you. I don't want a repeat of the ass-grabbing that went on at Andy's second birthday." Charlie is quick to remind Lex. "You free for lunch, Adriana?"

Charlie is distracted by Lex wrapping his arms around her waist.

"Get a room, you guys. Dry-humping in public isn't acceptable," I groan.

Honestly, they are such a pain to be around sometimes. You would think my brother is a teenage boy.

"I've been getting a room, by myself, since I have two of the biggest cockblockers to walk this earth," Lex complains.

"True story." Charlie laughs. "So, lunch?"

"Yep. I'll just say goodbye to Andy."

I walk over to where Andy is playing with a friend. "Hey, pooh-bear, Mama is going to work now."

He stops playing with the blocks and latches onto me again. It's short-lived as Amelia taps my shoulder.

"Aunty Ri-ana, look at my ball. Andy, come play ball wid me?"

"You wanna play with Amelia?" I whisper into Andy's ear. He nods slightly.

Amelia is tugging away at Andy, giving him no choice but to follow her. I watch them walk away until Andy stops, running back to me like he's forgotten something.

His big blue eyes are staring back at me, and I know this stare. I've seen it several times. It's the stare that makes my heart beat abnormally because the words he is about to speak are words that will stick with me for a very long time, if not *forever*.

"Mama, Daddy had to stay at work. Heaven was weally busy again."

My heart sinks deep into that dark abyss, shattering every which way as the reality of his words weigh heavily on my mind.

"Yes, Andy, very busy," I answer, pushing the loose strand of hair covering his face.

He runs off, and with an extremely heavy heart, I walk toward the exit leaving my baby behind.

TWO

Alone in the restaurant waiting for Eric and Charlie, I attempt to occupy myself by playing *Candy Crush*. It's the worst game ever, being stuck on this level for like two months. I'm cursing Rocky for sending me the damn request through social media causing this ridiculous obsession.

Ten minutes later, Eric and Charlie still aren't here. I throw my cell onto the table in frustration, crossing my arms as I wait impatiently.

I hate tardiness.

This time alone isn't good for me, today's events leaving me in the biggest funk ever. This is the first of many milestones Andy will celebrate without Elijah. Graduations, wedding—the list goes on.

I still recall his baptism, a request from my parents to avoid Andy living in 'limbo' if anything should happen. Then came his first steps, to his first birthday. Each one of those moments brought pain and joy all rolled into one emotion.

How dare he do this to us! I want to scream out loud.

I didn't sign up for this life. I was born and raised in your typical American family. I had a dad and mom who were the best parents a girl could ask for. My brother was your typical jock, a loving, smart-ass older sibling who had this protective nature over his little sister. Girls loved him, and so did my best friend.

We were your television sitcom loving family. You couldn't get any more typical than us.

Then I met this boy—Elijah Jean Evans.

I knew from the moment I met him that he was my future husband. So what if I was only seventeen and a virgin? He was great, and we were great together. Elijah filled my life with so many happy memories, and it wasn't until the first cancer scare did I realize how quickly it can be taken from us. Elijah fought hard, and my brother fought even harder to keep Elijah alive. After the battle was won, not once did I think it would come back, and most importantly, not once did I think my husband would stop fighting. Not even when he agreed to try IVF to conceive a baby.

At times, I'm angry at him, at God, at everyone. And other times, I just carry on as best as I can.

Glancing at the time again, I send Eric a text with a big fat 'Where the fuck are you?' Out of all people, he knows what I'm like, and knowing Eric, he'll come up with some pathetic excuse.

Letting out a huff, I busy myself with an email a buyer sent me about my upcoming spring collection.

Opening a boutique in LA is the best thing I could've done for Andy and me. I closed my store in Brooklyn, not because of the distance but of the memories of Elijah.

Back to designing and fashion, I'm in my element, and it keeps my mind distracted. Aside from that, I need an income. Lex being Lex, he offers to pay off my mortgage, but I don't want to be that charity case.

Since Elijah's plan was to leave us, I'm going to make damn sure nobody else has to provide for my son. Between daycare and my mom, I'm able to head into the boutique a few times a week, and I hired three younger girls to manage the store when I'm not around. Business is thriving. Celebrities in LA want to wear my designs. The red carpet has already showcased a few of my popular pieces. The demand is starting to build, so at night when I struggle with insomnia, I work on my designs.

I have a plan—a plan to move forward.

Until the day he walked into my life.

Julian Baker.

I have this awful habit of being a fate preacher to those around me. You know, that whole *'oh, it's so meant to be that you were in the right place at the right time'* bullshit.

Yes, I'm that annoying friend.

Yet, with my own circumstances, I shut it out. I was having a weak day, year, actually lifetime, the night I harmed myself. I'll never forget that moment, the pain of losing Elijah even greater than the actual day I lost him in the hospital. For the sake of my son, I knew I needed help, just not from anyone close to me.

Taking that first step was extremely hard. I had to reach out to complete strangers. I didn't expect him to be there, of all the places. *I mean really, universe, what the fuck is that about?*

At first, I had no idea it was him. Not willing to make eye contact with anyone as I shamefully sat covering my open wounds, ashamed and embarrassed I had resorted to this, knowing I had a son who needed me. The second time, I thought, fuck it. I'm here to make sense of my life. This fucked-up card Andy and I were dealt with needs purpose. That was the night I showed the world my mistakes. Scar after scar, adorning my wrists, a reminder of what my life had become, and fuck, was I angry.

It was the same night he first spoke, and, for the first time, I looked into the group and could not believe he was there. Of course, I recognized him, though just like me, he was beaten down. That once-bright and handsome man no longer lit up the room. He appeared paler than I remembered him but definitely bulkier. His arms and toned physique left the drag queen next to him hyperventilating like a bitch in heat.

Okay, and maybe I wasn't that immune to his looks. I mean seriously, even in his pathetic state, he still owned the room with his dashing face. The beard made him appear rugged, but it only added to his sex appeal.

I knew what happened with Charlie after Lex and Charlie got into a huge argument over the incident resulting in Charlie calling me in the middle of the night in tears. As usual, my immature brother couldn't curb his jealousy, and it took some serious ass-whooping to get him to see the bigger picture—his wife and baby were saved.

It wasn't an easy task recalling my conversation with him that night...

"Lex, he saved Charlie and the baby? Why can't you be grateful for that?"

We stand in the hospital corridor, the eerie silence echoing the heavy breathing coming from my brother. His knuckles are stark white, and he grinds his teeth against his jaw while trying to contain himself.

"Why do you think he was there, Adriana?" he says

calmly, followed by a loud bang of his fist against the wall. "Why the fuck do you think he was there?"

I saw the pain he was in by punching the wall to no avail. Fucking hell, now I was pissed off.

"Who fucking cares, Lex? What the fuck is wrong with you? You have a wife and baby," I yell. "Until you lose them forever, don't you even fucking dare complain."

His face softens, but it's too late. I'm worked up.

Fuck, he has pissed me off severely.

"I'm sorry, Adriana."

"No, you're not. You're a selfish asshole, Lex. Forget Julian. You don't ever have to see him again. Thank the Lord you're blessed with everything you've ever wanted. If you can't see that, then maybe you don't deserve this life." *I storm off down the familiar corridor, leaving my brother behind.*

My first instinct was to run, but the sadistic side of me, the 'new' Adriana, wanted to have fun and play games, torture Julian with my presence, anything to get my mind off my own existence. I learned at the first meeting, though, not to judge him. He's just like the rest of us, and we're all drowning. We wouldn't be there if it wasn't for that.

I never anticipated forming a friendship with him.

He makes it so easy for me to talk about Elijah, something I miss doing. My family walks on eggshells around me, Lex being the worst. I get it, you know, Elijah's death nearly cost him his marriage. I wasn't that stupid, I saw it happening, and part of me knew I had to get better to please everyone around me.

On the inside, I was dead.

And what frightened me is Julian creating a spark in me.

What started off as a game quickly bit me in the ass. Ignore his looks, his generosity, his intelligence, his compassion, and the fact he's the only person in this world I can't have feelings for. I'm bound to Elijah forever. Married to my soul mate, who was unfairly taken from his son and me. I'm a whore for feeling a spark two years later for a man my brother loathed.

A man who has a past of being obsessively in love with my best friend.

It was the exact reason why the night he kissed me, I ran away.

I hated myself for wanting to kiss him, for wanting him to place his arms around me and wash away the fear which consumes me each day.

I hated myself for the split second that I smiled when his lips touched mine only to be overcome and wracked by guilt.

And most importantly, I hated myself for crying throughout the night holding onto a wedding photograph when all I could think about was the look on Julian's face when I pulled away and ran.

It was a bittersweet moment when I learned he was moving to Australia. I thought, yeah, okay, you won't see him, and all is forgotten, but after the farewell at Hazel's, I already missed him.

No matter how much I tried to ignore the overwhelming feelings brewing inside of me, Julian is the only person who allowed me to be my complete self. Scars and all.

Not to be caught up in that moment, I said my goodbyes and walked away, followed by a sleepless night. It was around three in the morning when I climbed out of bed, walked over to my dresser, and pulled out the wedding album again. I turned each page looking at the photographs, smiling and remembering the day I had waited a lifetime for. It all felt so distant now. I didn't shed a tear this time, instead I walked over to Andy's room where I watched him sleep.

We deserved to start a new life, and it wasn't that I was looking for a father for Andy—I was lonely. I missed intimacy, the touch of a man on my delicate skin, the overwhelming feeling of having someone bury their body inside you, creating a frenzy within your body which can't be controlled no matter how much you try to fight it.

I miss having someone who understands my grief and remains patient with me throughout my outbursts.

Julian understands because he's been in my exact position. He knows how much it hurts to lose someone. Knowing how much he has suffered by watching Chelsea die in front of him, it makes me closer to him. I understand his flaws, his mistakes, and I understand why Charlie coming into his life took the pain away and why latching onto her became an obsession. Anything to take his mind off reality.

Yet, ironically, I became just like him. Latching onto him to numb the pain, but somewhere throughout the storm, what we had ran deeper than either one of us expected.

I'm pulled out of my daze when Eric sits down at the table and lets out a huge sigh. He pats his hair to ensure it's in place, followed by flattening out his perfectly pressed Dior suit. Today, he is wearing a pale blue business shirt which I recognize immediately from the Prada collection. He looks good, as always.

"Don't even fucking start, drama queen. You're late."

"Take a chill pill, Adriana. I had *the* worst day."

"What's wrong?" My stomach makes a slight grumble as I reach for a breadstick.

"Meh, work stuff, confidential. Where in God's earth is Charlie?" He grabs the napkin, gently patting his forehead to remove the sweat. I notice the nude powder transferring to the stark white linen cloth.

"OMG Eric, are you wearing foundation?" I gasp.

He places his finger over his lips and scans the room to make sure no one notices my outburst. "You don't have to broadcast it," he whispers. "I had a bit of an incident last night... using bleach."

I scratch my head in confusion. "Okay, um, what were you bleaching?"

"You don't want to know. Let's just say I forgot to wash my hands, and I accidentally got some on my forehead causing an allergic reaction. Hence, the need to cover up."

What on earth would he be bleaching? It wasn't the hair on his head. Oh gross, it was probably his pubes. OMG or worse yet his...

"I'm sorry I am late!" Charlie strolls in with the stroller and takes a seat. Turning to look at Eric, she notices his impatient stare. "What?"

"I need to speak to you about the case I'm working on," Eric says seriously.

"Okay, can it wait? I'm famished and have about ten minutes before she starts screaming again."

"Charlie, I'm on a deadline here. You haven't been in the office all week," he complains.

Oh crap. Here we go again.

"Are you kidding me? I've got a six-month-old who's teething and barely sleeping and a three-year-old still going through the terrible twos stage. Oh, and don't get me started on her diva behavior which has clearly come from your mouth, and I don't think I've slept for like three days."

She does look terrible, and as an aunt, I start to feel guilty.

"So just get Lex to help? What's the problem?" Eric huffs.

"Oh gee whiz, why didn't I think of that," Charlie sneers.

I intervene, "Okay, chill people. Charlie, let me take Ava and Amelia off you tonight. Go to sleep, or whatever with Lex... so awkward."

"Look, I appreciate it, Adriana, but..."

My pocket vibrates, and I know it's a text. My face breaks into an instant smile because I know what time it is Down Under. Charlie and Eric stare at me while I excuse myself. Eric is quick to open his mouth, and Charlie listens to him. I head outside the restaurant and pull my cell out. I'm giddy when I see the text sit on my home screen.

> **Julian:** *You will never guess what they made me eat today... kangaroo. Why on earth would you serve an animal that is part of your national emblem?*

I laugh at his text and click on the call button. The odd dial tone, one that has become quite familiar, rings, and within moments, he picks up.

"Hey, you," he greets me warmly.

"Did you have it with ketchup or a side of koala?" I joke.

"No, they serve it with vegetables, but let me tell you, I'll kindly refuse next time." He pauses for a moment. "How did everything go with Andy today?"

Julian and I chat almost every day, sometimes even twice a day. Since the moment he left, there hasn't been a single day that I haven't spoken to or texted him. I'm still waiting for a call from my network provider questioning all the unusual activity on my cell.

He knows how nervous I am about today after my mini-breakdown last night. We had spoken for two hours about the whole thing, and by the end, he calmed me down enough so I could catch a few hours of sleep.

"It sucked, but it's over with. Till next year."

"I'm sorry to hear that. Not having a dad, I know what it feels like. Chin up, okay? Perhaps a plate of kangaroo to cheer you up tonight?" He laughs.

"Gross. I'll politely pass. I better go, I'm at lunch. Text me tonight?"

"I'll be in a writers' conference today but will do when I'm back in." There's that pause again, and in this moment, my heart stills as I wait to hear something, words which send the butterflies into a chaotic blissful frenzy.

"And Adriana..."

The butterflies rev up their engines as my name rolls off his tongue. God, how can just saying my name affects me in a way that's so indescribable?

"Yes," my voice cracks in anticipation.

My ear is glued to the earpiece as I close my eyes briefly and focus on his breathing. It's uneven and quick. My throat dries up as I wait desperately for his feelings to connect to his voice.

"I miss you," he adds softly.

I smile, my body relaxing immediately. "I miss you, too."

We hang up, and I reluctantly walk back into the restaurant with no doubt the biggest smile on my face which seems impossible to hide. Charlie and Eric are in a heated argument but stop as soon as I sit down. Charlie is watching me, waiting for me to say something, but to annoy the fuck out of her, I sit and remain quiet. Very un-Adriana like.

"Everything okay?" she asks curiously.

"Yeah, peachy keen, jelly bean," I respond with a grin.

Ava's wail distracts Charlie. She tells us she is going to change Ava in the restroom and is quick to leave me alone with Eric. Eric is biting his tongue waiting for Charlie to be a good distance away from us.

"Adriana, look at you," he teases with delight.

"What? Spinach in my teeth?"

He laughs. "No, sweetie, you're happy."

"Eric, not now, please. We talked about this."

"I know. Nothing to be said to Charlie or Lex. Or Kate. Or Nikki and Rocky. Or anyone! You can't hide this forever, though."

Well, duh.

"Eric, I'll be quick before Charlie comes back. I've been thinking long and hard about something..."

He waits in anticipation, rubbing his hands together.

"I want to go to Sydney."

"Holy jizzballs," he gasps. "For how long?"

"I'm thinking maybe a week. Just for his book launch."

"You realize it's not a hop in the car, and I'm there in an hour?"

"No shit, Sherlock! It's always been my dream to open a boutique in Sydney, and I've been researching commercial real estate, so why don't I kill two birds with one stone?"

"Is that the official story you're telling Lex and Charlie?"

"Eric, don't start." My smile wavers while I bow my head, bouncing back and forth between happiness and guilt. "This is hard enough."

"I know that, Adriana, but, girl, you can't hide this

forever." He pauses, then places his hand on mine. "Whether you let the cat out of the bag now or in a few months, prepare yourself for the biggest ever shit-storm of holy shit-storms to ever grace this earth. We're talking, build your ark now because even Noah is looking down saying 'holy shit, you're screwed.'"

My blood starts to boil in anger yet I try to calm myself. This isn't Eric's fault. I'm a big girl, and I know what will happen when this gets out. If there's anyone to blame, it's me.

"Well, right now, I don't know what's happening. I just want to support him." I take a big gulp of water to calm myself a little, the room becoming hotter than usual. "Eric, this might not go anywhere, so why rock the boat?"

My shoulders droop almost instantly, my stare distant as reality knocks me cold. The thought of it not going anywhere saddens me more than I expected. *Stop overthinking things.*

"Will you leave Andy?"

"I've spoken to my mom, and she is happy to have him for five days."

"So, it sounds like you've got it all planned out. Just be careful," he warns.

"Of what?"

"I don't know, getting hurt. You know how much I like Julian since I've gotten to know him. He is practically like family to me since Tristan and I moved in together. But Adriana, he's recovering, too."

We see Charlie walking back with a settled Ava. "What did I miss?"

Eric blurts it out. "Adriana's going to Australia!"

I shoot him an annoyed look for putting me on the spot. Honestly, his behavior is so elementary school.

"Wow! That's far... why?" she quizzes.

"Uh... you know how I've talked about expanding my boutique? Well, there's a space I want to look at. There's a lot of demand within the Australian market, and I've got many clients who order from the States willing to pay the ridiculous shipping charges."

I hate lying to my best friend.

"Sounds like a great reason to go." She smiles, unaware of my extended lie. "When are you going and are you taking Andy?"

"This Friday. And no, Mom offered to take care of him. It's only for five days."

"Wait, this Friday? That's quick. Why didn't you say something earlier? Or is this one of those things that Lex has known about for ages but forgot to tell me, again?"

And the web of lies spins deepen.

"No, he doesn't know." Because if he did, he'd be on the first plane to Australia to murder Julian with his bare hands.

I quickly think of a reason why. "I'm scared of failure, Charlie. Opening the boutique is a massive dream. The other night I was thinking just take the leap, and whatever happens, happens."

"Adriana, it'll be fine. You're so talented, and there's a huge demand for funky boutiques just like yours," she says, resting her hand on mine to reassure me. "Just the other day I was reading an article about small boutiques pocketing nice profit from the upturn in the stock market."

"Nice story, Charlie," Eric drags. "Can you tell that to me with a menu in your hand? I'm starving."

Charlie lets out an annoyed huff.

"So, it's settled, I'm going to Sydney," I say loudly.

Charlie smiles back at me while Eric smirks.

"Watch out, Australia, Adriana's coming Down Under!" Eric roars.

Charlie bursts out laughing, but I know the meaning behind Eric's comment. *Muthafucking little shit.*

The truth? I'm nervous as hell.

You see, I've only ever been with one man. I was never the type to sleep around like everyone else I knew in high school. And to add, the man I had been with had only ever been with me.

Now, I'm kind of seeing—if you want to call it that—a man who has not only been with several, probably hundreds, of women, but has slept with my best friend numerous times and even proposed marriage to her.

Maybe this isn't the best idea.

But I miss him.

We haven't seen each other in four months. Will he expect me to jump in bed with him if I fly over to see him? Suddenly, the bile rises in my throat, and I quickly reach for the iced water to calm myself down.

Perhaps I didn't think this through properly.

Julian is a man, after all, and men have needs.

Needs I may not be able to meet.

And just like always, guilt rears its ugly head when I find a morsel of confidence. I'm sick of this carousel of emotions, desperate to get off this ride and wish the spinning to simply stop.

THREE

The furthest I have ever been from the States is Geneva a few years ago when Elijah was receiving chemotherapy.

I remember how draining the flight was, and on top of that, my emotions were a train wreck with the uncertainty of what was to be expected of me.

Australia is a ridiculous long haul.

A delayed flight and fourteen fucking hours airtime were exhausting, and thankfully, I brought my Kindle, immersing myself in reading some steamy smut. At the time, it seemed like a good idea, then I remembered who I was meeting, and sexually riling myself up, perhaps isn't the brightest idea I've ever had.

Six hours into the flight, the reality of how far I am from Andy has really sunk in, resulting in a quick dash to the restroom to sob in private.

I am drained.

Hitting the tarmac makes it official. I've landed, and now I have the task of getting myself to the hotel with little time to spare and glam myself up, getting ready to find Julian.

The hotel is located in the heart of the city, and I know Julian is staying at the same one. As soon as I check-in, I run up to the room, throwing my suitcase into the corner and hopping into the shower to wash off with a hope of waking myself up. I lost the concept of time, the change in time zones completely throwing me off, and my body desperate for sleep.

From the bits and pieces Julian has mentioned, the party is semi-formal. I settle on one of my new designs—a burgundy-colored floor-length dress with a split, made with chiffon fabric and a low-plunging V-neck. Despite my chest being small, the dress fits perfectly, and the design accentuates the curves of my breasts. I place a white-gold chain around my neck with a cross which hangs low, sitting right between my cleavage. To complement my dress, I slip into my silver Louboutin pumps.

Examining myself in the mirror, I don't look too bad considering I've barely slept, and the air inside the plane left my skin dry and tired-looking. I'm not a huge makeup wearer, usually applying only eye shadow and mascara but decide to add a bit of foundation with a touch of lipstick.

My hair has grown slightly longer, sitting just above my shoulders since the last time Julian saw me. The color is a mixture between cherry red and auburn. With not much time to spare, I run some hair product through my hands and smooth it in, choosing to leave it out instead of my usual messy bun.

I'm ready to go.

Breathe, one... two... three...

I grab my hotel key and head out the door.

The concierge escorts me to the private area which looks out onto the harbor. I thank him, offering a tip, which he kindly refuses. Gosh, what a swell fella.

From where I stand, the view is breathtaking. The venue is called the Palais, located in an amusement venue called Luna Park. The small seaside park reminds me of Coney Island—a rollercoaster overlooking the water, various rides including a Ferris wheel. Across the harbor is the iconic Sydney Opera House, and sitting high and mighty is the Sydney Harbour Bridge.

All of which, an experience I never thought possible.

I have an awful habit of crossing my fingers whenever I'm nervous, childish as it may be, and right now, nervous is a huge understatement. Behind these doors lies a feeling which frightens me. A feeling I've desperately tried to push aside because the moment I allow the thought to linger, the guilt will eat me alive.

I turn the corner, my heart hammering in my chest. My airways close in, and I think I'm going to run out of air until I see him, standing by himself staring out into the harbor.

He is perfectly still, dressed in his black suit, hair styled to perfection from the angle where I stand. Deep and lost in thought, he makes no move and fails to notice my presence.

Still thinking about my opening line, I watch him pull his cell out of his suit pocket, frantically typing away. The vibration in my clutch makes me smile. I thank the Lord I have my cell on silent.

Julian: *Did you know the Ovation of the Seas is the largest boat ever to enter Sydney Harbour?*

I want to burst out laughing at his text. As much as I tell him that his random facts serve no purpose, I love these texts purely because I never know what to say and guess what, the majority of the time I have no idea and actually learn something new. He is like a walking encyclopedia. I quickly think of a witty response.

Me: *You'd be surprised with how educated I am in boat trivia. Did you know Dionne Warwick sung the theme song to Love Boat for the final season?*

He reads the text, and I see his shoulders move up and down as he quietly laughs to himself.

Julian: *Now that you've mentioned it, it's stuck in my head. If I sing it out loud at the party, I think they'll ship me back to the States. I guess it'll distract me from this extremely uncomfortable suit I'm wearing.*

It's now or never, no turning back, especially when I flew fourteen hours to get here. I have to grow some lady balls, that's all there is to it.

Me: *Stop complaining like a girl, you look very handsome if I say so myself.*

As he reads the text, his body stiffens, and even from behind, I can see his chest rising and falling. He tilts his head slightly, allowing me to catch a glimpse of his profile. His eyes are closed, and with bated breath, I wait anxiously for him to notice I'm standing right behind him.

Like a flick of a switch, his eyes open, and his body turns to face me.

My heart is now in overdrive, beating wildly as the smile widens across his perfectly chiseled jaw.

"Adriana," he says, barely a whisper.

My body moves toward him, my knees threatening to buckle. Only an arm's reach apart, I stop before him.

"You said you needed a plus one. It was either Penny or me, and trust me, it wasn't that easy to convince Penny to stay home."

He places his hands in his pockets almost like he is trying to stop himself from physically reaching out to me. It's the small gestures like this making me want him even more. He understands me, has seen me at my worst, accepts me for who I am, and who I'll forever be bonded to.

Julian walks over to the table by the window and pulls a flower out of the large vase. Walking back toward me, he grabs my wrist and ties the stem into a knot, making a corsage.

"Thank you, plus one."

It could've been my heart thumping so loud or the blood pumping in my veins making me want to do the unexpected. The one thing I knew would change everything about who I was and what we were—I jump on my tiptoes placing my arms around his neck, embracing him tightly.

At first, he is still, then his body relaxes, and he moves his arms around my back and squeezes me tight.

Everything about this feels right, yet everything about it is *so* wrong.

How can I fall in love with a man who once hated my brother and loved my best friend?

Worse yet, how could I fall in love again?

And just like that, the pang of guilt hits me as the tears I try to hold in fall freely onto Julian's shoulder. Struggling to remain quiet, he's quick to sense my change in mood and pulls away. I hear the lift of his arm as he cups my chin and raises my face to meet his. The stare in his eyes eases my fear, the deep brown eyes watching me.

"We can take this as slow as you feel comfortable," he murmurs, never leaving my gaze. "Don't be scared."

"I'm... scared," I stammer, bowing my head while trying to piece my thoughts together. "I flew across the world to see you. Doesn't that count for something?"

"Yes. It means you're a supportive friend, Adriana. Don't put more pressure on yourself than you need to."

How does he always know what to say to ease my fears?

He raises his arm to check his watch. "It's time."

Holding out his arm in a friendly gesture, I link my arm into his.

"Julian?"

He stops and focuses his attention back on me.

"So, the paparazzi at this event..." I hold back, my paranoia on overdrive. The last thing I want is the tabloids to get wind of this and Lex finding out through some greedy photographer wanting a quick buck.

"Yes, if you're asking if the media will be at this event. It will go online and make it to the States, or shall I say to your brother's email? There's a possibility."

I pull my arm away not realizing I had done so until I see the look of disappointment in his eyes.

"I'm sorry, I didn't mean—"

He cuts me off, placing his finger on my lips, gentle, yet my body begins to feel things, a warm sensation spreading like wildfire.

"Let's just enjoy tonight, okay?"

We continue to stare at one another until his fingers

move toward my collarbone and lace the chain around my neck, tracing them down to where the cross sits inches away from the curves of my breasts. The tips of his fingers linger right in the middle, moving gently to pick up the pendant in his hands.

This is why you wear bras, stupid! Now the whole world will see you're aroused.

In a nervous move, I unexpectedly wrap my arms around him, burying myself into his masculine scent which is driving me insane. I feel his breath linger on my ear, sensing his struggle to hold back his feelings.

"Adriana... you look stunning," he whispers, resting his hands on my hips. "You need to let go of me, or else we won't be able to leave this room."

I can't be sure if it's the lack of a man's touch, or his words, which cause my body to go into a meltdown, and I may have felt something against me, something extremely hard.

His dick, Adriana. Fucking admit he has a hard-on.

I reluctantly pull away.

He opens the door with the most delicious smile plastered on his face. "You're going to kill me."

"It's nice to know I have that effect." I wink back.

"If only you knew how much, Adriana... If only you knew."

FOUR

The sun has set, the night sky illuminated by the vast range of buildings clustered in the city.
 I find myself drawn to the view of the bridge, the flickering lights creating a picturesque light show. I have to pinch myself. Never in a million years did I think I'd be fortunate enough to experience this dream.

But once upon a time, you and your husband dreamed this dream, and now you're here with another man.

I beg the voices to stop.

Walking into the spacious open room takes my breath away. Scattered around are tall white tables with leather bar stools surrounding them. The flooring is lit up like a neon light show, unusual yet very modern. There are large bi-fold doors opening onto a balcony, allowing a soft sea breeze to fill the room.

The room is totally stunning as is everyone in it. People in their gorgeous dresses and suits fill the room, and all of them are here to celebrate the man of the evening. *Julian.*

Julian mentions something about his publicist and gracefully excuses himself, promising to meet me back at the bar. I watch him walk away and assume the blonde latching onto him is his publicist. Letting out an annoyed huff, I move toward the bar.

It's time to get some alcohol into me, especially if I'm here to entertain myself, or so I thought until an eccentric-looking man stands beside me. Judging by his gray ponytail slicked back and his tan, making Mickey Rourke look like an albino, I'd say he's in his late sixties.

"G'day, darling. Whatcha got there?" He motions at my drink.

"Uh, some fancy champagne," I answer, lifting my glass.

"I can tell by your accent you ain't a local. Don't drink that stiff stuff. Bartender!" He whistles to the man. "Mate, give this girl a Tooheys dry."

The bartender grabs a glass and holds it under the tap. I see the foam filling the glass to the brim. On closer inspection, it looks very similar to beer.

The music is louder than I expected, forcing me to lean over and raise my voice. "I'm not really a beer drinker—"

The man roars in laughter. "Darlin', that's what they all say."

Four beers later, I'm as drunk as a skunk. The stuff tastes like shit, but Barry's hilarity entertains me. He's a storyteller, and something tells me that him wrestling with a crocodile is his biggest claim to fame.

"So which fella are you here with?" he asks.

"No fella, well, it's kinda complicated." I let out an unexpected burp, covering my mouth in shame.

"I got a nephew about your age, lives on a farm up north. I think you two would hit it off," he slurs.

"Aww, thanks, Barry, but I'm hoping this new guy is it. I mean, it's crazy complicated, you know? He dated... no sorry, was engaged to my best friend. My brother hates him to the core. It's insane, right?" I let out a hiccup, oblivious to my incessant rambling. "So why can't I stop wanting him? He is so delicious and smart. God, did I just say all that? What the crap is in this Tooheys?"

"Nothing that makes ya heart lie, young lady." He laughs.

I take another drink of the beer, unaware the warmth invading the space beside me is Julian. He stands almost touching my body, his aftershave close enough to inhale. I close my eyes for a moment, allowing the sensation to spread to areas in my body that lay dormant.

Holy shit, I can't avoid this.

"Everything okay?" He looks between Barry and me.

"Awesome. Have you met Barry? Barry, this is Julian," I introduce.

"Congratulations, mate. I read your book, and you, fella, are talented." He raises his glass to toast.

Julian is humble, thanking Barry and briefly chatting about the book. Maybe it's the four beers, or is that now five, which left me with the impression Julian doesn't want me alone with Barry. He stands over me in an overprotective manner.

Fuck, that's kind of hot.

Okay, it's pep-talk time, Adriana.

First, stop reading books with alpha males because it's fucking fiction. Except for my brother—he is alpha male to the extreme.

Gross, now you're thinking about your brother?

Shut up, brain!

I can see Julian is trying his hardest to keep his hands away from the small of my back. You know—that jealous she's-with-me gesture guys do. It isn't my imagination. I bet my life on it.

And maybe another beer too.

Julian's publicist walks over. I try not to listen to their private conversation, distracting myself with the view when I feel the palm of his hand on the small of my back.

Okay, brain, you won this one. Holy damn.

"I need to go do an interview. Will you be okay with Barry?"

I let out a high-pitched laugh. *"Barry?* He's as harmless as a crocodile in the wild!"

Barry raises his glass, roaring in hysterics at my pathetic joke.

"Slow the drinking. Okay?" Julian warns. He walks away once again with his publicist. *Slow down the drinking, pfft! Okay, Dad.*

"My nephew got no chance against him. Darlin', you got yourself a great catch." Barry grins.

"He is gorgeous, right?" I slur, watching Julian smile as he shakes the hands of some guests. "I mean like sooo damn hot, you just can't look away."

"Look in the mirror, darlin', you're a little firecracker if ever I met one." Barry winks, then announces he is off to dance, leaving me alone. Maybe it's the copious amounts of beer, but my eyes will not peel away from Julian and his publicist.

Okay, so she's pretty with her platinum-blonde hair cut in a sharp bob. She isn't exactly skinny, but she has the curves in all the right places, and when I say curves, I mean her boobs and ass are to die for. *God, when did I become an insecure loser?* She's wearing a strapless silver dress which falls just above her knees with killer legs and tall pumps. My focus moves toward her body language. She is practically throwing herself at Julian. That fake laugh, the arm resting on his forearm, all the typical flirtatious moves.

It's like she's trying to claim him.

The heat rises in my cheeks as the pit of my stomach aches in jealousy.

Okay, but he isn't mine. Why the fuck am I getting jealous? Maybe because he is hot, and every woman in the room has their panties in a fucking twist and then some.

Including yourself.

This unfamiliar feeling of jealousy is something I'm not accustomed to, and I hate that my train of thought leads to Elijah. I loved him. I had been secure in our relationship. Maybe back in high school there were some catfights, but for most part, I trusted him. Girls didn't throw themselves at him.

So, is this a trust issue? I consider the fact that Julian had been in love with my best friend and tried to ruin her marriage. Both of us have a past, a past filled with great memories involving other people. This isn't like when Elijah and I first started dating. We were kids with no past except for a few stolen kisses with other kids in junior high.

I shake my head in an attempt to clear my thoughts. An older gentleman takes to the stage and introduces himself as the head of Lantern Publishing Australia. He delivers a speech, praising Julian on his journalistic efforts which has brought him here today. After applause from the crowd, he welcomes Julian onto the stage.

Julian is calm, welcoming everyone in the room. His confidence astounds me, a far cry from the broken man I stumbled upon months ago. We often spoke about how life changed for him, but despite everything he endured, I can't be prouder than to see him building his future once again and doing it all on his own now. In front of this crowd, something about the way he owns the room reminds me of my brother.

"To be standing here today isn't only a dream of mine, but a reminder of our privilege. We live in a world where anything is possible. Our daily struggles are not the lack of water, food, or freedom. We're programmed to believe one person can't make a difference, however here I stand as one person. When you read their stories, your heart is reaching out to them. When you purchase my book, it's bringing fresh water to a village. For as long as I have a voice, I'll continue to share their stories and, in return, ask for your continual support. Thank you."

The crowd raises their glasses followed by another loud applause. A few drunk folks in the crowd whistle—of course, Barry is one of them. Blondie is quick to get her hands on Julian as soon as he walks off the stage.

Fuck that bitch.

Annoyed, I walk toward the lady who's distributing the books. I may have glassy eyes, but I can read the blurb. Julian is no doubt extremely talented. His book is a memoir of his time spent abroad. Reading the blurb alone leaves me all teary-eyed. I turn the page to read the dedication.

Dedicated to you.
My friend, my demon, my savior.

I shut the cover and hold it toward my chest. Quickly, I grab my purse to hand the lady a bill, interrupted as Julian's tight grip pulls my hand back.

"I've got a special copy for you," he murmurs into my ear.

Placing my hand into his, he leads me outside to the

balcony. Only a few people mingle, the majority have moved inside as a local band starts to play.

"Big night for you." I struggle to make conversation, the blonde playing on my mind. I want to ask him if he is fucking her. Surely, that isn't inappropriate? You're an idiot, and you are *drunk*.

"Yes, and I couldn't have asked to share it with anyone else besides you." He smiles.

"Or your publicist," I blurt out.

Fuck.

He distances himself, turning to face me while pressing his lips together. "You don't trust me?"

"You're so fucking hot, and every woman in this room wants their hands on you. I'm not stupid, you need sex, and I've had way too much to drink," I babble incoherently.

"Does every woman in this room want their hands on me?" His smirk leaves me breathless.

"Yes... no... I don't know. Is Tooheys really just beer?"

He nods his head in amusement and turns to face the water. We remain quiet for a while as we both stare at the ocean. He asks me if I want to dance. I nod, and we make our way back into the room. Placing his arm around my waist, he pulls me in as the soft beats of Michael Bublé play in the background. I lean my head on his shoulder and enjoy the music until the song switches and 'Unchained Melody' is played.

Our wedding song.

A familiar, anxious feeling rushes through me. The weight of my decisions, where I stand, who I'm with instantly riddles me with guilt, and without even thinking, I pull away and run for the exit. Julian quickly follows me outside, watching me struggle to gulp for air.

"Adriana... what is it?" he asks in a panic.

"I want to go back to the hotel."

"Okay, give me a minute. Stay right here, and I'll just say goodbye."

He enters the building, and with minutes passing, I walk toward the street and hail a cab back to the hotel as my tears fall freely—the weight inside my chest burdening my soul.

I hear my phone vibrate, but I ignore it, waiting until I'm alone in my room.

It's not a long ride over the bridge but long enough for my guilt to manifest into something bigger. When the hotel is in view, I'm relieved, paying the driver and exiting quickly.

As soon as I'm back in my room and the door closes behind me, I break down in sobs and fall to the ground. In a feeble attempt, I pull out my cell and read the text sitting on the screen.

Julian: *We need to talk.*

I don't respond, and it isn't long before I hear the gentle knock on my door. I'm scared to open it, scared to see his face and feel the conflicted emotions swirling around me. I'm unable to rid myself of the wave of pain which rises and falls, depending on the tide.

Unlocking the hinge, I open it slightly, not looking at his face. Moving aside, he brushes past me but doesn't enter much further. I lift my head to trace his body. His tie is removed, and the top three buttons of his shirt are undone. With his chest slightly exposed, a stir awakens, and again, I'm conflicted. It's been almost three years since I've been intimate with someone, and to make it worse, I have only ever been with one man.

One man.

The words ring in my head.

My eyes move up to his and reflecting back is worry. Great, now I feel like shit for making him worry about me.

"Adriana, what happened back there?" His soft tone calms me.

I don't say a word, sick of this rollercoaster of pain. I do the unthinkable and grab his jacket so his body is flush with mine. I don't give myself time to think, arching my neck as my lips trace his chin until they are firmly locked into his. There's no resistance, the sweet taste of his tongue circling mine. His hands cup my face, the intimate touch causing this meltdown within me. I hear him moan and feel his hardness press against my stomach. This frenzy that's consuming me forces me to move my hands toward his belt until I feel the warmth disappear from my face and his hands are gripping my wrist, pushing me away.

Out of breath, our lips unlock, and we're both standing still, chests pumping loud, eyes wide.

"Adriana, we can't."

Confused and rejected, I answer back. "Wh... why? I want this," I say unconvincingly.

He rests his hand on the wall behind me, towering over me in this tight confinement of the entrance. He closes his eyes, attempting to compose himself, fists clenching. "Because you're not ready. Whatever happened back there upset you. I don't want you to regret your actions."

"You don't want me to regret my actions?" I ask, taken aback. "Or are you scared you'll picture Charlie instead of me?"

I watch his face drop, his lips press tight as he holds in his anger. Instantly, I feel ashamed for my pathetic accusation. *What the fuck is wrong with me!* I reach out to him once again in an apologetic gesture, but he flinches, and I know I've caused damage which can't be erased no matter what I do right now.

"Here, this is for you. I'll speak to you tomorrow." He opens the door, and I stand there numb as it slams behind him.

My hands are shaking and within them sit his book. I walk over to the bed, falling instantly against the pillow as I allow myself to cry. Even in my exhausted state, the presence of his book beside me has me curious. I sit up against the bed and prop the pillows behind my back. Turning on the lamp, I lift the book and carefully open the insert. Written in bold is his personal message to me.

Adriana,
Good things come to those who wait.
I've waited, and you, Adriana, were worth the wait.
Yours, Julian.

FIVE

I officially have the hangover from hell.

The glare of the sun filtering through the window does nothing to ease my pain. Grabbing the pillow beside me, I throw it at the window, hoping for a miracle in which the drapes will shut by themselves. My head is throbbing, the foul taste of beer in my mouth urging me to run to the bathroom as fast as I can.

After emptying the contents of my stomach for what feels like an eternity, I hop into the shower to wash away the regret over what I said to Julian. It was uncalled for. I was a downright bitch all because I thought I am not good enough. If my husband didn't think I was worth staying alive for, then why would anyone else want me?

Stop with this self-pity crap.

An hour later, I'm standing in the hallway staring at his door, planning out my apology—word for word what I am going to say. Raising my hand against the door, I knock gently. Nothing. My mind immediately thinks the worst, and my knocks become frantic until the door opens.

Julian rubs his eyes. His beautiful disheveled hair a

result of me waking him up. My tongue is unable to connect to my brain as I find myself gawking at his chest. Standing in only his boxers, how can I not look. I mean hot damn, he's cut to perfection.

My eyes trace the lines of his abs.

One... two... three... four... five... six, I count to myself.

"Adriana, it's early," he mumbles, sleepily.

Lost in my abs daze, I quickly speak, "I... uh... I came to say sorry, Julian."

He motions for me to come inside the dark room. Walking over to the windows, he opens the drapes, then grabs a T-shirt hanging off the chair. I take a seat on the edge of the bed as he sits on the small tub chair by the window.

"What happened last night?" His voice is somber.

"I drank too much."

"Yes, you did. But what got you so upset that you had to run away from me?"

I nervously play with the ring on my middle finger, my eyes glancing to where my wedding ring used to sit. There was a time when anger consumed me overshadowing my grief and yearning to bring my husband back. The band reminds me of a life promised, and so, in the midst of my raging emotions, I removed the ring and stored it inside a small trinket box Elijah gave me in high school. I half-expected to feel a loss when I removed it, but it never came. What came was more pain, more anger, and resentment toward a man who isn't here to even defend himself.

"Our wedding song, it played. Your publicist... I don't know, there was just too much going on."

"My publicist?"

"She was all over you."

He remains silent, something he does often because he actually thinks about his words unlike myself.

"It's understandable that a song would upset you. Studies show that—"

I interrupt him in frustration. "Screw fucking studies. It hurt, okay! I hate that one minute there's this ray of hope, and then, *bam*." I raise my hands, the anger swelling inside of me. "Some stupid thing will trigger all the pain. I'm *so* over feeling this way. Sometimes I just want to forget he ever existed."

Silence.

"And stop being quiet. Just say it... say whatever it is you want to say."

"It's before eight in the morning. I'm tired and mentally drained. You're hungover and clearly tired as well. Nothing I say or do right now will please you, so if you don't mind, I really just want to sleep a bit more."

He takes his shirt back off and closes the drapes. Walking over to the bed, he pulls the covers off and climbs in, resting his head on the pillow, rubbing his face with his hands.

Great, what am I supposed to do now? The room is silent and dark, the jetlag settling in, not to mention I stayed up reading his book. I just couldn't put it down.

I'm not sure why I climb into the bed beside him and nestle my head into the crook of his neck. Something draws me to him, an unexplainable magnetic force. Gently, he places his arm around me, pulling me in. There's nothing sexual about this encounter, and for the first time in a very long time, I fall into a blissful sleep surrounded by the warmth of a man.

∽

"Are you sure this is just beef?" I use the fork and knife to cut the meat on my plate.

We wake up a little past noon, and Julian decides we both need some fresh air, plus he really wants to show me around Sydney. We end up at a restaurant overlooking the Sydney Harbour Bridge and Opera House called the Toaster. Apparently, it's supposed to look like a toaster, but for the life of me, I don't see it.

"How do you like the view?" Julian asks.

"It's beautiful. I mean, what you see in movies doesn't do it justice." I grab a mouthful of salad. "The weather is perfect, and the people are so relaxed and friendly. I really could see myself living here."

"It's beautiful. There's something calming about this place," he adds.

"Like the Aussie gals?" I say in my best Aussie accent.

"Your accent is terrible. Now tell me, what's this nonsense you're going on about my publicist?"

"She wants in your pants."

"She wants in my pants?" he repeats.

"Oh, puh-lease! Like you can't see that. Oh, Julian..." I mimic, "... let me touch your arm again and flash my boobs in your face."

His laugh startles me.

I cross my arms, not seeing the funny side of this conversation.

"Aww, is someone jealous?"

I know I'm pouting, and his cheesy smirk isn't helping me keep a straight face.

"Adriana, I don't want Giselle—"

"Great, Giselle. She even has a supermodel name."

He places his hand on mine. "Why can't you see the only person I want is sitting right in front of me?"

"Because the person in front of you is completely fucked up and doesn't feel worthy of anyone, especially you."

"Why me? I'm no saint," he admits.

"No, you aren't, but you have what every woman wants. And I want it..." I say the words I can no longer hold back.

I wait for his reaction.

His eyes are watching me, and they look alive. In this one look, in the middle of a crowded restaurant, heat travels down to the most sensitive areas of my body and is igniting a flame that's seriously burning out of control. With his forefinger, he traces my lips, making them quiver. As he leans in, his aftershave lingers, and I'm seriously ready to burst. His lips gently graze mine, and teasingly, he sucks my bottom lip. I trace my tongue along his without causing a huge scene. He pulls away, grinning from ear to ear, taking a sip of his wine.

"Wow," I mutter under my breath. "Is it just me or is it hot out here?" I fan my face, trying to cover the smile.

"Hot, yes. Very hot," he murmurs, seductively tasting his lips again. My eyes are drawn to the way his tongue slivers across his lips, wondering what else he could do with them.

"Okay, don't, 'cause that's unfair. Do you really want me to pull a Meg Ryan in here?"

"Let's see. Adriana orgasming in a restaurant? Hmm... I think I'd like that show in private."

Oh man, what a hot thing to say.

"More water, please," I call to the waiter.

"Still hot?" he teases.

Bowing my head, I suddenly feel shy. "Very."

We finish our meals and spend the rest of the day walking along the Quay. We settle on a spot, standing amongst the crowd as we watch all the performances. Crowds circle the buskers as they perform amusing tricks. One man is dressed and painted from head to toe in silver. He doesn't move an inch, kids laughing and trying to make him flinch to no avail. When someone throws coins into his hat, he will suddenly acknowledge their gesture, stirring the kids again.

As dusk sets in, the lights illuminate the city. Julian firmly holds onto my hand as we walk along the streets. It feels right, and it surprises me that it doesn't make me anxious at all.

"So, I was thinking, how about we take it easy tonight? Room service and a movie?" I ask casually.

Okay, so I can see how easily that can be interpreted as sex, but really, I'm tired. I see the cogs turning in his head and the general saluting me, ready to battle.

"Sounds like a good plan," he responds, without any further suggestions or sexual innuendo.

"But... but... I'm just really tired and want to hang out with you. I'm guessing it sounds like I want sex, but it's so not like that," I ramble on.

"Adriana." He laughs. "Relax. I'm exhausted, too."

Later, we sit on the bed surrounded by several dishes after being indecisive about what to order. I'm a huge eater despite my small frame. In fact, I entered several eating contests when I was a kid, even going up against my brother.

"How can you eat so much? You're tiny," he says, intently watching me devour the crème brûlée.

"It's the one thing which has baffled mankind. Trust me, I wish I could put on weight."

"First time I've ever heard a woman say that."

"Yeah, well, believe me, I'm so sick of hearing, 'you're so

thin... blah blah blah.' Even when I was pregnant with Andy, I barely put on the baby weight. Except my boobs. God, I'd be so pregnant again just to have boobs like that."

Julian grins and shakes his head in amusement. "Okay, so how about no boob talk while you're in bed with me, technically."

"Why?" I tease. "Can't handle it?"

I see him squirm, and I'm enjoying every second of his discomfort.

"You're mean. I'd like to think I have some self-control."

"You sound too cocky... excuse the pun."

I move the tray which sits between us, and in a bold move, I climb on top, so I'm straddling him. There's something exhilarating about taking control, succumbing to this uncharted sexual desire I feel toward him. The fire in his eyes is undeniable, and I can see him struggle to compose himself. I don't move, but his hardness is pressed firmly against me, certain that with one grind, he'll be undone, and I probably won't be far behind.

And that thought alone excites me.

He places his hands on my knees and slowly slides them up my thighs, pushing my skirt up and exposing my skin. "Adriana... you're pushing my limits."

"Maybe I want to push them."

"Be careful what you wish for."

His hand moves up to the back of my neck, pulling me down as our lips lock, and our tongues entwine. There's desperation as we struggle for air, not wanting to break the intensity fueling us. I cup his face, nestling his cheekbones in the palm of my hands. I want him, all of him, right here, *right now*.

I want him to be mine.

"Julian," I murmur. "I don't know if I can stop."

"Then don't."

His short answer only drives the passion further as I start to grind against him, letting him moan in my mouth. Knowing that I'm the one causing his body to cave at this moment, I feel myself crumble all around him.

This is it. This is the big moment I've been dreading yet yearning for at the same time. We remain fully dressed, dry-humping like a couple of teenagers, not stopping the rhythm of our bodies. The moisture between my legs is seeping out of my panties, making me wild and unpredictable. His hands have moved around to my buttocks, sneaking underneath my garment resting against my heated skin. With a gentle squeeze, I'm ready to convulse. I nudge his palms to move further back and caress the weak spot of mine so desperately needing attention.

As my hand slides down his torso, ready to embrace his manhood, the ring of my cell startles me. Reluctantly, I pull away, unwillingly biting my lip as I watch him watch me.

Worst timing ever.

Short of breath, I lean over and see my home number appear on the screen. "Sorry, it's my son. Do you mind if I place him on speaker?"

"Adriana, it's fine, just answer it." Julian stands and moves toward the balcony. Opening the door, he sits outside leaving me alone. I'm guessing the fresh air is beneficial for him.

"Mama!" I hear Andy's voice. *God, how much I miss him.*

"Pooh-bear!" I want to hold him, smell his hair, and smother my face into his neck.

"Mama, Amelia got an ouchie today. She jumped off da swings, Mama."

"You mean she fell, Andy," I gently correct him.

"No, Mama, she wanted to be Batman and fly. She was wearing her cape."

Good Lord, Charlie must have had a heart attack. Andy continues to talk about his friends, what he ate for dinner, how Ash dug up the backyard. I could've talked for hours forgetting Julian was just outside.

"Andy, can Mama talk to Grammy now?"

"Grammy went to the shops. Uncle Lex is here."

"Hey, sis, how is it Down Under?"

I see Julian shift uncomfortably outside, and I know that I can't take Lex off speaker as he'll ask why I did that. My brother is like an annoying detective, always thinking the worst. I have to make the call short. "All good. I miss Andy. Hope he is behaving. I'll be back on Friday."

"He misses you, too. So, he told you about Amelia? I swear, she doesn't have an ounce of fear."

I laugh. "I'm sorry, Lex. Is Charlie okay?"

"Apart from having a stroke, she's okay. I was all the way across town when it happened, and you know LA traffic. Nothing was broken."

"Give her a big hug and kiss for me." I pause, trying to think of a way to quickly end the call.

"Is everything okay? You sound a bit off."

"Just tired. You know, the time zones."

"How was the shop front you looked at? I've got a contact in Sydney if you need more assistance."

"Actually, I'm heading there tomorrow, but thanks anyway. Listen, I've gotta go. Gonna try to fit in as much as I can while I'm here."

"Oh, hang on, Adriana... Charlotte wants to say hello."

This is awkward, but Julian doesn't seem bothered as he continues to sit outside, now watching me. It bothers me that he isn't bothered.

"Hey, Thunder from Down Under! How is it?"

"Hey, Char, yeah, all good. Such a beautiful country."

"And the men?" I hear Lex mumble in the background. "Ignore him. So, is the country swarming with Hugh Jackmans?"

"Uh yeah... some very good-looking men around."

"Oh... *oh*! Are you with one right now, and that's why you have your awkward tone on?" she squeals.

I look uncomfortably at Julian, who appears amused with the turn of conversation.

"I gotta go. Kiss my son for me, okay?"

She whispers into the speaker, "You better tell me what's going on when Lex is gone. You're hiding something."

I say my goodbyes and hang up letting out a huge sigh of relief. "I'm sorry, that took longer than expected."

"You shouldn't apologize for wanting to speak to your son."

"Yeah, I know, but you know with Lex and Charlie..."

"Look, it's been a long day for both of us. I'm going to call it a night."

He stands, but before leaving, he bends down and plants a kiss on my lips. I want him to stay, but I don't want our night to end on a bad note like last night. He makes it quick, and is out of the room in a flash, leaving me alone again.

I move toward the nightstand and pick up his book. Continuing to read, I lose myself in his words, clutching onto his hopes and dreams, his fears and nightmares as if they are my own. With every page I turn, I find myself more astounded by his talent. He's going to be an international bestseller, no doubt about it.

Somewhere in the middle of the night, I take in his final

words, shutting the book as I let it all sink in. What the hell am I doing? I feel intimidated by his intelligence and the life he's lived so far. I haven't done half the things he's done, traveling across the world, helping those suffering. What have I done? I create fashion and live in a material world. He gives his shoes to poor villagers and walks a mile just to fetch a bucket of water for the sick.

It all feels so insignificant, I feel insignificant. My goals and my dreams pale into nothingness compared to his.

I lay in bed wide awake, unable to shut off my brain. I grab my cell to text him. It seems to be the only way to relay my thoughts without word-vomiting.

Me: *I finished reading. I am speechless, yes me. I can't believe how talented you are.*

Minutes go by with no response. When the screen lights up the room, I rush to read the text.

Julian: *Thank you. And the inscription?*

I think about his question. I want to pour my heart out to him and tell him how terrified I am of losing him, how my heart is confused and how much I want to admit I feel the same way, but the guilt consumes me whole and leaves me voiceless. Instead, my insecurities get the better of me.

Adriana: *Why did your mood change after that phone call?*

I wait and wait, with no response. I fall asleep to wake with the sun rising and the beep of my cell.

Julian: *It's your last day here, Adriana. Let's just enjoy the day.*

I'm hurt by his comment. He obviously doesn't want to talk about it. I hate the fact I automatically jump to conclusions.

The same broken record playing over and over inside my head.

I'm not worthy.

And maybe because he is still in love with Charlie.

SIX

Here's the thing about time zones—they suck more than a two-dollar whore.

I'm wide awake at this godforsaken hour, dressed and fed with nowhere to go. The sound of the street sweepers and garbage trucks can be faintly heard in the distance, and the sun is barely peeking beyond the horizon. As soon as the light floods my room, I make my way out to inspect the shop front, my sole purpose for coming all the way to Sydney, or so I told everyone.

Kenny, the realtor, is very accommodating and takes me through several properties. Each has their own unique quality, but I'm not convinced I've found the perfect spot. That is until he shows me a space in a popular area called Paddington. According to Kenny, Oxford Street is notorious for upmarket boutiques and is a popular shopping district for locals and tourists. The shop itself is gorgeous. So gorgeous, I can imagine my couture gowns showcased in the window.

Within the hour, I have a copy of the contract in my hand ready for Charlie to read over.

It's almost midday by the time I finish, and much to my disappointment, Julian hasn't called. *Okay, seriously, why didn't I just call him?* Within seconds, I ring his cell praying he will answer.

"Hey," he greets mildly.

"Hey, I thought we were going out today?"

The sound of wind interrupts the call. I can tell he's outside somewhere.

"Meet me at the beach." He gives me the details and specific instructions of where to meet, a popular beach called Bondi located about fifteen minutes from where I am. I'm quick to let him know I'm not dressed for swimming, and he suggests I hit up the surf shops opposite the street.

I find several shops and settle on purchasing a hot red bikini. With the correct attire, I'm ready to cool off as the sweltering heat starts to make me feel lightheaded. The Australian sun is a lot stronger than back home, the harsh rays almost burning my pale skin.

Julian is exactly where he said he'd be beside a yellow Kombi-van housing surfboards. As soon as he lays eyes on me, he is distracted, and the scruffy young-looking blond guy is quick to turn my way. After an introduction, Julian insists we take surf lessons, and when I say we, I mean me. Julian is already skilled in that area, whereas I totally suck and keep falling off the board. Thank God, we are practicing on sand, though it makes me look even more pathetic if that's possible.

Walking into the ocean, I feel the goosebumps all over my skin as the water makes contact. I'm amazed at how blue the water looks up close, and it's so clean. It's picturesque and calm until, of course, a wave comes crashing.

After almost gulping a mouthful of seawater, I catch Julian looking at me with a broad grin. His hair is slicked back, dripping wet, and totally sexy as hell. He hasn't shaved with day-old stubble giving him this rugged look that makes me want to shove his face between my legs.

Calm the fuck down.

"Yeah, I totally suck. Go on, laugh it up," I complain.

He encourages me to paddle my board again for a wave coming our way. The freedom of the ride is surreal until I crash and fall into the water again. Julian swims over and pulls me toward him.

"You okay?" His eyes narrow, followed by a quick scan of my body to make sure all limbs are intact.

"Better than okay," I murmur, looking directly into his eyes.

I see him struggle with being only inches away, and I close the gap, wrapping my arms around his neck as we float freely in the water.

"This bikini isn't helping," he strains.

I wrap my legs around his waist, and ding-dong, there it is.

"Well, how about I crown you as official Bikini Watcher? You let me know of any potential nip slips?"

"I'll gladly accept that role."

I make the first move, finding his lips with mine. At first, I sense resistance, but within seconds, his face and body relax in unison, and he is returning the passion. His fingers are gripping onto me with force as I tease him by applying pressure to his groin. With no one close by, his fingers move into my bikini bottoms as he caresses my ass with an enthused grasp. My lips tear away to make eye contact with him, the thirst reflecting back as I squirm into him and allow his fingers to move further down south. An impending wave is upon us, and the force of the current causes his hand to slip, gently grazing my swollen clit.

Oh my fucking God.

My head tilts back in pleasure as I grip onto his shoulders, digging my nails into his arm. I can fuck him right here, right now. Since when did I become an over-charged sexual lunatic?

And with that thought, in a split millisecond, my mind somehow wanders back to Elijah. The guilt consumes me again. Fuck! My body tenses, and my mojo is swimming away faster than the tide.

The instructor swims our way, and I welcome the interruption.

"You guys ready to head back?"

We follow him back to shore, drying off and heading separate ways to the change rooms.

Julian has a meeting in the late afternoon, so we agree to get together for dinner. I spend the afternoon shopping for last-minute items for Andy and everybody else back home. In the hotel, I struggle to get all the items in the suitcase, fairly certain I've doubled my luggage allowance. It feels surreal that tomorrow I'm leaving, trying my best not to count down the hours. I miss my baby, but being here, away from everyone and finally being able to breathe a little, has been therapeutic.

Julian organizes dinner at a revolving restaurant on top of a tower. The elevator ride shot my nerves to shreds, my fear of heights flooding me with anxiety as I stare out the window with the city at my feet. Occasionally, Julian pokes fun at me, but when he sees me on the verge of tears, he surprises me with a ridiculously over-priced chocolate cake that tastes like heaven on earth. It's orgasmic and can possibly be better than sex.

Well, you haven't had sex with Julian, and your brain seems to think that ten of these cakes still can't compare.

My body starts to shiver as the nerves rear their ugly head again. Julian is quick to notice and covers me with his jacket. If only he knew the real reason behind it.

Since it's my last night, I want to make the most of it. We pack in the most we can in the space of a few hours before my legs feel like jelly, and the exhaustion is beginning to take over. Our final stop is a park bench under the bridge. Sitting in silence, we watch the yachts and ferries sail by. A party boat with drunken loons sails past us, girls flashing their tits at Julian, much to my annoyance. I don't blame them, he is hot. One guy flashes his dick, causing Julian to frown as he covers my eyes jokingly.

"You look tired." Julian places his hands on my shoulders and rubs them, releasing the tension as he kneads gently.

"God, you give good massages," I moan.

"I bet yours are good, too."

"No, I've been told I pull a Monica in that area. You know, hard and tough."

He chuckles softly. "I love *Friends*. Some people like it hard."

I shake my head and let it fall, embarrassed by my comment. "I walked into that one, didn't I? Elijah hated *Friends*, but he was polite enough to keep his mouth shut."

"You don't talk enough about Elijah." His tone is serious and catches me off-guard.

"I assume you don't like it... you know, since things have picked up a little between us."

"Why? I can't be jealous of someone who isn't here. And besides, he was a great guy. Despite the situation with Lex, he still made the effort to talk to me."

"He did, didn't he?" I wonder out loud. "Can I ask you something?"

"Since when does Adriana Evans ask permission?"

"Okay, maybe not one thing. It's about Charlie." I bite my lip, waiting for his reaction.

With my back toward him, the silence falls between us as he pulls his hands away from my shoulders. I turn to face him, met with a disgruntled expression as his eyes stare blankly into the harbor.

"Adriana, why do you always have to dig up the past?" His tone is bitter, almost spitting out the words.

"Because I don't feel like we've really talked about it enough."

"Why do you need to know? Why can't you let it go? God knows I'm trying my best."

"Because this is hard. Every time we get closer, I think, how is this going to work?" I answer honestly.

"You don't think I think that, too?"

"Well, I don't know. You never really express your feelings. You do that annoying guy thing." I raise my hands in frustration, annoyed at him for not wanting to talk, annoyed at myself more for causing this friction between us.

"Then ask me whatever the hell it is you need to know, then the subject is officially buried, okay?"

It's my chance to ask the questions that have been bugging me, the questions which can ease my fears or increase my paranoia. Either way, I'm screwed. I know myself well enough to know I get worked up and jealous over the smallest of things.

"Did you know Charlie and Lex were an item behind your back?"

I watch him intently as he presses his lips together, continuing to stare into the harbor and refusing to make eye contact with me. His shoulders are tense, and the muscles in his arms are protruding from beneath his shirt as he grips onto the bench.

"Yes, I knew."

"Why didn't you confront her?"

"I did. She denied it."

"And you bought it?" I almost laugh but am quick to hold back, not wanting to bruise his ego any further.

"Adriana, does it matter? It's done." The malice in his voice stuns me. I retreat by pulling my legs into my chest. He glances my way, and I see his face soften. "Of course, I didn't buy it. She was always distracted. We stopped having sex, and she had an excuse for everything. It's what started my coke addiction again."

I feel lousy for asking the question, especially when I'm Charlie's friend, practically cheering on her infidelity all because I wanted her with Lex. I wouldn't have done anything differently, but I hate the fact that I played a part in hurting Julian.

"If it weren't for my brother coming back into her life, you would still be with her, probably married and with babies."

"What kind of a question is that?" he asks, annoyed. "It's like me saying to you if Elijah didn't die, *you* would still be with him."

"I just—" I stumble on my words. "Never mind."

"You can't just say never mind, Miss Always-Has-Something-To-Say. Life happens. Charlie isn't mine, and that boat has long sailed. The only person I want is the one person who keeps bringing that boat and my mistakes back." He takes a deep breath and lets out a sigh. "Yes, I loved Charlie, and if it weren't for your brother, we'd probably still be together, and yes, I'd have been happy. But I've moved on, Adriana. Charlie isn't my life anymore. When you accept that, maybe then, just maybe, we might have a chance."

He stands, walking away without a goodbye. My brain takes a moment to click and follows only when it realizes it's fucked up once again. Why am I so jealous and insecure? Charlie was never like this. She was always so calm and collected. Maybe that's why he loved her, and you, Adriana, are the exact opposite.

I hop onto my feet and follow him quickly. His stride is faster than normal, quick to get away from the mess I'm dragging him into.

"Julian. Wait!"

He proceeds to ignore me, and I increase my pace until I'm at his side, holding his arm and forcing him to stop.

"I hate that I can't stop thinking that you think of her when you're with me. I don't know what it is," I cry openly in thin, strained sobs.

His face softens. "I'm trying here, Adriana, but you're making it awfully hard for me. You don't think I think the same way about Elijah? That every time you push me away, I'm not good enough?"

I listen to his words. He's right. I loved Elijah. He was my husband until death do us part. I have a son. Julian will always be reminded of the fact that he isn't the first priority in my life. Now that I've taken a moment to think about his feelings, it's unfair how I'm behaving. "I didn't think about it that way."

"Well, I do, Adriana."

This is the thing about insecurities—it's the ugliest trait a person can have. The problem is no amount of reasoning or voices in your head can ease them for you. Even when another person tries to reassure you, the words are lost and have no meaning. Sometimes it takes another person's heartache for you to realize how stupid and insignificant your insecurities are. In this moment, Julian put it in perspective by allowing me to see a piece of him that's hurting. It's only now I realize he isn't immune to feeling insecure just because he's handsome and intelligent.

I grab his hand and lace my fingers into his, closing the gap between us. He doesn't say a word as we stroll the block toward the hotel. Inside the lobby, I continue to walk to the elevator, pressing the button to my floor. When the door pings open, I pull out my card and swipe at my door. My heart is running a marathon, the thump hammering so hard, my airways start to constrict in panic. I need to show him how much I care for him, he deserves that.

And it's my last night here. Now or never. Okay, maybe not never, but who knows when I'll see him again.

With a soft click of the door behind us, there's a glow from the city lights filtering in the room. I place the card into the socket and turn on one lamp. It lights the room enough that I can see him and not overly to the point where all body parts are under a spotlight. *Oh God... he's going to see me naked!*

Guiding him to the bed, I motion for him to sit, straddling myself over him. I wrap my arms around his neck, giving myself some control over the situation.

"It scares me that I've never been with someone like you." I'm frightened to say the words, pausing while I contemplate baring my soul. "I've only ever been with one man."

He draws a deep breath as I study his lips, watching as he bites on the corner of his mouth. His index finger traces my cheekbone, gliding the tip as he moves toward my mouth. I feel my lips quiver, but with one touch, he eases my jitters as his thumbs sweep my bottom lip.

"I won't hurt you, Adriana," he whispers gently and without force. "This is hard for me, too. Sex became an addiction at times when I couldn't get high. It's been a long time since I was last intimate with a woman if we're honest here."

I'm somewhat relieved he feels nervous and isn't pushing me like I expect many men would've done if locked away in a hotel room.

I let out a soft moan. "You have to be patient with me."

He sticks to his promise, kissing me gently to relax my body. The slower he is, the more it excites me. Tracing the top of my dress, I feel the straps fall down my shoulder. His lips move toward the base of my neck, placing kisses one by one, causing my skin to erupt into small goosebumps.

"You're so sexy," he murmurs, teasing my heated skin with his tongue.

My hands are shaking as I unbutton his shirt, exposing his chest in all its fabulous ripped glory. He is so fucking beautiful, it hurts. I run my hands along his torso and watch as his eyes flutter. Lifting me gently, he moves me, so I'm underneath him. With his body pressed against mine, I feel the weight of his body, watching as he releases the weight by lifting himself slightly, causing his forearms to flex.

Fuck me now, he's so hot. It's like movie-star hot. Everything about his body is so *perfect*. I crushed on many actors throughout my lifetime, but they have nothing on Julian. Geez, Adriana, an intimate moment and your brain is picturing movie stars. *What the fuck is wrong with you?*

I'm suddenly brought back into the now, lost in a sea of kisses, his mouth trailing lower and lingering near my breasts. I absolutely hate my breasts, my biggest insecurity, but something he does, the way his eyes dance with delight as he exposes them allows me to let go of any inhibitions.

His mouth is watering, and I wait in anticipation for his tongue to circle them. The second it hits, I arch my back and let out a loud moan, pulling his hair, wanting more.

He brings his lips back to mine, and before I have a chance to gulp for air, an unfamiliar object brushes past my entrance. I close my eyes as he gently toys with my sensitive spot and am very aware of what's going to happen next. My body is clenching, and he carefully eases himself in. I let out a small whimper.

As I realize he is entering me, the panic sets in. My brain, unable to shut off, is frantically comparing his size, his technique, and that the feeling becomes too much. Unwillingly, the tears fall down my face, and my moans become sobs.

Within seconds, Julian is aware I'm upset and stops. Remaining inside me, he catches his breath.

"Adriana, you want me to stop?" he whispers.

"I don't know," I mumble through my sobs.

He lets go, and his body falls on top of mine. I'm suffocating underneath him, but I am too timid to let him know that I am uncomfortable.

Julian pulls himself out of me, his cock resting on my stomach as I see him wince in pain. The guilt is smothering me to the point I can't breathe. Squirming around, I free my arms and pull my dress up to cover my chest, aware my insecurities and guilt have gotten the better of me. Again, it was bound to happen.

Slowly, he moves off me and is lying flat on his back, palms resting against his face. For some reason, when I look at him naked, he catches me, and I immediately turn away.

"I'm sorry, Julian. It was too much."

He doesn't say anything, and I give him a moment.

Fuck, I'm a bitch for making him stop halfway. *What*

kind of girl does that? You—you idiot. But with valid reason, right? Right at this moment, I need my best friend to talk me through this. She will make me see some sense. Except, that would never happen because your best friend has screwed the guy as well. God, this is just getting worse and worse.

We lay there for a long time in the dark in an awkward silence not saying a word to each other. He is still, and his arousal has sunk faster than the Titanic. I'm still soaked, uncomfortable as the wetness between my thighs needs some attention.

"You feel like going for a walk?" he says in an arctic tone. "I could use the fresh air."

"Sure. And I get it. Soldier needs to calm down," I joke to hopefully lighten the mood. He lets out a relaxed laugh, and in that moment, I know everything is okay between us.

Both of us get dressed, and I take a moment to clean myself up in the bathroom before we head out. It's late, just past midnight as we take a stroll in a park not too far away. The cool night's breeze eases my anxiety, and the mosquitoes are feasting on my pale skin causing me to scratch like a crazed lunatic.

Julian grabs my hand and starts to talk about his next project. I listen intently, taking in every word. He loves his work so much and is passionate about helping others. As I watch him talking, my eyes move to his body. His light blue Lacoste polo shirt is slightly fitted across the chest and is showing off his muscular arms. He has a bronze tan from the Australian sun, but I love that he has no tattoos, and you can see how perfectly smooth his skin is. His hair is messy, sex messy, and a mousy brown color with a few strands which appear almost blond. As he continues to talk, his mouth does this licking thing I could watch for hours on end. I don't think he realizes he does it, which makes it sexier. Everything about him screams sex, including the way his eyelashes curl as they cover his beautiful brown eyes. I want to run my tongue along every part of him, including his cock.

Okay, and here is the giant elephant in the room. *How ironic.* He's bigger than what I'm accustomed to, and I hate that the thought crosses my mind. Surely, I'm not the only woman who has thought that when they sleep with someone new. I mean, vaginas aren't different. They are pretty much all the same. Mind you, Rocky has told some horror stories about loose vaginas comparing them to a bucket of sand. I didn't get the comparison, and Rocky had to, of course, spend the following hour giving Eric and me a visual demonstration on a whiteboard which was entertaining, though I'd never admit it to him.

Bigger doesn't necessarily mean better. It's different. And I'm not used to different.

"You're so fucking hot, do you know that?" I utter suddenly.

He pauses the conversation about Eastern Europe. "Um, okay, interesting topic change, but thank you?"

"No, I'm serious. You're like insanely hot. I always thought that, even the first time I met you. I couldn't stop staring at you, which at the time wasn't acceptable since I was engaged, but seriously, you ooze sex appeal. I mean, I just want to... I don't know what I want to do, but fuck, you're *so* hot."

I catch him smirking, shaking his head in amusement. "You know what I love about you? You just say what's on your mind. You don't bullshit. You, Adriana, are like no one I have ever met. And for the record..." he continues, "... just so you know, not at all helping the soldier here."

Did he just say *love?* Quick, think of something! "Good, it's better he is hard."

His eyes dart to mine. The ambivalent expression is expected. After all, I just ended a very intimate moment by crying. With his free hand, he adjusts the noticeable bulge, squirming uncomfortably beside me.

I want him.

This time, I won't stop. I need him, all of him, to be completely mine.

SEVEN

I don't need to search far. This desire that I know I have within me is finally staking its claim.
 I am fearless.
I am bold.
I want him.
I am rampant, pulling his belt buckle toward me. Screw all this take-it-slow-be-gentle-with-me bullshit.

He can sense my urgency all the while trying to keep his distance and maintain his composure.

"I want you, Julian. Right here. Right now." I bite my lip as the throbbing between my legs refuses to subside.

"Adriana, maybe we should take it slow. It was only an hour ago that—"

My hand clasps onto his hard bulge causing him to gasp unexpectedly and tighten my grip.

"You shouldn't have done that," he grunts.

The animalistic side of him takes over, exactly what I am craving, and he pushes me against the large oak tree. I'm numb to the loose bark and its rough edges as my back is grinding against the trunk. Amongst the scattered trees, no one is in sight, and the thought of fucking him here, outdoors, is seriously loosening my inhibitions.

Struggling to remain quiet, I bite into his shoulder as my ear grazes his lips.

"I know you're soaking wet, I can smell it," he groans.

I clench at his words, and my bite is robust, not worrying that I may have hurt him. He doesn't seem to notice. His hands have made their way into my panties, his fingers caressing my swollen clit, followed by a slight pinch. My body reacts instantly, jerking forward as I beg him to slide them inside me.

"You want me," he begs me to say the words.

"Yes."

"Say it louder," he commands.

I raise my voice. The birds that are contently resting in their nests have flown away, echoing through the night.

He is merciless, rough, and demanding, sliding his fingers alongside my clit, gliding effortlessly as he drenches them in my wetness. I grip his hand with mine, and he stops midway. His eyes are wild and dominating, hypnotizing me with the fueled desire consuming him. I want his words. I want to know his thoughts at this very moment.

I guide his finger to the entrance, letting him explore.

"Adriana, I've thought about this every day. I've wanted you more than I have wanted anyone else."

"You want me?"

"Yes."

"Say it louder," I command.

He arches his back as he screams in agony, thrusting his fingers into me. I yelp in delight, directing him to go harder. The sensation tightens as he slides another finger inside me.

I demand more, and I watch him crumble. I feel the

power, the dominant side of me wanting him to beg to be inside me.

"I. Need. To. Fuck. You. Now." He is greedy, demanding, but we both want the same thing, and he takes control of my body. No gentle moves, no warning needed. In this oblivious moment, he has managed to unbutton his jeans, thrusting himself inside me in one swift move, pushing deeper than I've ever experienced.

The moisture between my legs builds as he thrusts further. Our eyes are battling with one another, the greed and lust equally fighting for the same finish. Amidst the frenzied passion, that need to bring us closer nags me, yet I'm in new territory, not understanding how to fulfill this void.

"This. You. Us," he moans. "Fucking perfect."

The swell in my belly forms, and I stare into the sky trying to delay the impending orgasm on the verge of literally throttling me.

"I can't get enough of you. I love being inside you."

The target is hit, and the word *love* makes me complete. I don't hold back. I warn him I'm ready.

"Together," he begs me.

I fight every which way to hold back a few more seconds, and in my greatest achievement ever, I feel his grip tighten all around me, his body clenching followed by a low grumble, and I release.

I see stars, they are bright and blinding me.

I'm barely able to breathe, gulping for air.

Holy fucking fuck!

He stays inside me for a long time, only pulling out when we hear a rustle. Fuck, I forgot we were in public. Probably some dirty old peeping Tom has jerked off watching us.

We both slump to the ground, my head falling into his lap as I attempt to catch my breath.

"Can I ask a question?"

"You have more questions?" He is surprised.

"I'll take that as a yes. Is it always like that... I mean, for you?"

"Always like what?"

"You know..." Suddenly I'm shy. "Like so unbelievably mind-blowing."

He stirs, adjusting his pants then pulls my body back toward him. Guiding my mouth to his, I taste him, and he is delicious. The sweat is covering his face, and I just want to lick it off. God, sex sweat is like the hottest thing ever.

Julian pushes against me. "I'm still hard, what is that telling you?"

"That you're a horndog who probably hasn't gotten laid in a long time?"

"Uh... well, I guess you're right about not getting laid in a long time, but that was my choice. I wanted you. I've wanted you since the night I went on that awful date, and I realized I was willing to wait until I had you."

"Okay, so here you go again saying insanely hot things which make me want to do extremely bad things to you. Can we please get out of here and go back to the hotel? I have a plane that leaves in ten hours, and we have a lot of ground to make up."

"Thought you'd never ask." He grins.

EIGHT

His body presses into me as the sheets become tangled between us. It's unfamiliar territory, and I find myself unable to stop the addiction which is soon becoming his body. Watching every move, every curve and flex of a muscle as he worships me and takes me to places I never knew existed. Sweat covers our bodies as we continue for hours until the sun rises, and the reality of my imminent departure feels heavy in the room.

I'm not tired, still on my sex high. How many times did I come? Fuck, who knows.

He pulls me in, and I spoon against him staring at the clock sitting on the bedside table.

"I have to get ready in two hours," I tell him.

He kisses the top of my shoulder. "A lot can be done in two hours."

I turn my head and smile. "How on earth does the soldier have it in him?"

"Don't you worry your pretty little head. The soldier is just waiting for the green light again."

He presses against me, hard as a rock. I feel the ache

between my legs, but I'm extremely sore. I don't want to refuse him, but I'm pretty sure my vagina resembles a battered lasagna.

I feel him curl into me, holding onto me tight. "Adriana, what's going to happen with us?"

Normally, I'm the question asker.

I remain silent for a few seconds.

It's a huge question.

"What do you want?" I whisper.

"I want you. All of you." He holds onto me even tighter, my circulation in jeopardy. "I'm not here to replace Elijah. I just... I just want you."

"It's complicated, right?"

"I hate that it's complicated." He turns my body around, so I'm facing him. "Do you want me back in LA?"

"Yes... but..." Hesitating, I see the hurt in his face. "My brother and Charlie are my life. I don't know how we'll work without causing a shit-storm of epic proportions."

"Neither do I, Adriana. I don't want you to be at war with your family, but your brother... you know my feelings on him."

"What about Charlie?"

"I'll always love Charlie, just not in that way. She is a good, kindhearted person. You know just as much as I do that it's impossible to hate her."

"She is too darn likable," I agree with a smile. "But my brother is my blood, Julian. I can't be asked to cut him out of my life."

"I'm not asking you to, Adriana. I'm telling you that you can't expect us to be best friends. If he knows we're together, there's a high chance he may disown you or kill me. I'm not sure which will come first."

"Look, he doesn't need to know right now. When you

come back to LA, let's just figure this out then. So, when is that?"

He laughs. "Smooth topic changer. I'm about halfway through completing the editing on my second book. My publisher wants me back in the States in about eight weeks."

"Eight weeks?"

"Yes, eight weeks. Why? You gonna miss me or something?" He smirks, prodding me with his finger as he tickles my rib cage.

"Smartass. Yes, I will, but right now, I also miss my son so much."

I play with a lock of his hair as he watches me intently. "Julian, what about Andy?"

"What about Andy?"

"I have a son. Does that bother you?"

"It doesn't bother me that you have a son. He's a great kid. I'm just not used to dating someone who has a kid. I mean, I've never had to factor children in, ever."

"Do you want kids?"

"Wow, heavy question when you're lying in bed naked with me."

"I'm no skanky floozy. I swear I'm on the pill, not because I'm sexually active but because I have woman issues. Which, by the way, is an FYI, even though you've come inside me like five times now. Yeah, thanks for asking." I punch his arm in jest.

"I did want kids."

"When you were with Charlie..." I trail off.

"Yes. I just haven't thought about it since then. I haven't been in a relationship, and it's not really something which bugs me."

"What if I told you I couldn't have kids?"

"Well, first of all, you have a son. And second, this is a lot to talk about, Adriana." I see him withdrawing.

"I'm scaring you, aren't I?"

"I'm not ready for marriage," he admits.

I'm slightly hurt, but what did I expect?

"God, I sound like one of those clingy, whiney women. Okay, let's rewind. What my big fat mouth wants to say is that if our relationship got to that point, and I couldn't have kids because Andy was a miracle, could you still see yourself settling down with me?"

"Still a big question."

I pull the sheets up, suddenly aware that I'm exposing too much, and I don't just mean bare flesh.

"Hey." He pulls me closer. "I don't mean to be a jerk. Look, Adriana, I wasn't in the best place when we met. In fact, I was in the worst place I've ever been in. I've always thought with my heart rather than my head. You bring up a side of me that... completes me. Yet it frightens me."

"Why?"

"Because you're not replacing anyone. For once in my life, everything I feel for you, I've never felt before."

"You don't think I'm scared?"

"I know you're scared. That's what makes this harder. I..." he pauses, then continues, "Let's just enjoy this time, okay?"

I want to know what he is going to say, but this conversation has taken it out of me. I still don't really know where we stand. I know, though, that taking this further is a battle itself, and life in LA will be completely different.

∼

We stand at the entrance of the secured terminal for international passengers. Somewhere between this morning and now, there's distance between us. He becomes silent, and I'm not prying. A part of me wishes there isn't this tension if that's what you want to call it.

"So, I guess this is it," I say.

We're surrounded by fleeing passengers, scurrying to get inside. Bags are being lugged every which way, even my own is crammed full of souvenirs for everyone back home. Julian is watching me, and I know him well enough to realize something is plaguing him. I'm about to lean in to kiss him goodbye when I hear my name being called, and a Japanese couple rudely pushes Julian and me apart.

"Adriana?" The voice comes from behind me. I turn around and see it's one of Lex's colleagues.

"Amanda? What are you doing here?" I ask nervously. Turning around, I see Julian has caught on and has moved a little further away.

"Unfortunately, I was here for my uncle's funeral."

"I'm so sorry, Amanda." I am still distracted, my eyes scanning the area, more people pushing past me.

"He was eighty-six. Lived a long life. So, wow, you're here! Where's Andy?" She searches around me.

"With Mom back home. I came here for work."

"Sounds great." She looks at the boarding pass that's in my hand. "Good, we're on the same flight. Let's catch up." She pulls my arm before I'm able to do anything.

Chatting away, her words become monotone, and I am frantically looking behind me. I finally spot him, the look on his face unreadable, and I feel guilty for not saying goodbye. No doubt Amanda will tell Lex and whichever way, I'm screwed.

The automatic doors slam shut behind us, and already, I

feel the tears build up in my eyes. I miss his touch, and I want to say goodbye to him properly. There's no chance I can turn around without security detaining me, and then the cat will be out of the bag.

We take a seat inside, and before we're due to board the plane, I pull my cell out hoping he has texted me.

Nothing.

I don't know what to feel. Surely, he knows we can't be seen together? Should I be angry or guilty for what I did?

I send him a quick text, knowing I won't see his response until I land in LA.

Me: *I hope you understand why I did that. She's Lex's colleague. I'm sorry we didn't get to say goodbye.*

Our flight is delayed an hour, and like a deranged stalker, I check my cell repeatedly.

Nothing.

I slump further into the seat, the hurt and pain fueling the nausea and anxiety. I have a bad feeling about this, and the worst part yet, this is just the beginning.

NINE

"Mama, do koala bears make sounds like dis... RRROAR!"

Andy is snuggled into my side as we lay in bed. The jetlag drains me, and I'm barely able to sleep on the plane. Now, with my baby in my arms, I feel at home, my eyes slowly dozing off.

"Adriana, why don't I take him so you can catch up on some sleep?" Lex is sitting on the edge of my bed, making a silly face at Andy, causing him to giggle.

"No." I yawn. "It's okay. I'll try to stay awake until tonight."

"That's ten hours away," he points out.

Shit, that's a long time.

"Hmm, okay, maybe you can take him for an hour..." I feel myself dozing off, but the chime of my cell goes off, and my eyes quickly open, frantically grabbing my cell to read it.

Julian: *You did what you had to do.*

Great. Now I feel like shit. I contemplate sending him a

text, but with my brother watching me, I decide to send it later. He must have seen my face change and immediately starts questioning me.

"Something wrong?"

"Was just waiting on some news from a supplier," I lie.

"What news?"

Nosy bastard. "About some new fabric. I'm tired, Lex."

He tickles Andy and asks him if he wants a piggyback ride. Andy happily agrees, and before they have left the room, the last thing I remember is the click of the door.

It takes me four days to recover and get back into the routine of things. Andy is extremely clingy, which is understandable, so I decide to keep him home to spend some time with him. Getting back into our normal routine is a lot harder than I expected.

Julian hasn't texted me after that, and I don't know how to broach the subject. I miss him a lot, I know that much. I want the Julian I know, the one who sends me random texts in the middle of the night making me laugh in stitches. We both need space, I guess. The days I spent with him were surreal and feel like a dream. We were both on vacation. Now, the reality of every day is a different scenario altogether.

On Friday night, Charlie invites everyone for dinner. I'm not going to refuse since it's Mexican-themed, and Charlie makes the meanest enchiladas I've ever tasted. Andy and Amelia busy themselves watching *Nemo* in the playroom, giving us adults some time to eat in peace.

Seated at the end of the table is Lex, beside him is Charlie, Rocky, and Nikki. Eric, Kate, and I sit on Lex's other side, hogging all the cheese while Charlie places the food on the table. She swats our hands, but poor-mannered Eric sticks his finger into the cheese erupting in a mini argument.

"Have I told you lately how much I love LA?" Rocky says, chomping on a mouthful of food.

"You spent the day at the beach. All you did was look at fake tits," Nikki huffed.

"Is that what you did at the beach?" Charlie turns to Lex.

Lex shoots Rocky a fierce glare. "I wasn't involved in that."

Rocky roars in laughter. "Dude, you were the one who pointed out that famous porn star."

Our heads turn to Lex, who not even with his smart mouth can talk his way out of that one.

"Oooh, which one? Is it the one with all the tats and the piercings on her hoo-ha?" Eric asks.

"Yeah... which one, *dear*?" Charlie quizzes Lex.

He pulls Charlie into him. I turn away, not wanting to witness their display of affection. It only reminds me of what I don't have.

"If you have something to say, you need to share it with the table," Eric chides.

Lex begins to open his mouth, but Charlie covers it with the palm of her hand. "He doesn't need to share it. Besides, you're eating tacos, Eric. Need I say more?"

"Dirty bastard." Eric turns to Lex. "Lucky we aren't eating fish tacos."

"Did I tell you about the time in college when I dated this girl, and her beaver smelled like—"

"Oh my God, Rocky, we're eating," Charlie moans. "And yes, you've told us that story before. You still have the full feast despite feeling like you were deep-sea diving in the docks."

Everyone at the table laughs, including Nikki. My laughter is short-lived as everyone happily chats away. I find myself spiraling into a funk, and the worst part yet, I can't even vent. Except with Eric, only now noticing that Tristan is absent.

"Where's Tristan?" I whisper to Eric.

"Oh, he had um... some errands to do."

"At eight o'clock in the evening?"

He nods, then swiftly changes the subject.

The sound around me drowns out as I swirl the food on my plate, unable to concentrate on anything but Julian. Why hasn't he called me?

"You okay?" Charlie mouths over the table.

"Just tired," I lie again.

Kate wipes her mouth, directing her conversation to me. "So, Adriana, tell us all about your trip to Sydney."

All heads turn my way. Lex places his fork down, giving me his undivided attention.

"It's a beautiful country. The weather is warm, and the people are friendly. The shop I looked at was to die for, just waiting on Charlie to read the fine print, and if all is well, I'm ready to sign."

"What else did you do?" Charlie asks.

Julian, I want to say. My sadistic side is laughing like a lunatic at the thought.

"Spent most of my time in the city doing tourist stuff. Oh, I took some surf lessons at Bondi. The water is—"

Lex interrupts me. "You hate sports, Adriana. Anything athletic. What possessed you to do that?"

I roll my eyes at him. "Lex, surfing isn't athletic. It's something on my bucket list, plus the teacher was hot," I add to make the lie more believable.

"Now you're talking," cheers Kate.

The ringing of my cell stops the conversation at the table. I lean into my purse and see his name flash on my screen. Lex is watching me intently as I grab my cell and excuse myself from the table, practically running outside.

"Hello?"

"Hey," he replies.

There's a lot of noise in the background, and I try to figure out where he is, but it slowly disappears.

"Where are you?"

"Publisher party." His voice becomes clearer as he moves to a quieter environment. "Adriana, I miss you."

I let out a sigh of relief. "I miss you, too. This week has been hard without you talking to me," I admit.

"I'm sorry, I was a jerk. It's been hard on me, too. I just... I am frustrated, you know?" he slurs his words.

"And drunk?" My conscience tells me not to ask if he's high. He said that he wouldn't touch that stuff again, and right now, I trust his word.

"Yeah, maybe a little. Adriana, I can't stop thinking about you. How beautiful you are, the smell of your skin, the way your face glows when I'm inside you." It may have been a drunken ramble, but it's exactly what I need to hear. I know I'm blushing, and phone sex is super-hot when you're not at your brother's house.

"I, um..." I lower my voice and move further into the yard. "I can't stop thinking about you. All of you. I'm shit at phone sex, but to make a long story short, when you're back, you're mine for at least the first twenty-four hours."

He laughs. "You're shit at phone sex, but knowing you want to fuck me for twenty-four hours straight satisfies me plenty."

I hear the door creak open. Nikki has moved onto the verandah, prompting me to end my call.

"Listen, I gotta go. I'll call you when I'm home, okay?"

"Okay, and Adriana?"

"Yes?" I reply quietly, eyeing Nikki as she waits for me patiently.

"Never mind."

I don't want to let him get away with that answer, but with Nikki hovering, I have no choice but to hang up.

I place my cell in my back pocket and walk toward Nikki. We both stand on the deck before Nikki talks. "Everything okay?"

"Yes, not sure why everyone asks me that. Did Charlie send you out here?"

She smiles, playing with her ponytail which distracts me. "Charlie is still probing Lex about the porn stars on the beach."

I laugh out loud, Nikki following, but my head is elsewhere.

"Adriana, I know we don't talk as much as we used to, but I'm here, you know. Any time you want to chat."

What's this about? Dog sniffing the trail? Okay, pretty fluffy cute dog sniffing the trail.

"Thanks for the offer, Nikki. Really, I'm okay," I reassure her.

"If there's something you need to get off your chest, I promise not to say anything to anyone."

I shoot back defensively, "Have you been speaking to Eric?"

"Uh, no, but I did run into Tristan earlier."

"Oh..." I play dumb. "How is he?"

"Good. He's perfect for Eric. Really grounds him. But listen, that's not what we—"

We are interrupted as the rest of the group walks outside. Rocky starts rambling on about something which leads to a conversation involving Elijah. Everyone stops and turns to look at me.

"I'd really appreciate it if you guys stopped doing that. I'm fine."

"Sorry," Rocky says.

"Let's go inside for dessert," Charlie says. "It's homemade blueberry pie and vanilla bean ice cream."

"See, this is why I love LA." Rocky places his arm around Charlie as the rest of the group follows. Eric stays back.

"I haven't spoken to you about your adventure Down Under. Give me the juice," he probes.

"Eric, this isn't the time. Not here, at least."

He lets out a loud gasp and covers his mouth. "You got laid!"

"Eric... shh!"

"Batman got some kitty!"

"OMG, Eric. That's so crude, even by my standards."

The back door opens once again with Lex carrying a bag of trash. He looks our way, his eyes darting with curiosity, and I know he really doesn't need to take out the trash. Considering he despises housework, it's blatantly obvious what he's doing.

"Let's go in. We'll talk later."

Back inside, everyone is happily eating dessert. I notice the time is after nine and tell everyone I need to head home to get Andy to bed. After a number of goodbyes, I head off home.

A little later I pull into my driveway but feel somewhat odd. Andy is fast asleep in the back of the car, and something warns me to look around. The neighborhood is quiet, a few cars parked on the street which belong to residents. There's a faint glow of light coming from the streetlamp. In the distance, I can hear the sounds of birds or even bats.

I focus on a rustling sound, the tree in front of the yard, and I see a shadow.

Holy shit, this is it!

I'm being stalked!

I am about to grab the broom on the porch, ready to defend us when I hear my name being whispered, and the shadow moves away from the tree, walking toward me.

Shocked, second-guessing my imagination, I walk toward the figure.

"Batman?"

His familiar laugh confirms my suspicion, and I immediately run toward him, jumping into his embrace as he squeezes me tighter than he ever has before. I bury my face into his neck, and his scent of aftershave reminds me how much I miss him.

"What are you doing here? I thought you were at a publisher's party?"

"I was. In LA. You never asked that, smarty pants."

"You got me there." I examine his face. Even in his intoxicated state, he is deliciously handsome. I'm unable to hide the smile on my face as he grins in return. Just when I thought all was lost between us, he places his warm lips on mine, and I melt into him.

Finally, he is *home*.

TEN

I creep down the stairway careful not to wake Andy.

As I reach the landing, Julian stands in the living room near the mantel, holding a picture of Elijah and me on our wedding day. I'm not prepared for Julian to be in my home, my conscience is smothered in guilt. It feels disrespectful. I still remember the day Elijah and I moved in. It feels like only yesterday we were making plans, and it all revolved around this house and our family. Now, here stands a different man, one I am romantically linked with standing patiently in this house, and I'm unable to string a sentence together, conflicted with emotions of guilt and the fact that I've missed Julian more than I realized.

He hears my footsteps and is quick to turn around, still clutching the frame.

"You looked beautiful on your wedding day, Adriana. Ethereal, in fact. Very happy." He doesn't make eye contact, and his smile fades as he places the picture back on the mantel.

"I was." I fidget with the pocket of my dress, uncomfortable with the conversation. Everything about this house represents my marriage. Every room, every piece of furniture is attached to a memory. They may be buried for now, but occasionally, they resurface and that part of me which tries to move on, takes a step back.

"Does it bother you that I have these photos lying around?"

"Bother me? No, he was your life," he mumbles.

His eyes move toward the countless frames which sit on top of the mantel. Several are of Elijah, many of Andy, and, of course, a few including Charlie and Lex.

When his eyes stumble upon our family photograph, they quickly divert, piquing my interest. Does it still bother him to see them together? I need to stop asking the question. I know perfectly well if I ask, he will get defensive like every other time I've asked, but do I ever listen to my instincts? No. That's what gets me into trouble all the time, serious foot-in-mouth.

I walk over to stand beside him, careful not to get too close. My self-control is poor, and even though he is within arm's reach, the guilt is like a big fucking cockblocker if ever I met one.

"I still remember my wedding day as if it was yesterday. I may have gone Bridezilla on everyone's asses." I chuckle mildly to lighten the mood. "Charlie was different, though. She didn't care about her wedding at all. It was fun planning that day for her."

"I can't imagine Charlie making a fuss. God knows she didn't with me." One could misconstrue his tone as bitter. I know he has been drinking, and my resistance isn't helping to brighten his mood.

I try not to let his comment get to me, but I'm not that strong. Does it mean he wishes that she *did* care?

He turns to face me. His eyes are bloodshot, a result of

the alcohol, but as usual, he looks utterly gorgeous dressed in a white V-neck T-shirt covered with a dark gray blazer. His slim, dark denim jeans accentuate his height and physique. He's so much taller than me, not that I'm a midget or anything, but I am not exactly Heidi Klum.

He places his hands in his pockets almost like he can read my thoughts by keeping his distance. I can't help but stare at him. Even in his intoxicated state, my jaw wants to drop to the floor as his beautiful face draws me in. His skin, the way his chiseled jaw shapes his face is disturbingly perfect. How can one man look like a fucking god and want me? I'm nothing special, and I definitely am not Charlie.

"I've never seen you as happy as you look in that photo." It's a statement, said flatly, as his eyes intimidate me with a deep stare.

I blurt out the first thing that comes to mind, resentful for the mixed emotions swirling around in my head. "Well, you lose your husband a week after you give birth, and it's kinda hard to smile again."

"Right."

Fuck. I see the hurt in his expression. The deep stare narrows as he blinks, and he turns away.

What the fuck is wrong with my big fat mouth? I want to slap it and send it to the naughty corner, tell it that Santa isn't coming because she's on the naughty list.

Why do I not think before I speak!

Yep, that's how much I hate myself right now. I just can't do anything right.

"I'm sorry. That came out wrong," I admit, trying to repair the damage.

"It came out the way you intended, the truth in its finest form. Listen, I should probably go." He fumbles in his pocket for something, producing his cell a second later. He refuses to look my way, busily typing away to someone.

"Where are you staying?"

"A hotel on the other side of town. I've got a meeting with a realtor tomorrow."

"You're renting a place?"

He nods. During my stay in Sydney, we talked briefly about the success of his book and what that meant for him. Being honest and open, he told me how he'd lost everything he had worked so hard for because of his addiction to cocaine. Being signed by a publisher gave him that financial boost he needs to get back on his feet. Renting, in my eyes, means only one thing, though—it isn't a permanent stay, and being in his profession, he can up and leave any time.

"Why don't you stay here?" I offer, careful to hide the desperation in my voice.

"Adriana, I don't—"

"I mean like on the couch? I'm sorry, I don't know what is happening here." It's unexpected, the croak in my throat forms, my words choking as that lingering tear escapes my eyes.

"You're upset because I'm standing in the home which belongs to you and your husband, and you feel guilty."

I look up at him as his eyes have found their way back to mine. I want to touch him. I need to touch him. I beg him with my eyes to embrace me, but he doesn't, and maybe it's for the best.

"How did you know?" I ask, barely above a whisper.

"Body language, plus hours of therapy with Hazel."

"OMG, Hazel. I haven't had a chance to call her since I got back. When did you speak to her?" I get off track, welcoming the distraction.

"This morning. I went straight there to see her and

spend some time with Blaze. God, I missed her." His smile returns, and I'm hurt it isn't me making that happen.

"Why didn't you come see me first?"

"Why? Because I wasn't sure I could handle it."

"Handle what?"

"Being back in LA where all my problems started. Seeing you and not knowing how you will react in our normal environment."

"And Hazel helped."

I love Hazel like my own mother, and now with a better understanding, it makes sense why he'd have sought guidance first. This is far more complicated than our relationship. I know firsthand how being somewhere can trigger all the unwarranted memories of a time in your life where darkness prevailed.

Breathe, Adriana. Don't make this all about you.

"I knew that standing beside you, not being able to touch you, would be hard. I never expected it to be this hard," he confesses.

"Please stay," I beg.

"It's too hard, Adriana."

"*Please?* On my couch. I know I'm not ready but knowing you're here, I really want that." He remains quiet, and I continue speaking the truth. "I *need* you here."

He thinks about my offer, then nods without saying a word.

We work silently together as I arrange the cushions and grab a blanket from the linen closet. Within moments, he has taken off his jacket and shoes and is lying on the couch. A yawn escapes his mouth as he rubs his tired face.

"You sure Andy won't come down?"

"No, he won't. It's Saturday, and besides, he won't go downstairs without me," I tell him. "He's afraid the boogey monsters prey on little boys. Blame Rocky and his *Ghostbusters* obsession."

I'm distracted momentarily by his penetrating stare, the desperation to be physical with me, but I restrain, unable to relax in my own home. I say good night without a kiss goodnight and walk upstairs.

In the confinement of my room, a single tear escapes again followed by a stream. Why does having him here make me feel so guilty? Elijah told me to move on, find someone who will love me. Does Julian love me?

Love is a terrifying word I never thought I'd have to say to anyone besides Elijah. The anger is starting to build. Why does this have to be so complicated? Why is it that everywhere I turn, I'm met with a battle?

I change into my tank and bed shorts before climbing into bed. My bed feels emptier than in the weeks after Elijah's death. I lay on my side staring wide awake at the ceiling, chastising myself for being gutless and for not being able to talk openly about my fears, afraid I'm pushing him away, so I send him a text.

Me: *I'm sorry I'm hurting you.*

I wait fifteen minutes. I contemplate going downstairs, but my screen lights up, and I take a deep breath before I read his response.

Julian: *It does hurt. But what's the point of pushing you? Sleep, we'll talk tomorrow.*

The answer leaves me wanting to ask more questions, but it's been a long day, and exhaustion rears its ugly head along with its BFF, guilt.

It hits hard, and Elijah invades my mind as it decides to take a walk down memory lane.

I rest my head on his lap watching paint dry, and I mean literally. We had just painted the walls in our apartment a shade of lilac, creating a small piece of heaven which was slowly becoming our home.

"Did you seriously think we'd end up together? I mean, you know everyone says high school sweethearts never last," I asked.

"Babe, we aren't like anyone else. We always had that connection not many people get, but you and me, we got it bad," Elijah said confidently.

He placed the remote of his Xbox down and stroked my hair gently. My body relaxed as his fingertip glided against my scalp causing my skin to shiver in delight.

"Charlie and Lex are like that. I feel it. I just shouldn't have been part of breaking them up." I sighed loudly.

"Adriana, don't feel guilty for that. They both needed to find themselves. And I agree, they have a strong connection. If only their stubborn heads would realize that."

"I feel sorry for Julian. I know Charlie loves him, and he loves her, but he just needs to let her be with Lex. God, he is hot enough to pick up anyone. Let go of her and find another beauty."

"Sometimes, it's not so easy to let go. He's a great guy and intelligent. Don't meddle, okay? It's called a love triangle. Triangle has three sides, not four," he pointed out.

I wasn't a meddler. Okay, maybe I was but only because I had good intentions.

"So are you! You distracted Julian in the restaurant so Lex and Charlie could talk, but I swear to God they fucked

in the toilet because Lex's forehead looked sweaty." I screwed my face up in disgust. Argh, he is your brother, Adriana! Wrong on so many levels.

"Julian is a great guy. He'll figure it out soon. Now as for you, have I told you lately how much I love you, soon-to-be Mrs. Evans?

I let out a small giggle. "Yes, last night during that long lovemaking session with those new oils."

"Well, I love you," he repeated.

I moved my body, so my face met his. His crooked smile awaited me as I ran my finger down his cheek. His quick bite startled me, and we both erupted into laughter.

"You and me, mister, for life. We can't be broken." I smiled.

"Impossible." He smiled back.

And we were broken,
 One year and forty-six days after that promise.
 To be exact.

ELEVEN

"Mama, Mama! Uncle Lex is here," Andy yells throughout the hallway, his footsteps smacking hard against the floorboards.

I groan and throw the pillow over my head at the noise. Lex here on a Saturday? What the fu... *Oh, shit!* I burst out of bed so fast, certain I've just given myself a nosebleed, kicking my toe on the bedside table, the pain ricocheting up my leg. There's no time to stop as I race out of the room.

Oh fuck, oh fuck, this is it... my life is over!

"Hey, sis," Lex greets me.

He is dressed in his gym shorts and a Nike tank. I don't know why I notice, but his hair is a goddamn mess.

I stop at my bedroom door.

"What are you doing here?" I ask in my most relaxed voice, which is so high-pitched I'm sure he will catch on to me.

"Just here to pick up Andy for the bike ride I promised him."

Bullshit. This is the first I've heard of it.

"Uh, since when? I had no idea..."

"Why? Is it a problem?" I know he is peering through my door, fucking nosy piece of shit! Julian must have left, thank God, but now I'm going to annoy the fuck out of Lex for thinking he can outsmart me.

I walk toward the stairwell, resting my hand on the railing.

"No problem. I'd have gotten Andy ready if I'd known, that's all. Hey, Andy!" I call out. He races toward me looking up with anticipation. "Can you go to my room and get your runners? You left them there last night."

He races into my room and yells from within. "Mama, no shoes!"

I answer back giving him direction, and he emerges a moment later carrying them.

Lex looks frustrated, and secretly I'm jumping for joy and poking a stick at him. Nosy bastard.

"You ready, Andy?" he asks.

Andy nods, and they walk down the stairs ready to leave the house, but not before Lex pulls me aside.

"Adriana?" His eyes are doing that annoying hypnotizing thing that works on all women besides me. I'm his little sister. He has pulled this stunt several times knowing very well it's a fruitless exercise.

"Yes, brother?" I bat my eyelashes.

He is pissed off, and I love pissing him off. Lex believes the world revolves around him, and his controlling nature is a force to be reckoned with. Intimidation may get him far in life but messing with his sister is a dead end.

"Forget it," he responds, agitated.

Closing the front door behind him, I race to the living room. Julian is long gone, not a trace he was here. Did I imagine it? Surely, he had to have been here. I walk around looking for something, anything, but nothing. The blanket and pillow I had lent him were back inside the linen closet.

Frustrated and seriously thinking I've lost the plot, I head to the kitchen to make myself a much-needed coffee. Next to my machine, I notice my shopping list. Huh, that's odd, I don't keep this here. I go to return it to the fridge but notice handwriting on the *to-do list* section.

Midday, Beach Resort Hotel, room 349.

My mind takes a moment to click. Shit! It's his room number.

My body reacts first in excitement, then prompts me to call my mom and ask if she can look after Andy. She is free until seven o'clock. Beggars can't be choosers, right? I then text Lex and ask him to drop Andy off at Mom's. Suddenly, I'm in my shower shaving every part of me. No time for a wax, knowing I'd regret shaving my lady garden two days later when I'm itching like a dog with fleas.

I head to my closet where I find a short floral summer dress and mix it with wedged sandals. My hair is done, and I glance at my watch—ten-thirty. Oh, who cares if I'm early. I'm eager to head across town and don't want to be late.

I walk into the lobby of the hotel conscious people are eyeing me like I'm Julia Roberts in *Pretty Woman*. With some direction from the concierge, I make my way to the tenth floor and find the room. Just as I'm about to knock, I notice a swipe card peeking out of the bottom of the door. My hands are shaking as I grab it and swipe it. The door unlocks, and I find myself inside the room closing the door gently behind me.

The room is dark—all the curtains are drawn shut, but the sound of the shower can be heard. I place my purse on the nightstand, and with my heart beating out of my chest, I open the slightly ajar door to a steaming bathroom. My vision is clouded, but I can see the silhouette of his muscled back. My jaw almost drops when he turns to the side, and I catch a glimpse of him stroking himself, eyes closed as he uses his spare hand to lean on the wall.

I'm ready to combust.

It's the most erotic thing I've ever seen, and without even thinking, I remove my shoes and climb into the shower fully dressed. With the water embracing me, I wrap my hand around his chest and lean my head against his back.

"I thought you'd come," he whispers.

"Not yet, handsome," I tease.

He turns around slowly and stands naked with the biggest hard-on I've ever seen in my life. I gulp in fear, yet uncontrollably, I drop to my knees and place my hand on his shaft. With slow strokes and maintaining eye contact, he groans under his breath and demands I take it all in. But I play hardball, teasing him with gentle strokes, watching his body tense with desire. His eyes open wide as he stares down and watches me intently, begging me now to take it all in, but I resist again, building up the pleasure. My mouth moves closer to the tip of his cock, and just when he thinks I'm about to suck, I pull back teasing him again, increasing the pace of my stroke.

"Adriana, take it in now," he whimpers.

I hold the control, and I know I'm getting off on it too, practically swollen and dripping wet despite the water cascading down on my fully dressed body. He sees me inch closer, and while I plan to hold back again, he's swift and demands me to suck on his cock, shoving all of him directly into my mouth.

Giving head isn't on my top ten fun things to do, but something about him, the way he makes it look so sexy and appealing, possesses me to take him as far in as I can. The tickle at the back of my throat causes me to gag slightly, warning me it's as far as it can go. His eyes flare at my ability to push him in further, the thrill indulging me to exceed my limits and open my mouth wider. I move my mouth in rhythm with my suction as I watch him melt around me. He is demanding me to pleasure him, and I give him all I have, and just like the gentleman Julian is, he warns me with a rugged threat it's all about to end.

I keep on going until he explodes in my mouth, banging on the wall of the shower as he releases into me and finds himself coming down from an extreme high. I lick the tip of his cock and move my way back up to him. He smashes his lips onto mine, caressing my face in an intimate gesture.

I'm about to tell him how much I missed him but am distracted by the removal of my dress followed by my bra and panties. Standing naked in front of him, he licks his lips in delight. Pressing my body up against the wall, he demands I raise my hands over my head, and I obey.

"So fucking beautiful," he groans.

I'm a little unsure of what to do, never been pinned to a wall before, but it doesn't take me long to figure out his next move as his tongue moves from my mouth, tracing my neck as he stops midway between my breasts. My nipples are erect, waiting in anticipation as his lips circle them, my eyes close allowing my senses to take over. I'm trying to hold back the impending orgasm, but fuck, fuck, fuck, it's all becoming too hard, including his delicious cock pressing firmly against my leg, begging to be noticed again.

His rolls my nipples between his fingers, tugging them as I beg for more. Words and emotions are leaving my mouth without my brain's approval. I feel dirty, and I fucking love it.

With his tongue now moving past my belly button, I embrace the pleasure he is about to bestow on me and wait impatiently as he kisses the insides of my thighs. He is taking his jolly old time, and this gratification stuff has run its course.

Perhaps he senses my frustration and smiles. "A little impatient, aren't we?"

I squirm again and blurt out, "You're killing me."

The smirk on his face widens, but he doesn't move an inch.

"I'm not kidding, and this is fucking unfair!"

He still doesn't move an inch. I mean seriously, I'm a bomb ready to explode, one button, that's all I am asking for here. There's no change, and that bomb warns me it's time to take matters into my own hands.

I pull my arms down and firmly grip his head, forcing his mouth between my legs, and the second his lips touch my sensitive spot, I let out the loudest groan, clutching his hair as my body threatens to give straight away.

A little longer, distract yourself. Quick, look around you!

Shampoo.

Soap.

Rainbows.

Rainbow showers.

Pee.

OMG, Eric!

Eww, gross.

A let out a huge relief as the thought of Eric is like a splash of cold water. I enjoy Julian devouring me, watching his tongue flick the tip of my clit. It's insanely hot watching him at my command, and I'm lapping up the attention until I feel a finger slide within me, and I know I have zero control.

Game over.

The water is stifling hot now. My body tenses as my chest rises and falls, and I warn him only seconds before I'm seeing fucking fireworks. I feel myself contract, and the pleasure consumes all of me, gulping a whole heap of water as my dry mouth screams in ecstasy. He moves his body up, satisfied with himself, and suggests we hop out. My clothes lie wet in a heap on the bathroom floor, but I don't care. I'm here with him.

We are entwined within each other as we lay contently in bed. My head is resting on his chest as I attempt to listen to his heartbeat. It's strong, and I want to ask it if it beats for me.

"You're too quiet," he says, kissing the lobe of my ear.

"I'm thinking."

"Wait. Stop the press. Adriana thinks quietly?"

I punch him in the chest.

"A little lower," he instructs.

I punch him in the stomach.

"Lower," he grumbles.

My hands move lower, accidentally grazing his hard-on. I'm no longer shy. I've become extremely comfortable with his body. With a tight grip, I begin to talk. "So, I have a question."

He rolls his eyes and moves, so he is on top of me. "I haven't fucked you. So, the question and answer portion are on hiatus until I've been inside you, you got me?"

I smile back, and he doesn't pussyfoot around with foreplay, entering me whole as I sink beneath him. Every thrust, every push, he whispers how much he needs me, and I return the sentiment. Consumed with raw passion, I beg him not to stop, never to stop being inside me.

We lose all sense of time, clinging to each other, desperate for the intimate connection both of us crave. With our bodies in perfect sync, I beg him to come inside me, demand he explode around me, and when he does, I follow shortly after, collapsing beneath him as I'm short of breath.

He pulls me back into him, and I wrap his arms so tightly around me, ignoring our sweaty bodies.

"Can we stay like this?" I murmur.

He lets out a short laugh. "Change of heart from last night?"

I sink into him deeper, wanting him to protect me and not let me go. "I was a bitch. I felt so guilty, you know? It was our house. What if he was watching me?"

"You think he's watching you?"

"I don't know what to think. It just didn't feel right, and I should've been more honest about my feelings rather than hurting you."

"I agree, Adriana. I need to know what you're thinking. You need to let me know when you're uncomfortable."

I smile in his arms. "So, about my question," I ask again. "And I hear that eye rolling."

He pulls me in deeper and places his hand on my breast in a non-sexual move.

"How do you feel about coming out to Charlie and Lex?"

Julian remains silent.

I give him a minute.

"Okay, I don't like silence," I complain.

"Adriana, it's called a thought process."

"Oh, bullcrap, you're fabricating your thoughts. What was the first thing you thought?"

"First thing? I'm not ready. Like the first time you eat spaghetti after vomiting it."

"What?" I laugh out loud.

"When I was five, I puked up spaghetti all over my bed. Couldn't touch the stuff till I was sixteen, and even then, it was with fear and trepidation."

My body moves up and down, laughing uncontrollably at his story. "Oh, that happened to me with strawberry ice cream. I couldn't touch the damn stuff till like twenty years later."

"So, you know," he confirms.

I do know. We aren't going to be welcomed with open arms. That's the bottom line. Just as Eric had said, an epic of shit-storms no matter how the truth unveils.

"Okay, so change of subject. Are you here for good, and what's the plan?"

"I'm here for the next month, then off to Morocco for a piece I need to do. I've found a place not far from Hazel's which is great since I can spend time with Blaze."

"When do I see you? How will this work? Will we just meet at your place?"

"Adriana," he says soothingly. "Calm down, okay? Let's just take it one day at a time."

"But... but... I need to—" I feel him throbbing against me. Fuck me dead. Wow! Okay, what was I going to say? "So yeah, anyways—"

"Do I need to fuck you again to shut you up?"

"Well, I do have more questions," I tease.

He doesn't ask and slides himself in from behind. "There's only one question I want you to ask, Adriana."

"What's that?"

"Ask me how I'm going to make you come."

My body quivers. "How are you going to make me come, Julian?"

He pushes me on all fours and positions himself behind me. With his hands firmly on my hips, he pushes against me at an even, slow pace. "I'm going to slide my finger into your ass and fuck you hard until you come all over my cock. Can you handle that?"

Hot damn. I nod.

"Say it out loud," he grunts.

"I want you to finger my ass and fuck me hard."

I feel him spit onto my asshole, circling it gently before he slides in. His pace increases, and I'm coming undone feeling that familiar ache form in the pit of my belly.

I want him to explore every part of me.

Heart, mind, body, and soul.

I am his.

He is mine.

And that's what he did for the next five hours until it was time for me to leave, back to my so-called responsible *life*.

TWELVE

I pick up Andy on my way to meet Eric, Tristan, and Charlie for an early dinner.

Lex flew to Manhattan due to some big mess. I'm not listening, to tell you the truth. It's what happens when Charlie rambles on about her husband.

The restaurant is a family-friendly eatery, bugging the shit out of Eric. Amelia and Andy are happily playing in the kids' corner as the waiter stands beside our table to take our order.

"I'll have the ham and pea soup for starters with a side of garlic bread, the steak and mixed salad for my entree. Oh, wait, can you add potatoes to that and sour cream?" The waiter nods, quickly writing on his pad. "Great, and for dessert I'll have the chef's surprise, but make sure it comes with two scoops of vanilla ice cream... oh, what the hell, make it three." I place my menu down to be met with gaping mouths.

"Adriana, are you feeding Africa?" Charlie asks.

"No, just famished," I practically sing out loud.

"That's a mighty big meal. Sounds like you had a busy day." Eric snickers.

I shoot him an annoyed look. What the fuck is he thinking? At least Tristan has the decency to keep his trap shut.

"Oh, for Christ's sake. Amelia has spilled some water." A fretful Charlie excuses herself to attend to her daughter.

"Okay, you better fess up, missy, because you look freshly fucked in every orifice," Eric points out.

"Eric, honestly. That's so crass," Tristan scolds him.

My cheeks begin to flush, no doubt visibly red from Eric's observation. "Yes, all right. Keep your big mouth shut or no deets."

"Geez, don't get all nasty on me," Eric gripes. "Look at you, you've got that glow. You know that jizz-splashed-all-over-your-face glow."

My shoulders rise and fall as I chuckle at his comment. Even Tristan isn't immune to Eric's humor.

"Tristan, maybe you need to block your ears for this," I warn.

"Please, I live with Eric. I can handle the smut talk."

"Okay, Julian is so fucking unbelievable I can't walk. I mean literally, I think my vagina is broken," I blurt out.

"Oh, hell no, you could've warned me, Adriana," Tristan complains.

"I did!"

He rambles uncomfortably about needing to leave the table and uses Andy and Amelia as an excuse to heads over.

"Oh, sweetie, I'm so happy for you!" Eric claps his hands and stands up to hug me.

"What's going on?" Charlie returns, eyeing us cautiously.

"Finally finished a design, that's all," I lie. "I had this creative block for months, and now it's all coming together.

"Right, I thought you were going to finally tell me who you've been fucking because I swear, Adriana, it's written all over your face." She chugs on her drink while waiting for my response.

Crap!

I can't tell her the whole truth, only because it will affect her marriage. Instead, I decide to give her a few tidbits, leaving out the most important part—Julian.

"Okay. Look, Charlie, it's not serious. It was a one-night fling, not even a fling just a make-out session, and please don't tell Lex. And I mean best friend pinky swear, sister-code swear on the Bible and your firstborn."

"Aww, Adriana, don't make me do all that." She frowns, letting out a breath. "What if he asks me?"

"You tell him you can answer the question, but you won't be held accountable for sexual images of his sister which may creep into his brain and require a gallon of brain bleach."

"Great response." She rubs her hands together in delight. "Okay, so gimme all the goss."

Andy moves toward us and asks to sit down. "Another time, perhaps."

"Okay, so guess what I've planned?" Eric says, barely able to contain his excitement.

We both shrug our shoulders. Tristan is already shaking his head disapprovingly—this can't be good. Eric is known to be wild and adventurous, but on a positive note, life is never dull around him.

"I'm having a little gathering at our place on Friday night. A very special guest will be attending."

"Eric, the last time you said that a shemale stripper turned up." Charlie winces.

I complain along with Charlie, "Yeah. Honestly, Eric, I don't like your surprise guests."

Eric throws his hands in the air like the drama queen he is. "Oh, let it go, will you? Yeesh! One time. Nope, something even better."

"Okay, is this a girl thing?" Charlie asks.

"It's for everyone, except kids."

Charlie and I both let out a groan at the same time complaining about babysitters and sleeping schedules. Eric, who doesn't like change one bit, promises it will all be worth it, and, in fact, it will be a bonding session for all of us.

We agree to go, though Charlie still has to convince Lex, the biggest complainer of all time.

Every chance I get during working hours, I race over to Julian's hotel, fuck him in ways my imagination dares only to dream about yet only for an hour before I'm due back at work. Three days straight, and I'm desperate for more.

By Friday, I am itching to get out but have an important deadline. I tell Julian it's a no-go since Friday is the day my assistant leaves the boutique at midday for an extended lunch until three in the afternoon. I busy myself preparing a sample for a buyer when I hear the door chime to be met with Julian standing in front of me.

"What are you doing here?" I ask, surprised, looking behind him in worry.

"Well, you couldn't come to me, so I came to you."

He is standing before me, wide grinned, dressed head to toe in a dark gray suit and light pink shirt. Armani. Okay, shit, focus and pick up your jaw from the floor.

"But someone could see you here." I panic.

"Adriana, you have exactly one minute to figure out where I'm going to fuck you."

Is he kidding? He doesn't have his kidding face on.

"You're not joking, are you? And why am I thinking of a place?"

"I'm not joking. I can smell how soaking wet you are from across the counter. Ten... nine... eight..."

I quickly look toward the door and see no one. I pull his arm to my back storeroom, and he doesn't wait, lifting my skirt and pushing me against the rack as soon as we're out of sight.

Note to self—*always wear dresses.*

He is already hard and enters me without warning, and I push back, the adrenaline running through me as he continues to fuck me when anyone can walk in. The thrill of being caught spikes my arousal, and my body is moving with his, pushing deeper into him.

"I can't go a day without fucking you. It's too hard. I need you, Adriana."

"I need you, too," I moan loudly.

His grip tightens, almost hurting me, and his movement speeds up. He brushes his lips against my ear and demands to come inside me. I nod, but he wants me to say the words.

I don't say it, I beg for it.

The ache down below is spreading all over me, and I clench in pleasure, biting his hand to keep myself from screaming his name. He wants us to be in sync, something I always struggle with, but with his magic fingers gliding across my swollen clit, I'm done faster than you can say *holy fuck.*

He fixes my skirt and kisses my shoulder as I control my breathing. I straighten my hair in the mirror on the wall and smooth out my dress when the chime rings. I motion for him to be quiet and stay put. As I walk back into the store, my heart falls out of my chest, smack bam on the floor, as I see my brother standing behind the register.

"Lex," I almost shout. "Why are you here?"

"Why are you shouting my name? I'm not deaf," he replies.

"Sorry, noisy aircon out back. So, what are you doing here?"

Act calm. Do not show any signs of paranoia.

"I wanted to talk to you about tonight. Do you always leave the store unattended?"

"No, dickwad. Cassie had to be somewhere, and I really needed to count something in the back, and besides, I have a door chime."

"Right. So about tonight. It's not a fucking drag queen party again, is it?"

"Shemales, not drag queens. Eric promised it wasn't." I distract myself by folding some garments in front of me, but it seems pointless as Julian's cum is oozing down my thigh. What have I gotten myself into? Why can't a vagina be like a Venus flytrap, once caught, it shuts. This is just plain uncomfortable, and my brother is in front of me. My eyes move toward my arms as they begin to redden.

"So, I'll bail. Charlotte can weather the storm."

"Whatever. You'll last an hour before the curiosity gets the better of you, and you do your whole I-miss-my-wife bullshit."

I need to wrap this conversation up, but Lex is getting comfortable resting his hand on the bench and pulling out his cell to type something. The anxiety was getting to me, and suddenly, the temperature in the room is stifling hot.

"Well, I haven't seen her much this week between me flying to New York and her helping Nikki with that pending case. Is it too much to want to spend quality time with my wife?"

"Uh, no..." I'm aware Julian hears all of this, and I am not too sure what he'll be thinking right now. Will he be annoyed? Angry? The last thing I want is to get into another argument when things are becoming great between us.

I see Lex's face light up, and his lips widen into a smile.

"What's so funny?" I ask.

He continues typing. "Oh, nothing."

"Whatever. Show me!" It's just like when we were kids. He knows how to push my buttons, and I used to hate it when he hid things from me. Classic example, when he was fourteen, and I thought he was smuggling Wonka bars into the house in a brown paper bag when my dad had banned all sweets for a month after Lex and I accidentally washed his wallet as part of our chores. I swore he was sneaking in candy and begged him to share it with me. He always refused, and so one day, I rushed home after school and raided his room only to find the latest *Penthouse* magazines.

Yet somehow, I still didn't learn my lesson back then or now, asking him to show me his cell.

"You want to see your best friend naked in the shower?"

"Oh my God, Lex! TMI! Get the fuck out of here, you freak."

"Gladly. I've got a wife who needs attention. See ya tonight, sis." He winks.

He walks out the door, and I let out a long-winded sigh. I give it a few minutes before I head to the back. Julian is standing there against the wall. I know he has heard it all, given that his face is blank. No smile or I-missed-you grin.

"I'm sorry, that was so awkward, and I know that must have been hard for you."

"Adriana," he grits.

"Yeah?" I mutter.

"How many times do I have to tell you that I want only you? The only uncomfortable thing about this is that I loathe your brother for holding us back. I want to go home to you and do dirty things whenever I please."

"But Charlie and naked..." I'm fucking rambling. *Why am I fucking talking about Charlie being naked!*

"Don't. Please."

"But you're not—"

"How many fucking times do I have to tell you it's over? I don't think about her that way," Julian raises his voice, throwing his arms in the air with frustration. "This has got to stop, you understand me?"

"Argh, I hate it, too. Okay!" I fall into his arms, desperate to feel secure.

Slowly, he wraps his arms around me, allowing me to bury my head into his chest. His lips kiss the top of my head. "I need to go."

I don't allow him to let go of me, not caring at this moment who walks in on us. "Don't go," I plead.

"I have a meeting. I'll call you later, okay?"

"Come over tonight?"

"You have that thing at Eric's," he reminds me.

"Oh, right."

"Tomorrow, okay? We'll make something work. I promise." He places a final kiss on my lips before exiting the store and leaving me on my own.

I plonk myself on the stool, slouching as I mentally scold myself for being a hormonal, jealous woman. Sometimes, I have no idea who I am. Almost like I have multiple personalities, and the worst one of them all is jealous Adriana. The thing that scares me the most is I never know what's around the corner. Our relationship is a roller coaster, and I blame myself. Julian does nothing but reassure me it's only me he wants, yet it isn't enough. What else do I want? That nagging voice inside me wants to ask him more questions. I feel like he's hiding something, but what?

I have no idea, and jealous Adriana will only disappear if I find out exactly what's bugging me.

THIRTEEN

The apple pie is placed in front of me served with a generous scoop of chocolate ice cream *and* covered in rainbow sprinkles. It's my absolute favorite dessert, and my go-to comfort food whenever I'm feeling down.

Rainbow sprinkles can easily be the solution to world peace. Sprinkle it on everything, and the world will be a brighter place. At least, that's what I thought when I was a kid.

Andy is standing on his tiptoes, peering over the countertop. Impatiently, he jumps up and down, forgetting to use his manners while forcing me to pull out the discipline card. He listens to my warning. After all, there are two scoops of ice cream on the line here.

Placing the bowl into his hands, my mom takes him to the sitting room and settles him in, returning moments later.

"So, honey, tell me what's been happening with you." Covering the pie dish, my mom moves it toward the side, leaning forward. She rests her elbows on the marble countertop and awaits my response.

I shove a mouthful of pie into my mouth, closing my eyes and letting out a satisfied moan. She smiles and waits for me to finish, using a spare spoon to scoop a small amount of ice cream from my bowl.

"Not much. I'm styling a few celebrities for that red-carpet event," I mention with a mouthful of food. "Oh, and Andy peed in the toilet for the first time."

"What? My baby peed in the big-boy toilet?" She leaves in a hurry, leaving me mid-conversation.

I use the time wisely, digging into this pie like it's my last meal on earth. My mom is *the* best cook ever. Not being biased, but if all women in America had a pie bake-off, she'd win in a heartbeat. With that in mind and knowing Lex will be here any minute, I pull the pie dish close to me and serve myself another slice. The selfish jerk will eat the whole plate if he sees it.

My mom casually walks back into the kitchen with a proud smile. Positioning herself as before, she gloats about Andy's achievement. "Oh, my little baby is becoming a big boy."

"Mom, don't get too excited. It happened only *once*. The ten times after that, he peed on the living room rug."

"Adriana, that happened with your brother as well. Took him weeks to gain confidence. He was peeing any place he could, all except the toilet."

"Gross. What about me?"

"My angel?" She laughs. "You toilet-trained yourself at two, no intervention from Dad and me."

I know I totally rocked, and just as I think that Lex and Charlie walk through the back door. Charlie wraps her arms around my waist, squeezing me into a tight hug, then walks over to my mom and kisses her hello. Charlie's stepmom, Debbie, is in town, offering to sit for her kids leaving them childfree for tonight.

Knowing Andy is here, Charlie goes in search of him, leaving us in the kitchen.

Lex pulls a stool beside me, almost knocking me over. Like a hungry wolf, he spots the pie, not even saying hello before he gets his dirty mitts on it. I scold him for being an immature ass, but he is too busy shoveling the pie in his mouth even to care.

Charlie strolls back in and takes a seat beside Lex. "Are you curious about what Eric has planned?"

My mom is quick to smack Lex's hand as he serves himself another slice. I complain I have none left to take home, arguing with Lex until my mom winks at me. That wink only means one thing—she has made another pie. My eyes quickly divert to the oven, and there, on the bottom tray, sits another dish. *Fucking score!*

"I'm only going to this because I don't trust Eric. He'll try to pull that male-stripper stunt like at your bachelorette party," Lex gripes.

"Nikki planned that. Not Eric." Charlie is quick to correct him. "Which reminds me, what's happening Saturday night? Are we on?"

Earlier this week, I got a call from a publicist wanting a few dresses for a red-carpet event. Of course, I was elated. It means exposure and a possible feature in a popular fashion magazine. In exchange for this, I was also offered VIP tickets to the afterparty. The hottest celebs will be there all glammed up, and when Eric caught wind of this, he was on my ass faster than a hemorrhoid. His words, not mine.

Charlie is over-the-top excited, surprising me as she rarely cares about anything these days but the girls. It doesn't take me long to figure out that the excitement derives from a certain Mr. Timberlake attending the event. That opened up Lex attending as well. I swear he has the biggest jealous streak, it's downright obsessive. He's all up in Charlie's ass about it, no surprises there, prompting me to ask for extra tickets.

"Yeah, it's on. The driver will be at your place at eight. I'll come around six and get ready there?"

Charlie nods and talks about the dress she plans to wear, prompting Lex to complain that the dress is too low-cut or some bullshit like that.

"Charlie has great tits. Get over it, loser," I say, shooting him a fake smile.

It's time to leave, and because we're driving across town, Lex suggests we go together. I don't mind, considering I hate LA traffic, and being a passenger means my hands are free so I can text Julian. I say goodbye to Andy and head outside to be met with a shiny red sports car.

"What the hell is this?" I ask them.

"A car." Lex snickers.

"Yeah, I get that. I mean whose is it?"

"She's a stunner, isn't she?" Charlie squeals.

I roll my eyes at the two of them.

Charlie and Lex have a crazy obsession over cars. I'm fairly certain they have more than four in their garage, not including Charlie's bike. Lex starts to talk stats, boring the shit out of me. The car looks hot, that's the extent of my car knowledge.

Lex opens the door, and I climb in the back. It's awfully squishy, and the newly-cut leather makes awkward sounds as I settle myself in.

We drive off, and within minutes, I pull out my cell to text Julian. It's much better than listening to Lex and Charlie discuss what happened on *The Bachelor* last night.

Me: *What's my favorite man doing? I'm heading to Eric's. Wish me luck.*

I see the bubble appear on the screen, and I wait in excitement for his response.

Julian: *Favorite man? How many men are you hiding from me? I'm sure you'll enjoy it. It sounds interesting if I say so myself.*

Get the fuck out of town! He knows what Eric has planned. I type as fast as humanly possible. I'm *the* most impatient person in the world.

Me: *Are you jealous of the string of men waiting at my doorstep every night? Tell me please what Eric has planned? Pretty please with a naked cherry on top?*

The bubble appears again. I tap my foot impatiently until Lex asks me if I need to pee. It's what happens when you become a parent, I guess. I answer back at him annoyed, and he carries on with his conversation.

Julian: *You'll pay for that joke the next time I have you alone. Naked cherry? Please don't start. I can't even remember when I saw you naked last. Wait, too late. I'm rocking a huge boner now, thanks to you. As for Eric's, good luck, beautiful.*

Me: *Oh my.*

I quickly text back.

Me: *It was only yesterday so don't flash those pouty lips. Mmm, okay maybe I need to stop thinking about your lips and your huge boner. If I told you I had the equivalent to your boner, would that persuade you to tell me what's happening tonight?*

Bubble... bubble... oh, hurry up!

Julian: *How wet?*

Dammit! I'm hot and bothered, and it's highly inappropriate to be feeling this way in the back of my brother's car. Much like that delicious apple pie, I couldn't resist and had to take another bite.

Me: *The next time we're alone, you'll see for yourself. Now, stop being all hot & sexy and tell me what Eric has planned!*

There's barely a delay before a picture appears on my screen. I smile immediately, a photograph of his boner beneath his jeans bulging out accompanied with his text.

Julian: *Your fault. Have fun tonight.*

Frustrated, I throw my cell in my handbag but quickly pull it out again to stare at the picture. *Damn!* I squirm uncomfortably as the warm moisture builds between my thighs. Okay, time to think about something else because tonight will be a long night, and this feeling below has got to stop before I combust on the spot.

I stare out the window and watch the scenery, oblivious that Lex and Charlie have stopped talking.

"Why are you so quiet?" Lex quizzes.

I turn to face him. "None of your business."

Okay, so he is annoying the fuck out of me, and it isn't helping that I miss Julian. The only reason I'm not with him right now is because of the person driving this car. Calm down or you'll give the game away. Charlie, on the other hand, has tried to call me several times to discuss my so-called fling. I either avoid her calls or tell her I'll call her back, busy doing something with Andy. It's only a matter of time before she will probe again but at least is smart enough not to mention this in Lex's presence.

"Fuck, Adriana, what's with you lately?" he barks.

"As I said, Lex, none of your business."

He starts to mouth off, and I mentally shut down until Charlie yells at both of us.

"God, you two, shut up already!" She cranks up the stereo until Bon Jovi's 'It's My Life' blasts through the speakers, drowning out his incessant chatter.

We remain silent for the rest of the trip until we reach Eric's condo.

Eric answers the door dressed in a purple kaftan lined with gold trimming. He is also wearing matching pants and is barefoot. Stylish, I have to admit, but *so* not Eric's style.

"What the fuck, Eric?" I stare down at my attire. My jeans and loose-fitting tank seem highly inappropriate. Did I miss the memo?

"Welcome." He places his hands together and greets me by bowing. He has officially lost the plot. Tristan is by his side and leans in to kiss my cheek. I return the favor and pull him aside for a quick second.

"Has Eric lost his mind?"

"I think so. It isn't the first time, though." Tristan laughs.

"What the hell is happening tonight?"

Tristan moves aside, and I see tea-light candles scattered around the living room. The lights are off, only the glow of the flames illuminates the room. Soft music plays in the background, and large cushions are placed around the coffee table. My God, it's like a setting to an eighties' porn flick.

OMG, is he filming a porno?

"Thank you, friends, for gathering here tonight."

Eric is somber, and I rudely chuckle out loud. Lex is trying to keep a straight face but is failing miserably. He's probably glad it isn't a stripper. Kate has arrived and plunks herself next to Charlie. I know she's here this week and acknowledges her presence by smiling. She shakes her head at me and mouths the words, "Eric's gone barmy."

I've no idea what that means, immediately shrugging my shoulders in confusion. Tristan sits beside me as we wait in silence. I want to talk to him in private, and just on cue, Kate starts talking to Lex, distracting him.

"Julian knows about this?" I whisper into Tristan's ear.

He nods, then leans in, keeping an eye out. "He was here last night. Eric told him."

"What did he say?"

"Honestly? He hopes that maybe this is what you need."

"I don't understand, Tristan..."

Tristan pats my knee, not saying any more.

The bell rings, and Eric rushes to the door. A lady, perhaps late sixties, walks into the room carrying a small travel bag. She greets Eric and asks where she should set up. Her extremely long gray hair falls past her waist and is tucked behind her ears. She's dressed in a long velvet maroon gown, and my eyes are drawn immediately to the turquoise ring sitting on her middle finger. The color and stone are hypnotizing, and I find myself struggling to look away.

She sits on the floor and places her bag beside her. We all remain quiet as she encourages one of us to step forward. Kate is sitting in front of her in a flash. The lady closes her eyes and mumbles to herself, circling her hands in front of her.

Oh, hell no.

She's a clairvoyant.

Where the fuck is Eric's brain at?

I don't believe in this mumbo jumbo.

Recalling the first and only time I visited a psychic, she told me that Elijah and I would have three kids, all girls, and that Elijah would get a job in Seattle.

And look how that ended.

I want to stand up and leave the room.

Does she speak to the dead?

Is that what Julian wants?

My pulse starts to race as the anger consumes me. Accidentally, I knock the table with my knee, startling everyone in the room. If she asks me to come forward, I'll tell her to fuck off. I'm not interested in hearing a money-making nobody tell me what my future entails, especially if it doesn't include Julian.

Kate eagerly awaits her future to be told, and much like me, Lex is annoyed at Eric for wasting our time.

I lean over to Lex and whisper in his ear. "Good luck, you know what Charlie's like with all this shit."

"I know. That's what I'm worried about," he says, barely above a whisper.

The lady, whose name is Clarice, begins to speak to Kate. "I see a lot of traveling in your future."

"Oh," Kate coos.

"You travel for work," Lex states the obvious.

Kate is quick to hush him.

"No. These places I see, they are exotic. At first, you're uncomfortable, but you are drawn to these places."

Kate's mouth widens into a smile, accompanied by an over-joyous Eric happy clapping in silence.

Clarice frowns, and Kate's smile dissipates. "I see a man. He is tall, dark, and is very reserved."

"American?" Kate asks.

"I see a strong ethnic background. Beware of him. He will abandon you and burden you for a lifetime."

"What the fuck?" I say out loud.

"Oh, blimey," Kate notes in dark amusement.

Charlie's eyes are wide with fear. "Your dark angel."

"Her what?"

Eric warns me to keep quiet. I mouth 'sorry' to him, but he has already focused his attention back on Clarice.

Clarice continues to talk about Kate's family, mentioning a few things that seem to excite Kate. After another ten minutes, Kate is done, and Charlie stands up to replace her.

"Don't think you're getting that shit done," Lex threatens her.

"Whatever. You'll be thanking me later." Charlie face-palms Lex and takes a seat in front of Clarice.

From past knowledge, I know that Charlie's mother is a believer in all this clairvoyant and mind-reading stuff. Though, in my opinion, I think it did more harm than good.

Charlie's mom would constantly tell her Lex was no good for her. As much as Charlie is strong-willed, it did affect her ability to forgive Lex for abandoning her.

"I see a man who worships you—" Clarice is interrupted by Lex.

"No shit."

Clarice shoots Lex an annoyed glance. "You're very passionate about helping others. I see your line of work moving toward that."

Charlie looks at Eric. They seem to have an understanding, but it's nothing new, really. I mean it's easy to generalize, and you can interpret it however you want.

"You have had a troubled past. I see a man who means a lot to you. He helped you in many ways."

Oh shit. Lex's palm that was resting on the coffee table clenches into a ball, his knuckles stark white. I don't want to look at him, but the grinding of his teeth is enough of an indication that he's angry as hell.

Clarice has to be referring to Julian. Okay, what was that you just told yourself about generalizing?

"This man. He returns, but not to hurt you. You must understand that."

He was returning—he *has* returned.

So, it's a coincidence, right?

Why the fuck am I listening to this shit!

Charlie refuses to look at Lex, focusing entirely on Clarice. The room is dead quiet, Clarice closing her eyes and tight-lipped, followed by a shrill of laughter.

"You're constantly tired, but for a reason. Your energy is redirected to others. Perhaps children. I see this expanding. It's unexpected and causes issues within your marriage."

"You've got to be kidding me!" Lex exhales.

"Oh, hell no." Charlie shakes her head.

Lex is mumbling under his breath until Clarice tells him to be quiet. We sit in silence once again but this time for ages. Clarice opens her eyes and stares directly at Charlie. They hold each other's gaze for moments on end. "I feel a presence coming through."

The room suddenly gets darker, or perhaps that's my paranoia, and all eyes are fixated on Clarice.

"This person was close to you, but only for a short time. She checks on you often when you need it most." Clarice talks about inner peace within ourselves and forgiving our past decisions that continue to burden us.

Charlie is trying her best to contain her emotions. I move and sit by her side, placing my arm around her. Tears fall down her cheeks, but she doesn't sob nor does she wipe them with her hand. Charlie's grandmother, who I assume is the person coming through, speaks through Clarice and says things that Charlie acknowledges are of truth.

Her turn is over, and Lex softens up, scooping a distraught Charlie into his arms.

Seriously, who does this lady think she is? I move toward Tristan on the couch as she bows her head. She starts to talk out loud, and I don't realize it's directed to me.

"There's someone else coming through... his presence is strong." She motions for me to sit, and I have no idea why I do. My body moves of its own accord. Her stare is so deep and penetrating, it intimidates me.

I'm terrified.

What does she mean 'his' presence is coming through?

Is it Elijah?

"I see a painting of apples. The apples are bright red, and the rest of the painting is black and white."

I take a deep breath, the nausea creeping in. Like the painting he gave me when he proposed. Okay, seriously, it could be a coincidence... but the apples. *The apple picking.* Julian has gone apple-picking with me. Had he seen that?

"I see blue eyes and a child. He talks to this child. The child understands him."

My eyes dart to Lex in panic. Did Andy hear Elijah's voice? Why doesn't he talk to me? Why don't I hear his voice? Charlie pulls away from Lex, motioning for him to sit beside me. He does, and grabs my hand, lacing his fingers into mine. I look up at him on the verge of tears.

"He tries to talk to you, but you don't listen," Clarice continues. "You're conflicted. You feel pain, but you also feel love."

A lump forms in my throat, panicking that the double life I'm living will be exposed, and Elijah will hurt and be disappointed by my behavior. My sweaty palms sit inside Lex's, but he doesn't seem to care, squeezing them tighter, reassuring me everything will be okay.

"You're confused, and the intensity is something you've never experienced."

Lex stares at me, confused.

"He is a flame, and you are drawn to him."

Tristan is wide-eyed and watching Lex's expression. Eric's mouth has dropped. Charlie is watching me curiously as her tears have subsided. My heart is racing a million miles a minute, a panic attack imminent.

"What does that mean?" I ask in desperation.

"It means there's always a calm before the storm. Right now, you're experiencing the calm." She must sense the storm is sitting in this very room, right beside me.

I swallow the lump in my throat which continues to linger, my chest rising and falling heavily as my breaths are few and shallow. I know he sits beside me, but I ask the burning question anyway. "Will it end well?"

"Let your heart decide. There's room to love again. This man, he is trying to tell you that."

There are voices in the background, yet I hear nothing. Lost in a whirlwind of emotions, I find my strength disabled, and my weakness overtaking. The feeling is familiar, and it's all part of that grieving process which still haunts me. The only thing is—being with Julian distracts me. It's almost like he protects me, but here comes Elijah, talking to me through a psychic, begging me to listen to him.

And part of me knows I'm not listening because I am scared he will tell me that Julian is a big mistake.

How dare I replace him.

I'm so lost in my thoughts, and before I know it, Clarice has left the apartment, and I've missed Eric's turn. I am sure he will re-tell the story a million times, so I make an excuse about being tired so we can leave.

In the car, we all stay quiet.

The night has set, and darkness has fallen on us.

Charlie turns around to look at me. "You okay, Adriana?"

"Yeah," I croak.

Charlie glances at Lex, then turns to face me. "You know if there's someone that you, um... are seeing... you shouldn't be afraid to tell us."

I exhale. "Sure."

Her face tells me she's hurt, and I'd be too if someone brushed me off like that. We've been best friends for such a long time, and I hate hiding this from her. But I have no choice.

"So, anyway, you want to stop at the drugstore now to pick up your bulk lot of condoms?" Charlie asks Lex.

"You don't believe that bullshit, do you?" Lex

complains, shaking his head, disagreeing. "No old lady is going to predict and rule my sex life."

"Do you want to have another baby right now?"

"No. We'll just continue doing what we do," he states confidently. "C'mon, Charlotte, I can't wear that shit."

Am I seriously hearing this? I feel I have no choice but to intervene. "Oh my God, please shut up! Lex, get over it. It's just a fucking condom."

He lets out a loud groan. "It feels disgusting, okay? No man wants their dick to be covered in plastic while fucking their wife."

"So romantic," Charlie responds in a sarcastic tone.

"Surely, when you're seeing someone new, it's okay?" I ask, my eyes widening when I realize I've said that out loud instead of inside my head.

"Why the question? It's not like you're a virgin, Adriana. Jesus, I can't believe we're having this conversation," Lex mumbles.

"No, but I ain't no town bike, either."

Charlie erupts into laugher much to Lex's annoyance. She takes a while to compose herself, and I can see she is struggling to keep a straight face. Grabbing her hair into her fist, she twists it around and arranges it in a bun. It's quite warm in the car, and like she can read my mind, she opens the window to let in the fresh air.

Why was I asking for an opinion from my brother? First of all, the light bulb has switched on in my brain, and I realize that Julian and I don't use them. I haven't been blessed in the fertility area, so I'm not worried about falling pregnant. It's that whole ex-lovers can of worms bullshit.

"We're all adults here, though some may not act like it," Charlie says, glimpsing at Lex. "What are you worried about, Adriana? Getting back into the game and what's the norm?"

"Well, take you, for example, since we're all adults and can talk about this in a calm manner." I wait for the bomb to explode, but he is ticking away in his seat, hands gripping tightly onto the steering wheel. "No surprises, Lex isn't your first, and there were others in between. Did you always use them when you slept with someone new?"

"You've got to be kidding me, Adriana. Charlotte doesn't have a past. End of fucking story," he snarls.

I swear I feel the car swerve.

"Oh, get over yourself, will you? So?"

Charlie isn't bothered by Lex as much as I thought she'd be. "I think it's common sense to use one if you don't know their history and if you don't want to fall pregnant."

"Yeah, I know that, but did *you* always use one?"

She rubs the crook of her neck nervously. "I can't remember."

"What do you mean you can't remember?" Lex shouts.

"Hey, don't yell at me, manwhore. There isn't enough time in a day to list off all your skanks," Charlie bites back.

"So, you're telling me other men have been inside you without a condom?"

I may have stirred the pot slightly. And when I say slightly, I have the biggest ladle known to mankind in my hands, and I'm stirring faster than a cyclone.

"You're riling yourself up over things which can't be changed," she warns him.

"You aren't answering my question," he grits.

"Oh fine, only one person. There I said it. Now move on because seriously, don't even start on me, or I'll bring up your past, and I swear, Alexander Matthew Edwards, you make Hugh Hefner look like a prude."

I sink into the seat. *Only one.* No surprises to who that was, an ex-fiancé comes to mind. Am I stupid or what? I didn't even ask Julian about the other women he's been with, and the fact that he is ridiculously good-looking means he probably isn't far off, if not on par, with manwhore Lex. I really need a distraction. Tonight has thrown me a curveball, and the mental anguish is just too much.

"So what kinda bad things has Lex done? Don't worry, I'm a big girl and can handle my brother's sordid past."

He is quiet and extremely pissed off at both of us. God, what an ass. I don't know how Charlie puts up with him.

"Let's see, apart from the obvious threesomes, to sex with random strangers across the world. Oh wait, and the infamous gangbang of 2007—"

"Oh my God, *Lex*! Are you kidding me?" Stunned, my mouth widens in shock.

"What? Where on earth did you hear that from?" Guilty as charged, the tone of his voice softens.

"A reliable source, so don't you dare deny it," Charlie huffs.

He is tight-lipped. *Busted!*

"C'mon, how many were there?" I pry, placing him under pressure.

"This conversation is past its expiration date," he says flatly, making a sharp turn as we drive onto my parents' street. "And Rocky is dead fucking meat."

"See, I knew it," Charlie brags. "Adriana, you may want to leave before I have a word with manwhore over here."

I say my goodbyes and quickly exit the car.

Lex is toast.

FOURTEEN

Lex's car skids away fast, leaving me alone in front of my parents' house.
    I honestly don't know why he got so riled up about Charlie and her past. He's the manwhore. A manwhore who participated in gangbangs. I'm not entirely sure what a gangbang entails, not being a huge fan of porn, but Eric is your walking encyclopedia for all things sex-related should I require more information. Gross but hilarious at the same time.

    My mom is sitting on the couch with a cup of tea when I walk in. My parents' living room is cozy and warm. It isn't the house we grew up in, but they make it feel like home. The tones are all neutral with a splash of color on the cushions. The mantel holds all the frames from our childhood and newer additions of the grandkids. My mom is obsessed with lamps—there's one in almost every room in this house including one made of seashells my dad absolutely despises.

    She pats the couch, and I take a seat beside her, resting my head on her shoulder. I feel lost and unsure of myself. Tonight's events are plaguing me, the thought of him watching me. That he is talking to Andy and most importantly, that he's trying to talk to me. I don't understand what she means about me not listening. I'm not hearing any voices, and I don't see any unusual signs.

"Mom, can I ask you a question?"

"Of course, honey." She places her tea carefully on the coffee table.

"When is too soon to start seeing someone else?"

She looks at me and smiles. "Are you seeing someone?"

"It's just a question," I mumble quietly.

"Baby girl, I know you better than anyone else. I can see you're happy, Adriana. Someone is making you smile, and as much as you'll hate me for saying this, you've also put on some weight. You look healthy and have a beautiful glow."

"On my boobs?" I ask in hope.

"Yes, they do look fuller." She laughs.

I laugh along with her, then let out a sigh, snuggling into her side.

"Honey, please don't be afraid to talk to me."

"I'm not, Mom, it's just complicated."

"It always is. Whoever is making you smile like this, please say thank you from me."

"I will do that." I smile. "Mom, can you promise me something?"

"What, honey?"

"Just promise me if you hear anything about this from anyone else, you hear me out first?"

She pulls me in closer and embraces me tightly. "I'm assuming your brother is the problem here."

"Yes."

"Adriana, Lex will always be protective over you. He and Elijah had a special bond. Just don't forget to give him a break, too."

"Mom, Lex won't understand."

"What makes you so sure of that?"

"One day we'll revisit this conversation, and you'll know why. It's late now." I stand and stretch my arms, ready to carry Andy into the car.

"I love you, honey, no matter what you choose in life."

"I know, Mom, and I love you, too."

I find Andy fast asleep on my parents' bed. He is curled up into a ball hugging his koala bear I got him from Australia. I watch him for a few moments, his eyes fluttering every so often, his tiny breaths making small sounds. He is muttering something very softly about white feathers and angels. *OMG, is this a sign?* I lean forward to carry him into my arms, and the moment I have my grip on him, he silences. I move my face toward his and inhale his scent —*my baby*.

I never would've dreamed or even asked for this life, but Andy makes every second worth living. I can't imagine my life without him, he is truly a blessing from above, and I have no regrets of persuading Elijah to do IVF when he tried to convince me it wasn't the right time.

I say goodbye to my mom and head home with a sleepy Andy talking to himself in the back seat.

It's very late, and I can't fall asleep. Tonight was overwhelming, and as much as I said I don't believe all that fortune-telling shit, it got to me more than I thought it would. I grab my cell and decide to text Julian. I'm not sure if I'll get a response, but I do ten minutes later.

Julian: *Why are you awake? I was just about to hop into the shower.*

Curiosity gets the better of me. It's late, has he been out? He didn't say anything to me when we spoke earlier. It occurs to me that he rarely tells me what he's doing unless, of course, I ask. We live separate lives, and the only thing we do together is have sex. Perhaps that's my fault, the desire possessing me in a way that is new territory for me. He's equally as demanding, unable to resist touching me whenever we're within arms' reach of each other.
Can it be that it's just sex for him?
I'm a plaything to occupy his time while he recovers?
I send him a quick text.

Me: *Why are you about to hop into the shower? It's 3am.*

There's no bubble, and I wait impatiently. If possible, I'm even more alert than before. My mind is conjuring up all these possibilities including the fact that maybe Julian isn't alone.

Julian: *I just came back from a friend's book launch in Malibu. Great party.*

The animosity starts to build, my words blurting out onto the screen before I even re-read them.

Me: *Party? As in girls?*

I throw my cell to the side momentarily to calm myself

down. Crossing my arms, I stare at the wall like it's my enemy. The curiosity of his response gets the better of me.

Julian: *Yes there were girls there. There are girls everywhere, Adriana.*

I don't respond, and I'm pissed he went to a party where, no doubt, girls will have thrown themselves at him. The vibration of my cell startles me, and I see his name along with the words FaceTime appearing on my screen. Great, I have to actually see him meaning I can't show how annoyed I am.

"Hi." I plaster a fake smile on my face.

"So, walk me through this, Adriana, because I do not understand what I've done wrong..."

I sigh. Do I tell him the truth? "I don't like it when you're with other girls."

He screws up his mouth and runs his hands through his hair. "There's always going to be other women around, just like there is always going to be other men around you."

"Yes, but I'm not super-hot like you."

"You don't think so?" He laughs. "Do you remember at my book launch when I came over, and you were chatting with Barry?"

"Yes..."

"The three male bartenders were gawking at you. I actually had a word with them."

"What? Wait... you did that?"

"Yes."

"Well, I was dressed up. I don't always look like that," I try to downplay.

"Do you remember when we were getting surf lessons

at Bondi Beach? The instructor asked me for your number in case you were free."

"Oh, well, I was in a bikini. Go figure."

"No, Adriana, you're stunning. Everywhere we went, men would turn their heads to look at you. You may not realize it, but I sure as hell do."

"I'm sorry."

"Don't be sorry." He grins, shaking his head slightly. "You are gorgeous. I can't stop men from looking at you as long as they know who you belong to."

"Well, how would they know if we can't be seen in public together?"

"Again, Adriana, you're calling the shots on this one, and I've told you numerous times, it'll come out eventually."

The decision to come out as a couple is too overwhelming. I don't know why, but I'm kind of hoping things will just work themselves out. There's a better chance of Eric turning straight than that happening.

"Were you really getting into the shower?"

A smile spreads across his face. "Yes. You don't believe me?"

"No, prove it."

His cell moves, and the screen has moved down his torso like a slow-motion video, and I'm fixated on his sculpted abs. What a fucking tease. I wait in anticipation for the main feature, licking my lips as the screen shows me the top of his pubic bone.

He quickly brings it up to his face. "You believe me now?"

"No, you just had your shirt off. Big deal," I brush it off, pushing him to show me the rest.

"Well, then, I better prove you wrong."

This time I watch with my hand rested on my thigh. He

doesn't waste time, moving the cell smack bam in perfect view of his beautiful dick as it stands hard, practically throbbing and calling out to me.

I almost drop my phone in shock.

"Cat got your tongue?" He laughs.

"Uh, more like cock got my tongue. That's unfair. You're parading around like that, and I'm not there." I sulk.

"Might have to take care of it myself, then."

"You're mean! Well, fine, maybe I'll need to take care of myself, too," I say, playing along with his game.

He walks over to the bed and positions his cell in front of him. His naked body is sprawled across the bed with his legs wide open. The moisture between my legs warns me I won't have to self-help myself for very long, the ache already starting to build between my thighs, traveling and branching out to every part of my body.

With his eyes closed, he strokes himself slowly, releasing soft moans as his pace increases.

Holy shit, this is unbelievably erotic.

And with that said, I position my cell exactly like his and show him that two can play at this game.

I don't know what it is about Julian. His raw sexual appetite pushes me beyond my sexual means. This situation right now is out of my comfort zone, yet, with him, my body screams for attention, and awkward and timid Adriana has officially flown the coop.

FIFTEEN

The drive up to Hazel's house is calming.

Andy fell asleep as soon as I turned the corner of our driveway. My mind is desperate for solitude. It's difficult being a single mother with an energetic two-year-old boy, and on top of that, I'm involved in a secret relationship, one that resulted in middle-of-the-night pleasuring sessions via FaceTime.

Even after last night's events, I don't feel any closer to making a decision. Several times, I've caught myself listening out for Elijah expecting him to speak to me just like the clairvoyant said. It isn't that simple, I guess, but unfortunately, the seed of guilt is growing, and it's taking me along with it.

I'm nervous having Andy and Julian together. It isn't the first time they've met, and Andy has talked a few times about Julian being Blaze's daddy. Of course, I bring Ash with us, happily lying in the back seat with Andy, head resting on his paws with his eyes closed.

We pull up to the house, and I take a few deep breaths. I give myself a moment before exiting the car, allowing Ash to run free. He is wagging his tail, happy to see his mother. I nudge Andy gently and whisper his name. He stirs slightly, then opens his eyes. He is dazed and confused but slowly works out that we're at Hazel's. I pick him up and carry him, walking along the pebbled path to the back of the house. As I turn the corner, the familiarity of all the old faces comforts me, and my fears subside.

Hazel is the first to greet me, immediately taking Andy into her arms. I wipe the hair away from his forehead and kiss him gently. She rocks him back and forth singing his favorite song as he sticks his thumb into his mouth sucking on it for comfort.

"Honey child, look at you. Damn!"

The clicks of the over-the-top platforms move toward us, and Penny is holding my arms out, inspecting my outfit with a nodding approval. "Girl, if I had a body like yours, I'd tell my man to watch out." She raises her eyebrow at Julian and then swats her hand at him in a friendly gesture.

My eyes are drawn to him as he stands against the wall, dressed in a denim button-down shirt folded midway up his arms, showing off his glorious forearms. His light tan dress shorts complement his shirt, and lastly, my eyes scroll down to his footwear, *Chucks*. Dear God, he's a walking runway model. I quickly move my eyes back up to his face, his perfect grin and dancing eyes are watching me in amusement. It may have been my deprived body, but I swear he licks his lips to tease me, biting his bottom lip as I continue to be rendered speechless.

He knows he has my attention—my knees threaten to buckle under his gaze.

"He is very aware of how hot and sexy his girlfriend is, and that she doesn't realize that men actually turn around to look at her."

A shy grin escapes me, my cheeks flushing at the sentiment. *Did he just say girlfriend?*

Penny is fanning herself in her usual flamboyant way. "Mmm... damn! Why can't a man say that about me?"

Hazel offers to take Andy inside for some milk, allowing us to have some private time. As soon as they enter the house, my body moves toward Julian. He places his hands on my cheekbones, kissing me deeply. Even with Penny watching, I find myself melting into him, my hands trying ridiculously hard to behave themselves.

"I miss you," he says with his lips brushing against mine.

"You mean you miss your girlfriend?"

He steps back with his palm cupped into my cheek. "I hate that word, but socially, yes, you are."

"Like OMG," I brag. "I got myself a boyfriend."

Penny is laughing until she realizes her wig has shifted, and in a blind panic, she is busily arranging it so it's back into position. This sight alone causes us to erupt into laughter. I rest my hand on Julian's chest trying to compose myself and also as an excuse to touch him again.

It's refreshing to be open with our friends. Penny has known we're seeing each other for a while. She isn't one to judge, and knowing our history, she embraces our relationship with open arms. Julian and Penny are great friends, and unlike others, she understands him and got to know the real Julian much like I did. He never treats Penny any less than she deserves. They resumed bingo night with Eric in tow, and Julian always speaks highly of their friendship. On a few occasions, he mentions writing a few pieces for an LGBTQ website, a topic he is extremely passionate about.

Hazel is also happy to see us together, giving much-needed advice to both of us on several occasions. Having lost her husband, I rely on her wisdom to help me overcome the guilt of being with Julian. I have to admit she is biased—Julian is like a son to her. She admits that having him around gives her peace—he has so many qualities like her son, and because of that, she has grown to love him like her own. How can you not love him? He is perfect.

"You understand we can't be so open with Andy, right?" I quickly remind him.

"Of course. We talked about this. One step at a time. I can keep my hands off you."

"Wait, you know how to do that?" Shocked, I withhold a smile and put on my poker face.

"You got me there." He wraps his arm around my waist, pulling my body in flush with his. "Two minutes, down by that bush, it's all I need."

I swat his arm. "Two minutes now? It's getting shorter and shorter."

"Like you can talk. One minute and fifteen seconds," he teases.

"You time me?"

He appears to be amused as the corner of his lips rise, flashing his beautiful teeth.

"Oh, that's nothing, honey. Once, I only looked at a guy's schlong, and I jizzed right on the spot," Penny admits.

"Wow!" I exclaim. "How big was it?"

"Okay, ladies. I'm going inside to fetch Andy. This conversation is all yours." Julian has left us, happy to walk away and avoid Penny's wild stories. They make Eric look like an amateur.

Penny and I sit on the wicker chairs as we both stare into the valley. It's a beautiful day, only a few scattered clouds in the sky. Hazel's house is located a fair distance away from the city, enough that the hazy smog has disappeared, and only beautiful nature surrounds you.

"There's something about this place that calms me, you know? I don't know what it is, but just when I think my life isn't worth living, this place reminds me how fortunate I am," Penny says wistfully.

I sigh dreamily. "Maybe it is not the place, it's the people."

She nods. "Honey child, you wanna talk about it?"

Penny is easy to talk to, non-judgmental and wise. She has led a rough life, one that has beaten her down in unthinkable ways, but if you know her, you'll know she is made of steel.

"Sometimes I feel like I'm living a double life. Actually, a triple life. Being a single mother is a lot. I mean, I'm so lucky to have my family and friends who help me out so much."

"Anytime you need us, we're here."

"I know." I pat Penny's arm. "And then there's Lex and Charlie. I love my brother. He has always had my back, sacrificed so much for me. And this is how I'm repaying him?"

"You can't always control who you love. God knows I can't."

"I feel guilty all the time, and the only time it subsides is when I'm intimate with Julian, and my body is possessed."

"Have you told him this?"

I shake my head. "It will come across all wrong. I can't think straight when I'm with him. He does things to me, Penny, things I've never experienced before, and it scares me."

"But in a good way?" she asks.

"In a great way."

"So, don't fight it. You've got a man who makes your toes

curl to the point you can't function without him. God only knows you deserve someone like him."

"But I feel so guilty that... oh, never mind." I can't even be honest with myself, let alone with Penny.

Andy comes barreling out of the house pulling Julian along with him. Tugging on my arm, he begs for my attention. "Mama! Blaze's daddy wants to go visit the pond. Please, can we go?"

"Julian can take you, and I'll meet you down there."

Julian happily agrees and follows Andy. I watch them walk away, Julian holding Andy's hand as they make their way down the hill toward the small pond. Blaze and Ash are excited to be in each other's company, chasing their tails in endless circles.

Penny poses a question. "What do you want, girl? You want a father for Andy?"

"He has one, Penny. He just isn't here. *I want Julian.*"

"So, have him. He adores you. You gotta see that."

"But look at him. He can have any woman he wants, why me?"

"So, let me get this straight. A beautiful man worships the ground you walk on, fucks you to oblivion, and you have to question why. Have you looked in the mirror lately?"

"It's hard to feel secure when the one man you loved gave up on you," I mumble.

We remain quiet, Penny fiddling with her hoop earrings as we both watch them down by the pond.

"He cares deeply for you. I mean, every time he talks about you—"

"Julian talks about me?"

"All the time," she reaffirms.

"What does he say?"

"Just this and that."

"Hey, what about girl code? C'mon, tell me." I try to persuade the information out of her.

"I promised I wouldn't tell, but let's just say you complete him." She smiles.

"I complete him?"

She nods. I stare out into the pond, watching Julian sit beside Andy as they throw bread at the ducks. I excuse myself from Penny and make my way down to spend some time with them. My footsteps are faint, and I stop not too far behind and listen to their conversation.

"That big duck's name is Fatty, and that's his daddy over there."

Julian chuckles, allowing Andy to continue talking.

"Do you know my daddy works in heaven?"

"I do know that. Heaven is a very special place. I have a friend who works there, too."

"Do you think your friend has seen my daddy?"

"Maybe. It's a very big place."

Andy turns his head to face Julian. "Have you seen my daddy?"

"A very long time ago. He looks just like you, kid." Julian ruffles Andy's hair.

"Daddy gone makes Mama cry. I don't like Mama crying."

A lump forms in my throat. Andy had seen me cry several times. I never realized how my emotions impact him thinking that because he's young, he won't understand.

"It's okay for your mama to cry. She just needs extra special hugs."

"I like giving hugs. Uncle Lex always hugs Mama when she cries."

I make a small sound causing both of them to turn around. Julian smiles reassuringly as I sit on the other side of Andy. Andy begins to talk about the ducks telling us the story about the family. Jesus, my kid can talk for hours. Julian doesn't mind, though, asking questions Andy loves to answer.

"Mama, can I ask Hazel for some chocolate chip cookies?"

I nod, and without a goodbye, he runs back up the hill. I watch him until he is safely in Hazel's arms again.

"He likes to talk," Julian says.

"Much like me?"

"Like mother, like son."

The ducklings are swimming behind their mother, and I watch in merriment as they nibble on the leftover bread floating on the water. "It's beautiful here."

"You're beautiful here," he says.

I rest my head on his shoulder. Underneath our legs, he entwines his fingers into mine.

"You're really great with Andy."

"You've done a great job raising him, Adriana."

"It's hard. I won't be in the running for Mother of the Year. I'm just doing the best I can."

"It's not supposed to be easy. You know if you ever need help, you just need to ask," he offers.

"I need you."

I feel him squeeze my hands. "We can't keep hiding this if that's what you want."

It's complicated, and his question warrants an answer. "I know that. It's just... you don't understand Lex like I do. He is my brother."

It's instant and takes me back as he pulls his hand away leaving me cold.

"I'm not giving you an ultimatum. I'm *not* that kind of guy. But you need to think about what it is you want because we can't hide this forever. What if Andy picks up on it, huh?" The arctic tone in his voice stuns me only because there's so much truth behind it. Andy tells Lex everything.

"I know. Stop pressuring me, okay?" I stand up and wipe my hands on my skirt. "There's no way in hell this will go down well with Lex. I need time to prepare myself. And I have to think about Andy. He adores Lex. I don't want my decisions to negatively impact him."

He follows my actions, standing up in a huff. His face contorts into rage. "How about your brother sees you're happy and for once stops acting like a selfish prick and allows you to live your life?"

I'm floored by his comment. He doesn't understand Lex like I do. After all, Lex is my flesh and blood.

"This is getting us nowhere," I sulk.

"You're right, it isn't."

He doesn't reach for me, and together we stand apart allowing this argument to cool off. Eventually, he drags me back to him and embraces me. I start crying, frustrated with this ongoing wall between us.

I never want Julian to let go of me, and he doesn't, even when Andy runs toward us.

"Mama, is Jay hugging you because you crying?"

I let out a small laugh at Andy unable to pronounce Julian's name. "His name is Julian, Andy."

"No, Mama, he said his name is Jay."

I look toward Julian, and it clicks why he said that. He doesn't want Andy to use the name Julian in front of anyone. Even though he's ready for us to come out, is he just as terrified as I am?

I lift Andy so he is between us. "Don't cry, Mama. Jay can make you happy."

I kiss his little hands and say it aloud. "Jay does make me happy. Very happy."

Andy squirms out of my embrace. "Okay, Mama. Jay, Hazel says we can take Blaze and Ash for a walk. Please?"

"Sure, buddy. You tell Hazel I said that's okay."

His face lights up with a smile, and before he runs off, he wraps his tiny arms around Julian's legs and hugs him tight. "You're a good daddy. Blaze loves you."

Julian beams, and then hugs Andy tightly in return. "Thank you, little man."

Andy has run off again to find Hazel. We slowly make our way back to the house and find Penny inside the kitchen frantically searching for hot sauce.

"Gee, Pens, you craving or something?"

"The only thing coming out of me is that leftover Taco Bell from last night."

I screw up my face. Penny is quick to raise her arms in frustration announcing that she's heading to the store. Picking up her keys from the table, she leans into my ear and says, "You can thank me later," before disappearing outside.

Julian pulls me toward the couch and makes me sit. He places his hand around my shoulder to close the gap between us, and follows with a deep and loving kiss. I find my hands moving toward his chest, latching onto his shirt. His tongue sweeps over mine as I moan into his mouth. His kisses range from slow to frantic, both of us desperate for more, but know we can't.

"You're killing me," he grunts.

"Uh, hello, you're killing me." I grab his hand and quickly shove it under my skirt sliding it into my panties. I'm fucking soaked. His eyes flare, and I see his body tense in delight.

"I need you tonight."

"I can't. I have that event I need to go to," I apologize.

He battles with my answer, his glance fierce and dominating. Julian is patient, yet at times he demands so much of me, and that patient side of him is overcome by jealousy and greed.

"I'm trying to be patient here. I need to be inside you every day, you understand. This has gone on long enough." The darkness in his eyes and tone of his voice alert me of his intentions. Holy fuck, every day, though? The reality of our life comes to a crashing realization when Andy's voice is on the verandah.

"Mama! Hazel is making popcorn and we gonna watch wah... wah hun... something bout spotty dogs, and there's lots of them and an evil lady who tries to steal them. Can I stay here tonight, Mama? Penny is staying, too!"

I walk into the kitchen where I hear Hazel humming along. "Are you sure he can stay? I mean, I know you said yes, but I feel guilty for burdening you. My mom is happy to take him."

"Sweetie, I've got his jammies in his drawer."

Andy has stayed over a few times already. He claimed the room that he said was his and now he has a drawer too. "I wouldn't normally go, but this event is a big deal."

"Now, you listen to me. You're a great mother. You've got family and friends who all adore Andy and just want to keep him forever much like myself." She winks. "I was thinking about taking him to the zoo tomorrow plus Miles' grandson wants to come."

"Henry will be here? Well, no twisting my arm."

I go back into the living room and sit down beside Andy. He's making Julian show him on his phone what a

Dalmatian is, and just like his mama raised him, along comes a thousand questions that follow.

I ask Andy again if he is sure he wants to sleep over, but he is distracted when Henry comes barreling through the door, and I become insignificant. I kiss him goodbye and am met with my face being pushed aside as he tells me he is busy and has to show Henry something. Hazel reassures me it will be fine, and Andy hasn't even noticed I'm still there, completely taken by a new set of toy cars Henry has brought over. I wave goodbye to Miles and Hazel, but not before I'm stopped by Penny.

"You go enjoy yourself with your man. Get that groove on, Stella!"

I laugh, giving her a tight hug.

The second we're out the door, Julian pulls me into his arms again, this time making me squeal.

"Hotel. Now," he demands.

"I can't. I've got to be at Charlie's in two hours to get ready."

"No isn't in my vocabulary when it comes to you spread out naked in front of me."

I wrap my arms around his neck. "Can I ask a question?"

"Is it about how many times I'm going to fuck you tonight?" He is deadly serious.

"Uh, no... but how many?"

"Get your ass in the car now. It's gonna get a hell of a workout tonight, lady."

I laugh then pause. Wait, my ass will get a workout as in anal? Oh, fuck! I fall into a panic at the thought. It's one thing to have a finger in there but a whole penis? Okay, seriously, I can handle this, it can't be that bad. Maybe even enjoyable. Oh, who am I kidding, I need major advice, and my bestie is totally off-limits. I can call Eric, but knowing him, he will get way too excited about it all.

Julian senses my trepidation as I squirm uncomfortably in the front seat. Quick to distract me, he places my hand firmly on his bulge. *It is rock hard.*

"Breathe, Adriana. You'll enjoy it."

SIXTEEN

The balcony door is wide open—a view of the ocean lies before me. The water looks crisp as the waves crash hard into the shore. The room is located on the tenth floor, well above the street noise and chaos beneath us on the boardwalk. It is your typical executive suite, modern and functional, not a single thing out of place.

The warm breeze engulfs me as I stand in front of the door, hands resting on the armchair facing outside. Julian's presence lingers behind me, grazing my backside at a slow pace. I wait for him to close the drapes, and when it doesn't happen, I suggest he do so.

"No," he responds firmly.

"No, you won't close the drapes?" I ask.

His hands curl around my hips, directing them into him as he pushes his groin against me.

"You won't let the world know about us, then let me have this, Adriana."

I'm still confused about what he's asking for. We're standing in the doorway to the balcony, and stupidly I am assuming that we'll fuck inside the room with the drapes shut.

"Let me make it nice and clear for you to avoid any confusion," he continues, moving closer to my ear. "I want to fuck you, right here, in broad daylight. I want everyone to see you belong to me."

It takes a moment to sink in, and the second my body registers his commands, that familiar rush down below builds, torturing me with pleasure.

"People can see us." The nerves are driving me to whisper.

"That's the plan."

My eyes divert to the sidewalk, and while we're quite high up, I can still make out the array of people walking down the street. My sensibility is pushed aside as his hands wander to the front of my jeans, careful to zip them down. In one swift move, they are around my ankles and pushed aside.

Although he is behind me, I'm quick to notice his shorts lay on top of my jeans, wearing only his boxers. Still only in my tank and panties, the touch of his fingers brush against my front, causing me to buckle into him. He catches me, applying pressure as a moan escapes my mouth loudly. Like every other time he has touched me, my body has taken control, blood pumping hard in my veins allowing the adrenaline of pleasure to consume me whole.

However, this time he ups the ante.

His hands make their way back up to my face, roughly sliding his index finger into my mouth, forcing me to suck. I do so, building up my saliva as my lips wrap around his finger sucking it with ease.

With his left hand, his palm glides across my backside, and in a quick fistful, he grabs my panties forcing them down to my ankles. I shuffle to free them, excited and impatient for his next move.

"Tell me I'm the first to be inside here." The low rumble escapes his throat as he applies pressure at the entrance.

I nod, but he is unsatisfied, his demands repeated. "Tell me out loud."

The pleasure and pain all roll into one, encouraging me to respond boldly, "Yes, Julian, you're the first to fuck me in the ass."

He stiffens, but it's short-lived. His grip tightens, almost hurting my small frame. I don't know what to expect and wish I had some time to prepare by studying porn or something. He takes control not allowing me any more time to think. Taking a deep breath, he continues to circle the entrance, smothering it with the moisture between my legs. The tip of his arousal toys my entrance excitedly, my body tensing in nerves, and as soon as he senses my tension, he rubs the small of my back and whispers for me to relax.

He doesn't enter quite yet, focusing on my swollen clit, rubbing it fast and steady. Every inch of my skin is covered in goosebumps, holding back the impending orgasm. I give him a signal, a slight push back to suggest I'm ready. With his hand firmly on my hip, he guides himself slowly into me. The pain ricochets, and a small cry escapes my mouth. Terrified, I'm on the verge of telling him to stop, worried that there's no chance in hell his gigantic dick will fit in my ass. It's impossible, right? It will tear me apart! And then worst yet, what if I needed to... *Oh my God, shut up! Shut up!*

"It'll hurt at first, but I promise you it'll feel good." He pushes a little further, my body continuing to tense. I take deep breaths, failing to relax. I grip his wrist, a sign to stop.

"You trust me?"

"Yes," I whimper.

"Then let me have all of you, Adriana."

He begs of me what I already want to give, and with that, I take control, easing myself back into him ignoring the deep, throbbing pain and allowing his whole cock to sit inside my ass. The moment I've taken him all in, a moan escapes followed by slow movements. He talks me through this experience, every thrust, every sensation, and I lose myself to his words, using them to enhance the torturous pleasure that he promises I'll experience. The pressure of his cock entering me whole consumes me, the ache of my clit begging to be touched.

He reads my body like it's his own, guiding his hands to my front, and with just one brush, I brace myself for the finishing line.

I want all of him, and I'm not afraid to tell him. "I want you inside me, everywhere on me."

His ragged breaths and rough handling demand I tell him where.

"I want you inside my mouth."

He moans.

"I want you inside my pussy."

He grunts.

"I want you inside my ass."

He growls forcing himself deeper, hammering his body against mine. We're equally as desperate for each other, ignorant of the loud echoes heard by the people below. He pleads with me to come with him, and I know I'm close, the ache in my belly rising at a fast pace, ready to let go when the sting of his palm smacking my ass speeds up the momentum, and I cry out loud, shocked at how much I enjoy the pain.

I beg him for more. Grabbing my ass into his hands, he squeezes tight and releases, slapping me hard again.

I yelp again at the sting, begging again.

This time, the slap of his hand echoes against my skin, and with only one eye open, I'm certain that people below have heard and stopped to find out where the commotion is coming from. Never have I felt sated and free at the same time, letting go of all my worries and losing myself completely to him.

Leaning forward, he bites into my shoulder and tells me he can't take it anymore.

It's all I need to hear, riding the orgasm as my walls contract, and he tells me he can feel it against his cock, and follows right behind me. His final thrust is hard and fierce, and I release a lengthy moan, collapsing into his arms as we both come down from the intense high of it all.

"Fuck," I huff, breathing unevenly.

He places his hands firmly on my hips, warning me he is pulling out. I wince at the twinge and threaten to collapse in exhaustion as he pulls himself all out.

A tissue box lies on the bedside table. He grabs a few and cleans us up. I don't ask any questions, yet he knows I'm mortified and embarrassed. Being such a gentleman, he reassures me it's nothing bad and guides us to the bed, both of us falling into a crumpled heap. That was intense, and just like he promised, it aroused me in more ways than I can ever imagine.

I snuggle into his side, burying my face into his skin. I run my tongue along his nipple, tasting his sweat.

"One minute, Adriana. I *must* be good."

I swat his arm. Cocky bastard knows he is. "Well, since you soon followed, I must be *real* good."

He stretches my arms above my head and lies on top

of me. Positioning his face directly above mine, his piercing stare melts away my concerns, my worries, and guilt.

"I mean what I said. I need to be inside you every day, Adriana," he tells me.

"I know."

He is talking to me not only with his words but with his eyes. They are showing me what I need to see, a part of him that he's been hiding. "I've never felt this way about anyone."

"Like what?" I ask.

"Complete."

There's that single word again, one word that holds so much meaning. "But why is it any different to Charlie?"

Oh, there I go again. Fuck you, brain!

His expression is bleak, and he falters. "I don't know. It just is, okay?"

"That's not an answer."

"I'm feeling very vulnerable here. I just fucked you, I'm lying here naked, and you want to talk about my ex-girlfriend?"

"Fiancée," I remind him.

He pulls himself off me, dragging the sheets to cover his body. "I don't get you. What does it matter anymore? I thought we were past this."

"I don't know. I just want to know why you think it's different?"

A sinister laugh follows. "You don't trust me, that's it?"

"Of course, I trust you," I holler in frustration. "I'm just all over the shop, Julian. I didn't tell you what happened last night."

The room is silent as he waits for me to continue. "The psychic basically said this was real... we are real."

"Of course, it's real. What did you think it was... *a fling?*" He appears to be offended.

"I don't know anything!" I yell at him. "I can't stop thinking about you... *all the time*. I'm jealous when you go out without me. I hate that girls throw themselves at you. I hate that I don't know what your life is like outside of our time together, and you never tell me where you're going, and again that you're with other women. I hate that everything in your life is temporary... house, car, and I don't know if you're sticking around." I let out a breath, and just when he is opening his mouth, I continue. "I hate that I feel guilty because sex with you is the best I've ever had! That makes me a whore and dirty."

He is lying on his back, staring straight at the ceiling.

"I hate that you hide this relationship and that you think when I'm with you, I'm doing it to be close to Charlie," he admits, still keeping his distance. "The only reason I don't tell you where I am is because I'm afraid of smothering you. Feeling independent and not tied down gives me a sense of control because honestly, Adriana, *we,* our future, rests in your hands."

I'm about to open my mouth when he cuts me off.

"And most importantly..." He lets out a final breath, almost as if the weight of the world rests on his shoulders and he's about to set it free. "I hate that you can't see I've fallen for you."

My heart is beating at record speed.

He has fallen for me?

I climb on top him, forcing him to connect with me, baring my body and soul. His eyes meet mine, and I see sadness, guilt, and anger all rolled into one stare. Yet still, I'm unable to turn away, drawn in like a magnetic force, the power of love bringing hope and pain at the same time.

"You scare me, Julian. I'm not supposed to find someone so soon. You don't understand the things you do to me."

"I do understand. You do the same to me. I'm not supposed to find someone so soon, let alone it be you. Out of all people... *you.*"

I angle my body forward, tracing my finger along his lips.

I've fallen for him too. I can no longer deny it.

"Do you know how fucked up this is?" he says in a decidedly odd tone.

"Jerry Springer fucked-up."

"Not that fucked up." He laughs.

I lean in and rub my nose along his, moving my way toward his lips. Our tongues entwine, gently and passionately, enough to show me how real this all is. His hands run down my back, combined with a gust of wind that sweeps through the room. I shiver uncontrollably, prompting him to wrap my body in his arms.

With my head resting against his chest, I finally decide. "I'm telling them tomorrow. You're right. It's gone on long enough, and if we both want to make this work, we need to be honest with everyone."

Julian doesn't say anything, continuing to play with my hair.

I raise my head slightly. "Are you worried?"

"That your brother will punch me in the face again?"

"He did that?"

Julian nods. "Look, Adriana, I can handle Lex."

"Lex is... well... Lex. He will stop at nothing to protect Charlie. I just want to warn you he may drag up the past."

I hate the fact that it will probably result in just that. Lex is ruthless, overprotective, and always gets his way.

"We all make mistakes, he's not exactly a saint either," he answers bitterly.

"What do you mean? What did he do?"

"It's all in the past, Adriana, where it should remain."

Frustrated, I blurt out the obvious. "He's a selfish bastard for not realizing that without you, Charlie and Ava would be long gone."

"It's a double-edged sword. It's taken me a very long time to see the good in the situation. You saw me at my worst."

I have, and I'm so proud of him for coming this far. Just like me, he has endured so much, and overcoming the death of someone you loved is the biggest hurdle one can accomplish. Charlie has experienced that, and deep down inside, I know she will be okay with this.

Looking toward the clock, I tell him I need to leave shortly.

"That's twenty minutes," he states. "If you're going to be around hot Hollywood actors tonight, I need you to be reminded that you belong to me."

"You don't have a jealous streak in you."

His smile widens but disappears instantly.

"Baby, I got a jealous streak, all right. You may not see it, but trust me, it's there." His hands trace my collarbone until they have found their way to the crook of my neck, and with a tight grip, he warns me. "I'm going to play dirty now. You will be sore, you'll feel my touch all over you every time you move. Don't ask questions, Adriana. I'm going to do what I please, right here, right now."

I don't ask a single question, and for the next hour, he fucks me so hard my body writhes in pain, the agony and pleasure take me to imaginable places, submissive to his demands.

I know I'm late to the party and covered in red marks, but I don't care.

He promised to make me sore.

He promised to be all over me.

I can't move a single muscle.

And I can't be any more content.

SEVENTEEN

"I'm sorry I am late!" Bolting through the doorway and completely out of breath, I rest my hands on my knees on the verge of collapsing to the floor. Seriously, I need to hit the gym to keep up with Julian's stamina.

Charlie stands in front of the mirror, dressed in a black silk robe with her hair and makeup done. Thank God she isn't dressed yet.

"Adriana, since when are you *ever* late? I called you ten times."

What's my excuse? I had the whole drive over here to think about something, but no, my head was daydreaming like a lovesick fool freshly fucked by my boyfriend. Oh, that sounded really nice in my head.

"Just got caught up, okay?" I pull my dress out of the garment bag. It's one of my newer creations, and one that I've worked on for months. The dress is tight-fitting and hugs my body sitting mid-thigh. My favorite part is the intricate lacing of the top layer covering from my collarbone down to my arms. The shade is electric crimson, much like my ass cheeks after a good slapping, and is sexy as hell.

I love how confident the dress makes me feel, or maybe it isn't the dress, rather the most drop-dead gorgeous man to walk this earth telling you that you *complete* him.

"Love the dress. That shade is gorgeous." Charlie runs her fingers along my arm, admiring the lace. "So, where were you?"

"I need to shower," I tell her.

"No time for a shower." She makes me sit down on the vanity stool and starts working on my hair.

I squirm uncomfortably. My ass is sore as are my thighs, my arms, and every part of me.

"You smell like sex," Charlie says flatly.

"What?" I yell out loud. "Well, so do you."

"Most likely. My husband gave me a good pounding, a much-needed one."

I cringe, screwing my face in discontent. "How many times do I have to tell you, I don't need that kind of information?"

"You said I smelled like sex. I'm just confirming your suspicions. Now back to you. C'mon, Adriana, why won't you tell me who it is?"

I remain silent as she styles my hair. Not giving her a response just yet, I wait until she is done. Giving her the nod of approval, I inch closer to the vanity and start working on my makeup.

"Are you being safe at least?" she questions me further.

I feel stupid for forgetting to bring it up. It's just, I get lost in the moment, and any rational decision flies so fast out the window with no hope of coming back.

"I've got it under control," I lie.

"Adriana, do you know who he has been with? I mean, these days guys are sleeping with anyone they can get their hands on."

Well, he's been with you, Charlie, I want to blurt out yet somehow my filter actually works and does not spit out the obvious.

"Thanks for the reassurance."

"Why won't you tell me?" She is standing there, hands on her hips.

"I will, just not now. Give me time, okay?"

"But you tell Eric?"

"I didn't tell Eric, he just happened to be there. Look, it's a really a long story, and I'm just drained."

She doesn't say a word, shaking her head in disapproval. Her long, black satin dress is hanging from the hook. Taking it off, she slips in on quickly, then proceeds to slip into her pumps. Walking over to the vanity, she searches for some jewelry, and when she finds what she wants, she puts it on. Without a word, she leaves the room.

Lex yells out to me that the limo has arrived. I glance at myself in the mirror, not bad at all, and grab my cell to take a selfie, immediately hitting send.

The limo ride is quiet. Lex is busily responding to emails while Charlie stares out the window. I don't want to draw attention either, so I take my cell out of my purse and find a text sitting on the screen.

Julian: *You're beautiful, Adriana. And mine.*

I smile at his words, responding quickly.

Me: *You're all over me. I didn't get a chance to take a shower and for the record, I can barely walk.*

The bubble is back. Lifting my head only slightly, I see

Charlie watching me bewildered. I pretend I don't notice, focusing my attention back onto Julian.

Julian: *I want you back here no later than 2am. That gives me plenty of time to make sure you can't walk.*

I accidentally laugh out loud, covering my mouth the moment I realize I've done so. Since I'm speechless, I send him a smiley face.

"Okay, I'll bite. What's with you two?" Lex asks, not even bothering to look our way as he continues to type. He's sitting between us dressed in a black Armani suit and crisp white shirt. He isn't wearing a tie, his shirt slightly unbuttoned. Women everywhere throw themselves at Lex. It's been like that his entire life, blessed with good genes and, unfortunately, a stubborn attitude to accompany it.

Neither one of us says a word, and thankfully, the limousine arrives at the event shortly after.

We hop out to be met with cameras flashing like a light show. Every paparazzi and his camera are desperately snapping away, hoping to cash in, and with any luck, a possible wardrobe malfunction.

Eric and Tristan are standing at the entrance, both looking smart and almost matching. I have to admit, Tristan is one good-looking guy. According to Eric, he needs a major wardrobe makeover and a few sessions at the gym. I only met him after Eric sunk his teeth into him, so I can't comment. One thing that never struck me before is the similarities between him and Julian. Of course, I know they are related, but I swear with a nicely fitted suit, you can really tell they are family.

We greet them hello, Tristan pulling me aside sensing the animosity between Charlie and me.

"What's going on with you and Charlie?"

"She knows I'm seeing someone and is annoyed I won't tell her who."

"Fair enough. You can't hide it forever, Adriana, and I know Julian well... he won't allow it for much longer."

"I know."

Inside the event, celebrities gather in groups as the DJ mixes fresh beats. The room is decorated in a modern theme of blacks and reds which gives it a sensual feel. The space is dimly lit, only the bar illuminates the room because that's where all the important stuff is held, including some much-needed alcohol.

Eric can't keep still, dragging Tristan around to introduce himself to actors. A few people come up to chat with Tristan since he has done a few acting gigs, and word is getting around Hollywood.

Lex and Charlie are busily chatting to some people I don't recognize. I hate being the third wheel or fifth wheel, in this case, making my way to the bar to drown my sorrows. Three martinis later, the party has livened up. I make my way to the dance floor to dance with Tristan. It doesn't last long, though, Eric claiming him and getting into a kissing frenzy in the middle of the dance floor. I turn around, and a familiar male is standing in front of me. I recognize him from one of those crime television shows on cable. He isn't too much taller than me, dirty blond hair with deep green eyes. He asks me if I want to dance. Sure, why not?

We have fun but maybe he's a little too touchy-feely, and just when I probably should've told him to back off a little, my cell vibrates. I excuse myself, much to his annoyance, and open the text message.

Right there on my screen is the picture Julian took of us lying in bed just before I left the hotel. I'm wrapped around his body with my face against his, both of us smiling into the camera. I knew at this moment, I don't want to be here or anywhere for that matter, *not without him.*

I make my way over to the table where Lex and Charlie stand. Both of them have shots in front of them, taking turns as they laugh. Lex drapes his arm around Charlie, pulling her in as they passionately kiss. He leans into her ear and whispers something to which she laughs. Watching them makes me realize who fucking cares if Julian is part of my life. They have each other, they are happy.

Lex slides over a shot, and I don't hesitate to drink it. He motions for a bartender to hit us up with another round. It's very rare to see my brother let loose, and judging by the way he's all over Charlie, he has had quite a bit to drink.

This party has run its course, and even with the extra shots coming my way, I'm no longer entertained by the Hollywood crowd. I take out my cell to see the picture again, but Lex swipes my phone off me.

"If you won't tell me who the hell you're seeing, I'm finding out for myself. " He doesn't have to search far, and like a slow-motion movie, I watch his face drop instantly, suddenly morphing into anger. His lips are pursed, the vein on his forehead practically jumping out to me and slapping me across the face. The look of pure rage meets me in the eye, and he growls, "Outside *now!*"

I continue to stand, not giving in to his stupid request until he grabs my arm forcefully and drags me through the crowd. I beg him to stop, his tight grip much like a Chinese burn. He doesn't even have the decency to ask people to move politely, rudely shoving me until we hit the exit sign. The second we're outside the side entrance, he lets go, and I catch myself just before I stumble to the ground.

"What the *fuck* is this?"

I rub my arm noticing the red marks on my skin. "Well, now you know."

It's a stare-down, and I refuse to back off. Charlie pummels through the doorway, barely able to walk after the copious amount of shots she's had. "What the hell is going on?"

Lex has not backed down, his glare is fierce, and his normally emerald green eyes are onyx black. The look of death. I cross my arms, refusing to allow him to think he can control my life.

"Why the fuck didn't you tell me?" he shouts at Charlie.

She looks my way, shrugging her shoulders. "Tell you what?"

"Like you don't know." He lets out a nasty laugh.

"I have no idea what you are—" Lex shoves the cell into Charlie's face, and it takes her a moment to register. With her eyes wide, she lifts them to meet mine. Does she understand now? Shocked and confused, she stutters trying to form a sentence.

"Adriana," she whispers.

"Cut the I-had-no-idea bullshit, Charlie!"

Oh crap, he only ever calls her Charlie when he sees red. How dare the dickhead take it out on her. I can't believe we're related, honestly.

"Don't you think if I knew it was Julian that I'd have said something to you?" she responds exasperated.

"Why would you? You're probably happy that he's back in the picture. Always loved him, right?"

Charlie is furious. "How fucking dare you say that about me."

I know Lex is drunk, which doesn't help the situation.

"So, let me guess, Adriana, he found you and swept you off your feet? Promised to respect Elijah, told you he was over Charlie." The anger and hate consume him, turning him ugly. I don't even dignify him with a response.

I have to stand my ground now. "I'll tell you what, Lex, you have no idea how hard it's been for me, and frankly, I don't give a goddamn *shit* what you think."

He follows with another hateful laugh. "So just fuck him and get it over with. I'll be ready and waiting when he starts his move on Charlie, which I'm sure she will gladly welcome."

I hear the slap of a palm.

Charlie has struck Lex on the face.

Holy fucking hell!

Lex grabs her forearm, his grip tight, but she doesn't complain.

"Let go of me." Her bark warns him to back the hell off.

He lets go, then follows by punching the brick wall, screaming in agony and frustration. Charlie walks over to me and hugs me tight.

"Let's go back to your place," she tells me.

Lex swiftly turns around, the blood pouring from his hand as his evil laugh echoes through the alleyway. "And so, it starts. You going to call Julian over so you can all hug it out?"

Charlie releases me and walks toward him. She lifts his hand to examine it, just a few minor scrapes and nothing serious and drops it immediately.

"I'm staying with Adriana tonight. Don't follow me. Don't call me," she says in an eerily calm voice. "I don't want to see or speak to you till you've calmed down, you imbecile."

"Charlotte, you can't fucking stay there. You're my fucking wife," he almost spits.

I'm too exhausted to say any more, Charlie looking just as defeated as I feel. She links her arm in mine, and we start to walk off until she stops a few moments later, turning around to face Lex one more time.

"I've never felt so disrespected in my life as I do right now. You practically called me a whore, Lex, and you know what the worst part is? I still fucking love you."

She turns back around, and I'm stunned by her words. *What on earth have I done?* This is entirely my fault. At what point did I think it will work itself out? The sorrow and shame accompany me as I walk hand in hand with my best friend down the dark alleyway. I know I have to warn Julian, terrified Lex will get to him, and God knows how psychotic my brother can be. With my free hand, I pull out my cell. Charlie understands what I'm doing, and she lets go of my arm. It's simple but straight to the point.

Me: *Cat's out of the bag.*

My cell immediately vibrates as Julian's name flashes on the screen. I pick it up, defeated and tired.

"I'm coming to get you."

"I'm fine. It's just been a long night."

"You can't be alone right now," he tells me.

I look over to Charlie, her smile reassures me. "I'm not. Charlie is staying with me tonight. I'll see you tomorrow, okay? I really need some time with my best friend."

I know he is smiling. I can tell by the softness in his voice. "I understand. I'll call you tomorrow."

He hangs up, and I place the cell back in my purse with a huge grin on my face despite the showdown happening only moments ago.

"That's Julian for you. A levelheaded, understanding man." Charlie softly laughs.

I nod, and just when we turn the corner, the loud echo of a glass smashing on the wall startles us.

No doubt my brother, the polar opposite of levelheaded, has something to do with it.

EIGHTEEN

Charlie sits on my sofa, sinking into the cushions as the weight of tonight's events finally hit her.

With her shoulders slumping, she throws her cell across the coffee table. It slides against the wood and stops as it hits a magazine. The momentary silence is welcoming until the cell dances across the table, the screen flashing as I see Lex's name appear again.

Tonight, I learned something new about my brother. Aside from being a possessive asshole, I saw an ugly side to him I've never seen before—his ability to hurt those he loves the most. His temper exceeded my expectations, and the last person I thought he'd lash out on was his own wife.

I place the cup of coffee beside the cell within Charlie's reach. She mouths a "thank you" as we both try to sober up. I've been waiting a while for this conversation, but now that it's going to happen, I have no idea what to say. What can I say? This is the man Charlie once saw herself spending the rest of her life with.

"Your brother is a dick," she says angrily.

"Your husband is a dick," I reiterate.

She lets out a long sigh and turns to face me, pulling her legs up against her chest cradling the steaming cup. "God, Adriana, why didn't you tell me?"

"Did you not see what happened back there? I was trying to protect you. I'm not going to fuck up your marriage by making you hide a secret from your husband."

"But, Adriana, this is huge. I mean... *argh*... so many questions, no idea where to start," she mumbles, then back to staring at the coffee table lost in thought.

There are so many questions—some that need answering and some that don't.

"Charlie... this is awkward," I tell her, breaking the silence between us. "I'm not stupid, you know. You guys were going to get married."

"Yes, we were," she says with a slight croak, fiddling with the band sitting on her wedding finger.

"Wait! Are you still in love with him?" I feel the bile rising in my throat. Fuck, where the hell did that come from? What an idiotic thing for you to ask. This is Charlie—she is married to your lunatic brother.

My mind is a complete and utter mess, and more than anything, I wish Julian were here to ease my rampant thoughts with his presence.

"Adriana, what's wrong with you? Honestly, you should not be allowed to drink." She shakes her head disapprovingly. "I love your dumbass big brother. Nothing, and I mean *nothing*, will ever change that. As for Julian, I love him as a person. I can't erase the past, plus he saved... I can't even begin to think..." Her eyes glaze over, and I quickly rub her knee to calm her down.

"Don't think about that, Charlie. He did save you. Julian is..." I can't complete my sentence, consumed by a warm feeling spreading all over my body, creeping up until it's spread across my face morphing into a wide cheesy grin.

Charlie is quick to notice. "How? When? Start from the beginning."

She props herself up, and I begin to tell her about the first time I attended the support meeting. I contemplate leaving out the part about harming myself, but if Charlie is to truly understand how Julian and I became close, she needs to know the entire story.

"Adriana," she chokes, her tone rattled by my admission. "Why didn't you come to us?"

"I was ashamed." I bow my head in disgust, reminiscing about the time I had hit my lowest point. To think of the damage it would've caused Andy is heartbreaking. "Julian was there, he saw how much of a dark hole I was in. He was equally in that hole with me, and he just got me, you know?"

"I understand. Julian has always been caring and has this nurturing side to him."

I nod. "We were friends foremost, and he encouraged me to face my fears. God knows I had plenty of them."

"Will you tell me about them?"

I take a drawn-out sip of my coffee, allowing the liquid to swim down my throat until it settles in the pit of my stomach.

"I missed Elijah so much, yet I was so angry at him for leaving us." Venting my frustration and anger, I struggle to continue as Charlie waits patiently. I barely find the courage but know it's time I finally let go of my demons. "Joining that support group allowed me to vent without any conviction or someone trying to fix it. Julian saw it all, but most importantly, he encouraged me to talk about Elijah in a positive way. The more I did that, the more it allowed me to move on."

"It makes sense. I feel like terrible for not helping you more," she admits.

"You couldn't have helped me if you tried." I place my palm over her hand. "Julian knew my pain, he was living it himself."

The cell starts to dance across the table once again. Charlie's quick to ignore it and carry on with our conversation. "Adriana, is that why you went to Sydney?"

"Yes," I confess.

"Okay, um... how serious is it?"

"I... uh..." I quietly fidget with the rim of the mug, running circles with my index finger. "Seriously, Charlie... *I think I*... never mind."

"You love him?" She is stunned, waiting on edge for confirmation.

"I don't know. He makes me feel so alive it scares me. I'm not used to it. Elijah was different. Sometimes, I feel so guilty for moving on, but if I think about leaving Julian, I just can't."

"Adriana, you were with Elijah since you were seventeen. Whether it's Julian or someone else, you would've felt guilty regardless. To me, these last few weeks have been a joy to see you this happy. I take my hat off to anyone who can put a smile back on your beautiful face and the light back in your eyes. I knew it was a guy, just never in a million years thought it would've been Julian. Excuse my language, but motherfucking shit, this is unbelievable!"

I laugh softly, looking for some comic relief. "God, this is so *Days of our Lives,* isn't it?"

"No." She smirks, almost spitting out her coffee. "More like *The Bold and the Beautiful.*"

We both chuckle reminiscing about Ridge and Brooke on *The Bold and the Beautiful*, counting the number of husbands Brooke had and how many times she married Ridge. Jesus Christ, now that was a soap opera.

"We talked about you and Lex, how we were going to come out. There never was a right time or place. God, Lex is going to be a nightmare, isn't he?"

Her cell vibrates as if on cue.

This time, Charlie grabs it in frustration. "Calling like a deranged lunatic does not fly with me."

There's silence, followed by Lex swearing profusely on the other end. Guttermouth! It's one of those you-better-wash-your-mouth-out-with-soap moments. He's digging a deeper hole for himself, that's for sure.

"Are you done carrying on? I'm staying at Adriana's tonight. You need to sober the fuck up before I get home tomorrow." She doesn't wait for a response, hanging up the call before he gets another word in.

Switching the cell off, she turns to face me. "Sorry, where were we?"

"About Lex being a nightmare," I remind her.

"Oh yeah, well, you know him. He'll get on his jealous high horse for a while, so don't expect to be double dating anytime soon."

That sums up Lex, all right. I don't expect them to be best friends, but surely, both of them can be civil enough if in the same room with each other.

What planet is my brain on? Pigs have a better chance of flying.

"Charlie, is this awkward for you?"

She shuffles closer to me, resting her head on my shoulder. "To be honest, a little, but I don't blame you, Adriana. Julian is... well, Julian."

"Intelligent, sexy, caring, funny..." I realize I'm saying the words out loud.

"Adriana, you're smitten."

"I've got a lot to be smitten about." I raise my eyebrows at her.

"Oh, can I ask?"

"What would you like to ask, Charlie?" I grin at her mischievously.

"Never mind. You've got the grin of a woman who looks *very* satisfied."

"Gee. I have no idea what you're talking about."

Charlie looks disappointed but is smart enough to know that the sexual part of Julian's and my relationship is best not to be shared with her. "It's okay. I guess this is one part of your relationship that you get to share all the juicy details with Eric."

I give her a sympathetic glance. She changes the subject asking me about Sydney. I tell her about all the amazing places Julian took me to and a little bit about his book release party. I'm about to mention my meltdown that night when a loud bang startles us. Within seconds, a much-disheveled Lex is standing in my living room. In the two hours since I last saw him, he looks like roadkill. Armed with a bottle of whisky, his bloodshot eyes tell me he hasn't stopped drinking.

"I hope you weren't stupid enough to drive here," I say out loud.

"I'm not as stupid as you, Adriana. I've got common sense."

Annoyed by his abuse, I'm quick to open my mouth before Charlie interrupts me. "I told you I was here. What do you want?"

"What do I want?" The sinister laugh returns. "For my

life to continue on as is and not have to worry that my wife is hanging out with her ex at my sister's place. I mean fuck, lucky guy bags two chicks, yes?"

"You're such a jerk!" Charlie yells.

I place my hand on Charlie's shoulder. "Charlie, don't bother. I'm going to make myself something to eat and head to bed. Will you be okay?"

She nods, and I head toward the kitchen. My walls are not soundproof, and eavesdropping is impossible to avoid as I make myself a quick sandwich.

Lex's voice comes through first. "What the fuck is wrong you? Why are you defending them?"

"Because she's happy, Lex. Unless you're blind, even you have seen how much she has changed."

The noise stops, only silence lingering.

"I don't want him near you. You understand me?"

"You need to sober up and go."

"Do you understand me?"

"Tomorrow we'll talk about this, but for tonight, don't expect me home. Don't expect anything from me after how you've treated me tonight."

"Charlotte..." I hear his voice soften, "... I need you to come home."

"Lex, please just go. I'll be home in a few hours. Sleep this off, and we'll talk about it then," Charlie responds, defeated.

The sound of the door slamming shut echoes down the hallway. Charlie walks into the kitchen, taking a seat beside me. She doesn't make a sandwich, instead lazily grabs a slice of bread and shoves it in her mouth whole. I pour her some juice, and she drinks it in one gulp. Just like me, she looks wrecked.

We finish and turn off the lights, heading upstairs.

Climbing into my bed, it brings back memories of our childhood and the countless sleepovers we had. It's as if she can read my mind, and she brings up the old days.

"I remember sleeping over at your house when we were like eight, and we had just watched *Nightmare on Elm Street*. Lex tried to spook us by wearing his Freddy Krueger mask."

I laugh in response. "I think I shit my pants, God honest truth."

"Gross, and I thought you had just farted in fear of your life."

We both fall into a fit of laughter, bodies shaking as we try to compose ourselves.

"Sometimes, I'll have these weird flashbacks and be like, wow, I had a crush on Lex way before we actually hooked up. I remember how every time I came over, your mom would make me a peanut butter and jelly sandwich and sneak in extra jelly. One day she wasn't there so I tried to make it myself. I must have been like ten or so. I wasn't getting it quite right." She laughs to herself then continues, "Alex, *not Lex,* walks in and catches me doing it. He is rambling on about his peanut butter and that nobody touches it, so to annoy him, I dunked my finger in his peanut butter."

"Oh God, what did he do to you?"

"He said to me, "bet I can gross you out more," then grabbed my hand and sucked the finger that had peanut butter all over it."

"How did I not know this?"

"Because I was so grossed-out and embarrassed. Remember, it was the day I left your house crying."

"Oh!" My memory is coming back. "That was the day

Lex said you had mono and not to bring it up because you had shit your pants in the kitchen."

"Are you serious? What an asshole!"

"You married him," I remind her.

"Yeah, he's my asshole."

Shaking my head in disgust, I turn to look over at the clock. It's just after two. If tonight didn't play out like it did, I'd have been in Julian's bed making sweet love until I couldn't walk, just like he promised.

"Adriana, give Lex time, okay? It's no secret how much he despises Julian given the past. I hope that eventually, he'll come around but just don't expect miracles overnight."

"I know, but now it's out in the open. Julian and I can just be a normal couple, no more hiding."

"And what does Andy think about him?"

"Andy loves him. I mean, Julian is great with Andy."

"That's what I was worried about," she confesses.

"Isn't that a good thing, though?"

Charlie exhales loudly. "I know he is your brother, and you know him well, but Adriana, he loves Andy like his own. I may not be the only issue here, but the fact that another man walks into your life and Andy falls in love with him."

"I never really worried about that," I admit.

"Tonight, he was an ass, but maybe, and only a suggestion, both of you should stay away from each other. Just think about Andy."

She has a valid point. Now that Julian and I are out in the open, I want to devote as much time as I can to him. Avoiding Lex won't be a problem, just seeing his face sent me into a fit of rage after his outburst.

"I hear you. Plus, I've got a boyfriend to go play with."

"Oh, yes, you do. A great one at that," she adds.

I stare up at the ceiling. It's pitch black. Even at this godforsaken hour, I'm wide awake. All right, I blame the coffee.

"Charlie, if Lex didn't walk back into your life, do you think you and Julian would've worked out?"

She keeps quiet, and I suspect she may have fallen asleep until the blanket shuffles.

"The way I felt about him back then, I'd say yes." She pauses, then continues, but this time her voice is timid, "He was perfect. He just wasn't Lex."

I nod, even though she can't see me. Charlie and Lex always have this unbreakable bond, and even after how awful Lex treated her tonight, I can tell she misses him and wants to go home.

"Maybe you should go home to your husband."

"I probably should but let him sulk a bit longer. No need to stroke his ego and run back to him like a pussy-whipped wife."

"Err... shouldn't it be dick-whipped wife?"

"Oh, right." She laughs followed by a yawn. "Well, I ain't dick-whipped... okay maybe just a little, but if you saw—"

I grab my pillow and muffle her face, and she squirms to break free. "Don't go there, Charlie... and I mean seriously, if you go there, I'll tell you about the time your stepmom, Debbie, told me about what your dad likes to wear in the bedroom."

"Oh, hell no!"

"Good night, Charlie."

She mumbles good night, and within a few moments, her tiny breaths are the only sound I hear.

Me, I'm wide awake, listening for Elijah.

Nothing.

Closing my eyes, I try to relive my memories of Elijah, just like Charlie did with Lex—back to high school, the first time we met at the football field. Yet every time I try to focus on his face, it's just a blur. The memories which haunt me are unpleasant—his sick face, his weak frame, and the worst one of all, his barren expression before he passed on. I place all my effort into forgetting these memories, and what makes it hard is that it stops me from living the life he wants me to live.

Move on, he said.

He made it seem like such an easy task.

It's a broken scene, and as much as I try to reminisce, all I can see is Julian's face.

It was just before ten when Charlie and I woke up. Already showered, I throw on a pair of yoga pants and my favorite retro tank with a Guns 'n Roses logo on it. My hair has grown, so I pull it up into a ponytail and slip into my sneakers. I figure today's a new day, and I should start my workout regime. That is until I find some leftover Dunkin Donuts in the kitchen.

Maybe tomorrow.

The doorbell rings just as I'm about to grab a second donut. With Charlie in the shower, I am assuming Lex is ready to use his manners and apologize for his bitch-fit last night. I open the door to be met with Julian standing on the porch. *Oh crap.* My body has mentally thrown itself at him, smothering him until he can't breathe, but in reality, I'm standing here not moving a single limb.

"Can I come inside, or would you like me to go make friends with the lady across the street?"

That nosy Mrs. Randle from across the street is peeking through her lace curtains. It isn't like I have men here, but then again, between Lex, Eric, Tristan, and Rocky, perhaps her twisted mind will think I run a burlesque house.

I motion for him to come in. "Charlie is still here. Is that okay?"

He nods and smiles reassuringly. Maybe I'm more nervous than him.

I grab his arm and pull him toward the kitchen when Charlie's footsteps bustle down the stairway. "Wow, Adriana, how good is that strawberry body wash. I should recommend it to a lady in my gym who has the stinkiest vag —" She halts at the bottom of the stairs, keeping her expression to no more than a faint smile.

"Was going upstairs to get you, but—"

She interrupts me, smiling warmly at both of us. "No. Hey, it's okay. Hi, Julian."

"Hi, yourself." He grins back at her.

Oh, this is awkward.

"So, how you been?" Charlie asks politely.

"Great, and you?"

"Yeah, good."

We all fall into a digestive silence until I open my mouth. "Okay, this is awkward. And I mean more awkward than the scene in *America Pie* where Jim is caught humping the pie."

Julian and Charlie laugh in unison, breaking the tension in the room.

I realize the only person making this awkward is me. I wrap my arms around his waist and snuggle my head into his chest. He smells like aftershave—sweet, cool, and sensual. Dressed in a white polo and navy dress shorts, his tan looks nice and even. I missed him.

"Oh, shucks, you two." Charlie beams. "No awkwardness from me, okay? And I reiterate... *me*."

"Thank you, Charlie. It means a lot to us," Julian says.

"I know you got my back. So, are you going straight home?" I ask.

She nods. "Yep. Hopefully, the beast has sobered up and not trashed our house."

"Call me later, okay?" I let go of Julian to hug Charlie.

She squeezes me tightly and whispers in my ear. "I think this will work out."

I smile at the sentiment, letting go of her. She steps forward and makes an effort to hug Julian. At first, he seems conflicted, but I see his body relax.

"It was nice seeing you again. Take good care of my girl, okay?" She pulls away and says goodbye, exiting through the back door.

Relief washes over me, and I immediately feel like a weight is lifted off my shoulders. Okay, maybe only one weight. My hands entwine with his as I lead him up the stairs to my bedroom. I said I was uncomfortable having him here, but my body needs him more than ever. He is quick to discourage me, but I hush him, closing the door behind me. Inside the room, my drapes are wide open with the sun filtering through. I tug on his shirt, pulling his body in flush with mine. His eyes are boring into me, filled with hunger and thirst, the same strong emotions which consume me. He tilts his head moving in, brushing his lips softly against mine. It travels directly to where it intended to go, the fire of passion ignites in just one kiss. My mouth moves back to his, nibbling his bottom lip with a gentle tug. His moans are trapped in our kisses, urging me to take a few steps backward until we've both fallen onto my bed. I pull away for a brief moment, staring directly into his eyes.

"Make love to me. Here. Please."

And just when he opens his mouth to say something, my cell rings, the loud noise bouncing off the walls. I excuse myself, worried it could be Andy. I roll over until I'm within arms' reach of the bedside table just in time to see the name Mary Jean flash on the screen. *Just fucking great.* If I don't pick up the phone, she will call like a crazed stalker ten times in a row.

"Hi, Mary Jean." I mouth to Julian "I will be quick."

"Darl! How is my gran-baby? Can I talk to him?" she almost shouts.

"Andy's great. He isn't here with me. Slept at a friend's house last night."

"Well, why would he need to? You're his mama..."

This isn't the first time Mary Jean has put in her two cents worth, and judging by her raised tone, she may have slipped some bourbon into her morning coffee.

"Listen, I need to go. How about I give you a call tonight when he's home?"

Seems like a good compromise, but typical Mary Jean has to ramble on. I listen for another two minutes before I quickly say goodbye, hanging up the call. I switch the cell to silent, not to be interrupted.

"We should probably talk," Julian insists.

"Probably, but I'd prefer to have you naked on top of me whispering sweet nothings in my ear."

With a wide-eyed grin, he rolls me back toward his body, pinning me underneath him. "Finally," he whispers.

And finally, just like he wants, he makes love to me on my bed.

It's exactly what I need, what we both need. I feel free, and my body is finally letting go. My mind wants to follow, but the sight of a raven sitting on my window ledge startles me. It's odd, and I haven't even seen one near my house. At least, not that type of bird. It doesn't leave, continuing to stand on the ledge.

Why won't it leave?

Then it dawns on me, remembering what my mom had once told me. The raven is known as a messenger bird, but what the hell does that mean? Was it coming here to warn me or guide me?

It doesn't matter. It's here to communicate with me, and there's only one person trying to do that, and only one person I'm not able to hear.

Elijah.

NINETEEN

We stay locked in the bedroom for two hours.

To say I'm sore would be an understatement. Every attempt to move a limb will have me laughing in hysterics, and even that task is painful. Between my legs are red raw, and I mean I can't even wipe myself with toilet paper without wincing. Julian's well aware of my physical state, but do you think that stops him? No. Apparently, my ass needs a workout, a very any-hole-is-a-goal situation.

"Why aren't you sore? Do you have an invincible penis? Should we get it a cape and mask?"

His chest rises and falls as he twists a lock of my hair between his fingers. "Adriana, that last move almost broke me. But fuck, what a nice sight of your ass."

"We could end up on *Sex Injuries in the ER* or whatever that show is called."

"I wouldn't be surprised if we do. You're quite bendy and flexible, and my super-penis is not."

Embarrassed, I blush at his comment. "I'm sorry."

"Considering I almost blew when you did that thing

with your leg over the side, it's a talent. No need to be sorry."

"You won't be saying that when you're on national TV."

I try to move my body so I can kiss him, but I've lost the will to move and fall onto my back. Julian laughs at me and reminds me to get to the gym if I want to keep up.

Who would've thought two hours could do so much damage to one's body? I remind him it's almost time to pick Andy up from Hazel. He's just as anxious to see him, and even suggests that we take Andy out afterward. It's a great idea and makes me very happy to spend time with my two favorite people. The only thing bugging me is the sight of that raven. *Google.* It holds the answers, but with Julian constantly by my side, it's best that I research this in private.

After the big showdown at the party, no doubt Lex will avoid me at all costs, he's stubborn and extremely hot-headed. According to Eric, he's also blacklisted since he knew what was going on. The only person who isn't is Charlie. No surprises there, the moron thinks only with his dick.

Our relationship coming out is a huge deal. One would think it means we have the freedom to see each other whenever and wherever we please. Quite the opposite—we barely have time to see each other. Julian has endless meetings with his editor this week, being offered another book deal plus the *New York Times* wants to offer him a permanent column. Life for him has really taken off, and no one is as deserving as he is. It does, however, mean he has decisions to make with what direction he wants to take his career in.

When he mentioned the *New York Times*, my heart sunk thinking he will need to move back to Manhattan, but he's quick to tell me they are happy for him to stay in LA and fly over once a month. It seems like the perfect opportunity, yet he's unsure if he wants to go back to working for a newspaper having enjoyed his time writing his book.

I, on the other hand, have become so busy trying to launch a new line. After the red carpet, my designs made it to *Vogue* and caught the eye of a few major labels in Paris. All of which want to schedule meetings with me, and given the difference in time zones, I find myself up at all hours trying to fit in work whenever Andy sleeps or is at daycare.

Between the madness, Julian and I will text or call, but we just aren't in sync.

And the sex... well, that's on hiatus.

We're both busy and just can't get anywhere within a reasonable time. Physically, I miss him. It's like going cold turkey. He fucks me into oblivion and then nada. Okay, not nada, I did manage to blow him quickly one day on my lunch break, and the only reason it didn't end in a happy ending for me is because an important buyer arrived early. Talk about leaving me high and dry, or more appropriately, lower and wetter.

Everyone has found out through the grapevine about our relationship. My mom is quick to call, and over the phone we had a lengthy discussion. She admitted that it all makes sense and understands why I was reluctant to come out in the open. After speaking to my dad, they both agreed that they want to meet Julian and thought it was a good idea to have a family dinner. I told her Lex wouldn't come, but she was quick to reassure me that he already agreed.

What the fuck? What game is he playing?

Friday night, seven on the dot, Julian is standing with me on the porch. Andy is shuffling between us, busily telling Julian about Gramps and Grammy. I take a deep breath, but my airway feels tight. It could also be this dress which no longer fits loosely. So, I've gained a few, it's what happens when you're in love. *Wait, did you just say that out loud or in your brain? OMG, look at him... his face hasn't changed. Phew, okay, close call.*

"Are you nervous?"

"Adriana... I'm thirty-three, it's not like I'm in high school. I've been through a lot worse."

I turn the handle on the door and push it open. Andy beats me to it, yelling for my parents as we enter the house. Mom is first to come out, wearing her apron. The aroma of pot roast is lingering in the air, and my taste buds go into overdrive. She wipes her hands on her apron as my dad walks in behind her. With both of them present, I introduce Julian. Being a perfect gentleman, Julian hands a bottle of wine to my mom and politely kisses her on the cheek. She seems incredibly pleased, shooting me a wink when he turns to shake hands with my dad.

My mom ushers us to the living room, both of us taking a seat on the couch. It doesn't last long as Andy sprints into the room, pleading with Julian to come see the playroom. Of course, Julian agrees and excuses himself to follow an overly excited Andy.

"He's lovely, Adriana." My mom beams.

I go to say something, but Julian walks back in the room with Andy. The anxiety creeps up again, and just when I think I can control it, Amelia darts into the room and finds Andy.

They are here.

What's the worst that can go wrong here?

Lex probably won't talk to us, sulking with his they-have-a-plot-to-ruin-my-life attitude. Distraction will be the key to surviving the night.

Amelia is engrossed in this new Batman figurine, so it's

best to ask her a question just to clear my mind. I regret it almost immediately—this girl can talk, and I mean nonstop ramble that starts off with Batman to her trip to the museum to what she ate for lunch. For once, Andy is listening intently. His eye is on the Batman which no doubt will result in a tug-o-war later.

Charlie's voice filters through the hall, and she enters the room with a baby carrier minus baby. Greeting everyone, she says hello to Julian in a casual way. She too looks on edge, and the reason why walks into the room carrying baby Ava. It's impossible to be mad as Ava lights up the room with her infectious giggle. She's almost eight months and has started to crawl. Unlike Amelia, she is a placid baby, happy to sit still and watch others. The older she grows, the more it's obvious how much she looks like Lex. Those emerald green eyes are the dead giveaway, and poor Charlie, none of her genes carried over.

Lex is looking smug, wearing his jeans and black hoodie. He greets my parents as usual but fails to make eye contact with Julian or me.

Andy runs up and wraps himself around Lex's leg. "Uncle Lex. Why didn't you take me to soccer?" Andy complains.

"Sorry, Andy. I was busy."

Fucking jerkoff. It's one thing to be pissed off at me, but how dare he lie straight to Andy's face.

The guilt must have hit him like a ton of bricks, his expression changing from wry to just plain old guilty. Serves him fucking right. Andy walks off with a sad face, almost in tears as he jumps into Julian's lap and sucks on his own thumb again for comfort. The second that Lex sees Andy do that, his face falls, and pure hatred is steaming off him. The tension is so thick you can't even cut it with three chainsaws.

My mom, also sensing the glum atmosphere, suggests we head into the dining room to eat.

Despite the nerves, I'm famished. The food is spread out on the table and looks scrumptious. I take a seat beside Julian, Lex sitting directly opposite me. It's either that or directly opposite Julian. The kids are on the little table beside us, even Batman's got his own chair.

We eat in silence until my dad begins the conversation. "So, Julian, Adriana tells me you travel quite a bit as a journalist. Tell me, have you ever been to Tanzania?"

"Yes, sir, about six years ago. I was part of a documentary which filmed people affected by diseases and how their current healthcare system can't cater to the number of patients who need to be treated."

"Please, call me Andrew." My dad wipes his mouth with his napkin. "Quite impressive. I'll be setting up a medical center in late fall. Would love to speak to you in more depth about what I should be expecting."

"Of course, Andrew, I still have footage and notes."

I look up at Lex. He has barely eaten and is swirling his food around. The conversation is probably a sore point, considering he gave up practicing medicine to become a billionaire. That's entirely his decision and causes headaches for my dad, especially since he bent over backward to get Lex a job at the hospital.

Charlie is quick to compliment my mom. "Emily, you've outdone yourself again. This pot roast is delicious."

"Thank you, honey."

Lex finally takes a bite. "It was Elijah's favorite."

Everyone is quiet.

Fucking asshole pulling out a comment like that.

"Adriana mentioned it was your favorite as well," Julian points out, challenging Lex.

Lex practically bangs his fork against his plate.

Charlie mouths "calm down."

Under the table, Julian squeezes my thigh, relaxing me a little. If Julian has no problem with this, then why should I? The only moron at the table is the one sitting across from me, refusing to make eye contact again. *God, he is behaving like a petulant child.*

"So, Julian, where did you grow up?" my mom asks as she serves some green beans to my dad.

Julian places his knife down politely. "In South Carolina. Stayed there till college."

"What college did you attend, son?"

Oh, my dad called him son. Lex's face is furious, the grinding of his teeth can be heard a mile away.

"Studied at Harvard, then moved to New York to find work."

And then he met Charlie.

Looking across the table, Charlie shifts uncomfortably until Lex purposely drapes his arm across her shoulder. *So fucking juvenile.*

My dad talks about Harvard, and it seems to interest Julian. There's a lengthy discussion held about the curricular activities, and during this time, the kids leave and are watching a movie in the playroom. The conversation then steers to New York as my dad probes Julian about his time spent there and his work with the *New York Times*. I motion to my mom to halt the conversation, and with feeble attempts, he still carries on.

"New York is a great home base for journalism. What made you move to Los Angeles?"

Lex laughs and rudely interrupts them, "Yeah, what made you move to *Los Angeles?*"

Julian takes all the questions in his stride, not flinching once. "I was done with New York, wanted a more relaxed lifestyle. I used to surf a lot, and it seemed like a good choice at the time."

"Well, I'm glad you decided to come here." I rest my hand on top of his.

"Did the two of you meet here in California?" my dad asks, slightly confused.

"Uh... no, Dad. The first time we met was in New York at a charity ball."

Charlie has a blank face, refusing to comment. Lex is lapping up the attention, his arm still around Charlie. He might as well pee on Charlie to claim her as his, that's how territorial he is.

"I met Elijah a few times. He was a great guy." Julian smiled.

Both my parents nod in unison, happily smiling at both of us.

"So why don't you tell my parents the real reason you left New York?" Lex pushes him.

"Are you kidding me, Lex?" I blurt out.

"We're a close-knit family. If Julian's going to be part of it, surely they should know?" he says innocently.

"Lex, please stop." Mom shakes her head, disappointed. "Julian, I want to apologize for my son's behavior."

"Emily, it's to be expected. To answer your question, Lex, I wasn't coping well with the death of a friend, and recent events caused the pain to resurface. I thought it was best to start new."

"And go after Charlotte?" he states.

"Oh my God, Lex, will you just drop it?" Charlie pleads, fed up with his ludicrous behavior.

My mom lectures Lex and is clearly standing on her own as my dad is drinking his wine, looking somewhat amused by Lex.

"I'm not just going to drop it, Charlotte. It's fairly obvious why he's here."

And here we go.

"Wow! I knew you were a selfish asshole, but I didn't think you thought that little of me." I pull my chair back and leave the room in a huff, walking outside to the backyard.

The fresh night air calms me down to the point I'm no longer seeing red, just a bright shade of pink. It's not long before Julian comes outside, sitting down beside me on the step.

"We always knew this was going to be difficult, Adriana."

But why is it only Lex making it difficult? He's my brother, he saw firsthand the pain I endured losing Elijah. Why can't he just be fucking happy for me?

"I just hate that he makes me feel like I'm nothing. It's all about Charlie. He hasn't once stopped to think that maybe I'm just as good as Charlie."

"It isn't a competition." He pulls me onto his lap, and I wrap my arms around his neck, resting my head on his shoulder. "I don't blame him, you know. I'd be the same in his position."

"Wait? You would?"

"Think about it, Adriana. I wasn't a saint, and for a long time I did try to steal Charlie away from him."

"This isn't helping me."

"Just let him do what he needs to do. For now, let's focus on us, okay?"

And that's the great thing about Julian, he's rational, and even at the worst of times, he makes me see sense. The door creaks, and I turn around to see Charlie standing behind us.

"Hey, kids. Thanks for leaving me in the lion's den."

I know she is joking, her half-smile reassuring me that she can handle it. Charlie's strong. She doesn't let things get to her like I do.

"Julian, Andrew wants to know if you would like to join him in the den, something about a documentary on some disease thingy."

"Sorry, beautiful." He kisses my forehead, and I climb off him.

As soon as Julian is gone, Charlie speaks, "Adriana, just ignore Lex. There's no point arguing with him. It'll be a waste of time."

"But surely that must have been uncomfortable for you? What gives him the right to treat Julian and me that way in front of my parents?"

"Yeah, it was. My hands are tied here. I want you to be happy, but I can't control Lex."

She's right. Charlie may be his wife, but Lex has always been stubborn. She has a hold over him, but this is one of those times where he refuses to listen to anyone or thing besides his psychotic head.

"Has he been treating you badly this week?" I ask, guilty she has to put up with him.

"Yes and no. He's got his mood swings, that's for sure. But for the most part, quite the opposite, he has been more demanding, um... *physically*."

"Huh?"

"I don't need to spell it out for you," she huffs, her eyes

widening while watching me. "You don't really want to hear it, do you?"

"Who cares? It's no hidden secret that he's apparently a god in the bedroom."

"I never said that!"

"Oh... maybe *Eric,* then."

"Ever since I came home from your house, any quiet moment we have alone he ravages me. And I mean ravage to the point that it's like back in New York when we had just started up again."

"Well, maybe that's his coping mechanism."

"It's his way of controlling what he believes is his."

"No surprises there. Oh well, it's nice, I guess." My tone flattens.

"Adriana, what's wrong? I mean, apart from the obvious?"

Should I tell her about the doubt creeping in? How that raven spooked me, and all I can think about is Elijah? In some ways, Charlie is so lucky to have it all. She has a man who will move heaven and earth for her, two beautiful children, money, the works. Jealousy is an ugly trait, and one not to be had toward your best friend.

The door opens, and we both turn to see Lex. He asks Charlie if he can have a moment with me. She stands and leaves, closing the door behind her. Lex keeps his distance, standing behind me while I continue to sit on the step avoiding his presence.

"I've got nothing left to say to you."

"Adriana, why do you have to make my life so fucking hard?"

I turn abruptly. "Your life?"

He keeps quiet. So quiet only the owls loitering in the trees can be heard.

"Out of all the people in LA, why him?"

I stand up in a hurry. "I'm not wasting my breath. I don't expect you to understand. All you really care about here is Charlie. Not me."

I walk back inside the house. It's quiet.

In the living room, my mom, Charlie, and the girls are watching a movie. Standing around for a few moments, I easily get bored and go in search of Andy.

In the den, my dad and Julian are watching a documentary, engrossed in a lengthy discussion about the African government. It's probably best I leave them alone, and just as I'm about to walk out, I catch a glimpse of Andy sitting on Julian's lap with his head resting on his chest, happily sucking on his thumb, *again.*

The strings to my heart are pulled every which way, the contentment on Andy's face indescribable. This isn't all about me, this is about what Andy needs as well. Everyone needs a father, one who can take you to soccer practice or coach little league, teach you all about the birds and bees because Mama knows it's the most awkward conversation of all time.

I wander back to the living room but remember I need to grab something from the guest bedroom. Making my way past the bathroom, an unusual sound escapes the room. *What the hell is that?* It's more of a moan, and just when I'm about to open the door, it becomes too clear.

"Charlotte, you are mine. You *fucking* understand me?"

It's followed by a low rumbling moan.

You've got to be kidding me!

I run out of the hallway fast, determined to erase the image creeping into my brain along with the sex moans. Dear God, please give me amnesia now. I'm out of breath by the time I enter the den, letting Julian know it's time to leave.

By the time my dad and Julian have said their goodbyes and arranged to meet up to discuss his trip in more detail, we're in the hallway when a very flustered Charlie turns the corner. She avoids eye contact, and when she goes to hug me goodbye, I place my palm in front of her, stopping her.

"No thanks, God knows what's all over you."

With that comment, her face turns beet red. Even Lex looks pleased with himself. I don't say goodbye to him, and Julian knows not to even attempt but does say farewell to Charlie. It pisses Lex off, and his smirk falters into a bitter expression.

Outside, we walk along the path until we reach the car. With Andy strapped in, I let out a sigh of relief when I sit down. I shiver in disgust at the thought of them going at it in the bathroom. It's not like they are horny teenagers, they have a whole house to themselves and sleep in the same bed every night.

"Why the shakes?" Julian asks as he reverses the car out of the driveway.

Without even thinking, I burst out, "Argh, just... *gross*... catching Lex and Charlie going at it in my parents' bathroom. I mean, where's the respect?"

A silence follows, and Julian's face shows no expression. His grip on the steering wheel looks tighter than usual. I expect him to say something, but he doesn't for the entire ride home. Andy is the one talking, and as soon as we park the car, Andy is quick to speak, "Jay, can you please read me a story tonight? The one with the puppy losing its mama?"

Julian releases his belt and turns to face Andy. "Sure, kiddo."

He ignores me, and I'm taken aback.

Inside, Julian is reading to Andy in bed. It isn't long before Andy asks, "Jay, will you stay here in my bed? The monsters talk to me, and I'm scared." Julian nods and pushes his hair aside.

I stand outside the room, wanting to ask what the hell happened in the car. Why did he have a problem with Lex and Charlie having sex? Yeah, it was gross, but why did it bother him this much that he has to give me the silent treatment? He falls asleep beside Andy, and I don't have the heart to wake him.

I climb into bed and hope that he will sneak in during the night.

It never happened.

TWENTY

There's a corner in my guest room upstairs with the most magnificent view of my neighbor's backyard, replicating an oasis.

The trees are leafy, green, and spread throughout the manicured garden enhancing the main feature—the Olympic-size swimming pool. On a warm day like today, I'm really trying to suppress the urge to strip off and jump into the pool. The pool may have been the main attraction but superseding that would have to be the young pool boy. He's easily in his early twenties, a tan to die for, and snake hips which will get any libido up and dancing. The first time I saw him, I knew Eric would be all up in that like an ill-fitting swimsuit, so I call him immediately.

Never in my life have I ever known Eric to be on time for anything, so you can imagine my shock when the doorbell rings fifteen minutes later. The profanities Eric can think of for a man-part never cease to amaze me.

Much to my disappointment, pool boy's off duty today. It doesn't stop me enjoying the view, though, and with my headphones on, the shuffling of my music drowns out the silence allowing me to work on some new designs for beachwear I've been playing around with. Somewhere during 'Footloose,' I feel a gentle tap on my shoulder. At first, my imagination does that 'you're cuckoo,' and I ignore it, but it becomes heavier, and I turn slowly to see Lex standing behind me. Startled, I pull off my headphones and drop my papers and pencil on the floor.

Crouching down, he assists me in picking up my papers as I mumble under my breath. "What are you doing here? You scared the shit out of me, Lex."

I place everything on the side table and walk away, ignoring that he's following me downstairs to the kitchen. He stands in the archway, and I open the dishwasher and start unloading.

"I'm here to pick up Andy."

I don't look at him, taking the plates out one by one. "Well, he's not here."

"He has soccer training in half an hour," he points out.

"They changed the time. It started an hour ago, and besides, Julian took him."

The earth may just have shaken with the rage flooding Lex's veins. This is mainly my fault. Early this morning, I suggested Julian take Andy to soccer. Once Andy had it in his head, he wouldn't let up, even getting himself dressed as best as he could. Soccer for little ones mainly consists of running around and tantrums. It isn't competitive and a great way for them to learn how to play sports.

Lex always takes him to soccer, except for last weekend, and that's his own stubborn fault for using Andy as a pawn in this twisted situation.

Amongst the clink of the dishes, I can hear the sound of him grinding his teeth, his eyes are closed and fists clenched tightly against the wall, and he lashes out, "Why the hell aren't you with them?"

"Not that it's any of your business, the smoke alarm is faulty, and someone is coming over to look at it."

He is glaring at me, eyes blazing trying to intimidate me, and I ignore him much to his annoyance. That used to work on me, but I'm not ten anymore. The doorbell rings on cue, and I walk past, knocking into him on purpose.

Thank God, the electrician is here.

"There's my beautiful daughter-in-law!"

Mary Jean pushes past me, carrying an overnight bag. *Oh, fuck no.* She places it down and hugs me so tight my body is mushed into her boobs. The cheap scent of her drugstore perfume invades my nostrils as I struggle to break free.

"I bet you're shocked to see me so soon?"

"Yeah, shocked would be one word for it," I respond plainly.

She pulls my arm toward the kitchen, and the second Lex is in sight, she lets go of me so fast, smothering Lex in an over-friendly hug which is borderline dry humping. He's uncomfortable and awkward, trying his hardest to pull away. *Sucked in. Serves him right.*

"What brings you to LA, Mary Jean?" Lex asks politely, using his arm to create a respectable distance.

"Well, I haven't seen my grandbaby in almost two months, and every time I try to call this lady, she's busy and can't talk."

Dammit. We could've avoided this if I had just called her more often. Too bad you were thinking with your vagina rather than your head.

Mary Jean scans the room. "So, where's Andy?"

I shoot a glance at Lex who's obviously relishing in my

awkwardness, waiting for me to respond. I'm about to open my mouth when Andy comes running through the house. Covered in mud, his blond hair is almost brown, and his face is streaked with dirt. Grass stains cover his knees, but he couldn't have looked any more pleased with himself.

"Mama! Mama!" He stops in his tracks when he spots Mary Jean. With a wide smile, she beckons him. Quick to run into her arms, she smothers him with kisses despite being covered in dirt.

Julian soon follows, walking into the kitchen, spotting Lex first. Immediately, his face drops, his smile is soon replaced with an arctic glare, and the room temperature rises as the tension hits an all-time high.

The uncomfortable silence is soon broken by Mary Jean's flirtatious flick of the hair. "Who's this fine young gentleman?"

There's no better time than now to reveal the truth. "Uh, this is Julian, my um... *boyfriend.*"

Mary Jean is crestfallen. Her cloudy eyes stare back at me in disbelief. "Excuse me, your what?"

"Julian, this is Mary Jean. Elijah's mother."

Julian greets her politely only to be ignored. He isn't fazed. Moving toward me, he rubs the small of my back to ease my worry.

"Andy, go upstairs to your room, and I'll be there in a minute to give you a present, okay?" she tells him.

"Kay kay, Grandmama." Andy doesn't leave immediately, hopping from foot to foot, then bolts out of the room announcing he is Superman, prompting Mary Jean to focus her attention back to us.

"Don't you think it's a bit too soon to be moving on? Did Elijah mean that little to you that you can move on so quickly?"

"Elijah meant everything to me. But it's been almost three years," I stutter.

Julian reaches for my hand, placing it in his. "I had the pleasure of meeting your son a long time ago. He was a great man. Adriana and Andy were blessed to have him in their lives."

Mary Jean's face softens. "He was a great son, too. I don't know why they had to take..." She breaks out into sobs. I grab a tissue from the counter and hand it to her. With a gentle smile, she settles down.

"You know what else, Mary Jean? Julian is Charlotte's ex-fiancée," Lex tells her.

Mary Jean stops mid-sob, the thirst for gossip an obvious distraction.

"Nice introduction, Lex. It's always fun to reminisce," Julian bites back.

Mary Jean starts asking questions. I'm annoyed at Lex for bringing it up and extra annoyed with Julian for his insensitive comment.

Does no one at all care about me? It's always about fucking Charlie!

I let go of Julian's hand and move toward the cupboard, grabbing myself a much-needed drink. With my back facing them, I close my eyes to calm myself down.

Lex announces he is leaving and reminds me about Rocky's birthday tomorrow night. I don't respond, nor do I turn around, wishing they would all disappear and leave me the fuck alone.

Mary Jean grabs her bag, complaining about her sore back. Julian, being polite, offers to take it upstairs. They disappear for a while, presenting a perfect opportunity to raid my cupboard and take a Valium.

"What's tomorrow night?" Julian creeps up behind me.

He doesn't touch me like before, leaning against the opposite counter.

"Remember I told you about Rocky's birthday party? It's being held at one of Nikki's client's homes in the Hills."

"Oh, right, the costume party? I don't feel like going," he responds flatly.

"But it's the first time we're going somewhere as a couple, and I thought you already had your costume which Andy helped pick out?"

"Yeah, of course, he had to pick Batman. It's a given, isn't it?" The bitterness to his tone catches me off-guard as does the sudden change of heart.

He doesn't say anything, and I continue on, "Is it because Lex and Charlie will be there?"

"I'll pick you up tomorrow, but I'm not riding in the car with them."

"But a car's coming to pick all of us up, so we can drink."

"You're coming with me, or I don't go." He walks over, and just when I think he'll change his mind and apologize for his odd behavior, he kisses my cheek and tells me he's leaving.

As the door clicks shut behind him, I try to make sense of the conversation. I'm not quite sure why all of a sudden, he is demanding and fighting me. The change in personality has left me baffled and questioning our relationship. He always said that Charlie and Lex wouldn't be an issue, yet he seems to be going against what he said, and it feels like they are the biggest hurdle in our relationship when realistically, it should've been Elijah and Chelsea.

Mary Jean makes a humming sound as she saunters into the kitchen. Grabbing a cup, she pours herself coffee and leisurely takes a seat at the table. Her company doesn't allow for me to brood any longer and pouring myself a cup, I sit beside her and start chatting.

"Darl, I came here to ask a favor from you. I don't like to ask these things, but something has come up, and I'm short of cash."

I hate conversations about loaning money. They are always awkward and create unnecessary tension. "How much do you need?"

"Five," she says. "If you've got it."

"Hundred?"

"No, thousand. Look, if it—"

I raise my hand, interrupting her. "Mary Jean, it's fine. I'll transfer it tonight."

"Darl, how did I get so lucky to have you as a daughter?"

When Nikki said the party was at a mansion, she failed to mention the mansion belongs to an A-list celebrity, and the house is insanely huge. It looks like it goes on for miles, every room exceeding the next. It's newly built and surrounded by glass with a gorgeous view of the city skyline. People are crammed everywhere, making it quite difficult for us to stay together which is probably for the best.

Guests in their costumes keep Eric and I entertained, laughing to complete embarrassment for the man dressed as a tampon. Our group theme was superheroes and villains. I was first to claim Catwoman, the extra tight suit a struggle to get on, and it probably isn't the smartest idea since peeing isn't an option.

"Do I look gay in this costume?" Eric turns to ask me.

"Eric, you're Robin, isn't that a given?"

"I'm going commando," he almost yells into my ear.

"Why? Honestly, don't go busting a move, or you'll get sweat patches on your ass like that Spiderman over there." I point to the dance floor, and Eric looks mortified.

"Look at my hunny, doesn't he look gorgeous?"

Tristan is standing with us dressed as Thor. His muscles are exposed, and with a mallet in hand, Eric looks like he is ready to combust on the spot.

"He does look yummy." I grin, raising my glass as Eric follows, and we clink to cheers.

Julian is standing by my side, drinking gin. Dressed as the Dark Knight, my lady parts are drooling as his eyes are shadowed by the mask, and the idea of having him fuck me in that costume is the only thought running through my head. My body moves into his as my lips move close to his ear.

"Is there a clause in the rental agreement that does not allow for sexual activity in the suit?" I whisper.

With a tight grip, his hands slide to my backside and slip just underneath my ass. "I'm happy to lose my deposit." The delectable sound of his words travels way down below. *Holy Batman, how the fuck do I get this suit off.*

I move my mouth to his and lock him into a kiss. All seems to be forgotten. The tension has finally passed, and knowing he is relaxing, is having the same effect on me. Eric clears his throat as Charlie and Lex are walking toward us. Dressed as Wonder Woman, Charlie looks sexy as hell. The costume fits her perfectly, showing off her naturally round breasts. I'm surprised Lex allows her to wear that—she's an image of every man's wet dream, *including your man*. Don't go there. I wait and watch Julian's face as he notices her attire, my stomach doing backflips as I see his eyes move down her body. He is quick to turn away, downing a glass of gin in one go.

It was bound to happen, I suppose.

And the jealousy rains in, marking its territory once again.

I wrap my arms around his waist forcing him to touch me. Underneath the painted face, Lex is dressed as the Joker, grimaces at my affection toward Julian, totally oblivious to his wife being gazed upon by her ex-fiancé.

"The birthday man is here," Rocky roars, flexing his green arms as he gets into character. With his bulky frame, he looks so much like the Hulk, and Nikki beside him does her part as Poison Ivy. She looks amazing in her short green dress and long ginger-colored wig.

Rocky gets the photographer to come by and take snaps as we pose in comical positions. Eric starts to complain again that he should've dressed in something more comfortable like the tampon man.

"Dude, I guarantee you, that guy ain't getting laid tonight," Rocky reassures him.

Tampon man has attracted ladies, purely for selfies and comical relief. His attempts to get phone numbers look far-fetched. No lady wants a reminder of Aunt Flow.

"What a shame Kate can't make it." Eric pouts.

Kate had a last-minute family emergency in the UK and had to fly out last night. It means the office in New York will be without her, and Lex will need to step in. According to Charlie, he isn't exactly pleased about having to go to New York for a week and leaving the family behind, but Kate is also family to them.

Tristan announces he has found us a great table, right in the middle of the action. We take a seat, and I make sure

Julian is as far away from Lex as possible. Countless waiters are circling the party.

Eric, as always, is quick to stop the cute young one and grabs us glasses of champagne. I need more of these if I want to get through the night. With the music blaring, people start dancing around us. Charlie pulls Lex away, both of them disappearing into the crowd. I catch a glimpse of them dancing. Charlie probably has had too much to drink, allowing Lex to practically fuck her on the dance floor.

Julian takes a drink, draping his arm around my shoulder.

"So, Morocco in two weeks, Uncle Jools?" Tristan asks.

"Watch your mouth, kid," he chastises. "Still undecided."

"Would a certain hot lady have something to do with it?"

"Maybe... depends if she starts behaving *or misbehaving*."

I go to open my mouth as Charlie and Lex stumble back to the table. Instead of sitting down, Lex pulls Charlie onto his lap, parading an open-mouth kiss. I turn away, and notice Julian's face is blank.

"Hey, Eric, I forgot to thank you for Clarice. Who would've thought some old lady would control my sex life?" Lex deadpans.

"Geez, Lex, you can still have sex and not get pregnant," Eric informs him.

"Wanna make a bet?" Lex challenges him.

"Well, you know you don't always have to enter the house via the front door, don't you?"

I burst out laughing, almost snorting out my champagne. The laughter doesn't subside—it's classic Eric!

Even Tristan is unable to control himself, both of us near tears.

"I'm entering every way possible." Lex places his hands onto Charlie's face and kisses her deeply, unable to keep his hands to himself.

This is getting old.

Yes, we're all adults, and yes, on more than one occasion our sexual quirks have been talked about in an open forum. This, however, is dangling the carrot in front of the rabbit.

Julian drinks his gin along with several others and calls the waiter over once again. Grabbing two more glasses, I expect one is for me, but he is quick to down it in one go.

Tristan looks over to me with a worried expression. Something isn't right.

"Dude, that's hot." Rocky is distracted by some ladies who walk past wearing short latex dresses. They wink hello, and he winks back causing Nikki to pull him onto the dance floor.

The champagne is settling nicely, and with my body already swaying of its own accord, I grab Julian's hand and pull him onto the dance floor. The DJ mixes in the songs as Rihanna's 'Only Girl in the World' starts to play. With his body against mine, he presses against me and moves his hips to the sound of the beat. I'm buckling underneath his touch, weak and full of desire. It only feels like us on the dance floor, and for once, for just a split second, I feel like the only girl he's ever loved.

But illusions are distorted, and reality is like a giant slap to the face.

Lex and Charlie aren't far from us, and once again, Lex is devouring his wife like no one else is watching, sliding his hands to places that should be left for the privacy of their own home. If it were anyone else, I'd continue staring, but

I'm disgusted at their behavior. I know it's just a giant pissing contest rather than just PDA, and plus, it's Rocky's birthday party, after all.

A few songs later, Julian asks to excuse himself leaving me with Nikki. Rocky has abandoned her to go dance with a group of his friends, and surprisingly, she allows it. Being with Nikki takes my mind off things. We dance for fun, copying moves from our favorite movies like *Grease* and *Flashdance*. Even Tristan and Eric join in, and with all the laughter and fun, I forget about Julian leaving.

I tell the guys I'm going to take a break and head back to our table to grab a drink. Water would've been the best option, but I stop the cute waiter and grab two flutes of champagne, almost chugging down the whole glass by the time I'm back at the table. Charlie is jumping around and begging Lex to dance again. He declines as she pouts, leaving him to join everyone else on the dance floor.

"I think I'm going to go find Julian," I say.

"Why bother? He didn't want to be here in the first place."

"He's just going through some stuff." I'm not sure why I'm defending him. Even I don't know what he's going through.

"The same stuff he was going through when he was stalking Charlotte?"

"It isn't like that, Lex. You don't understand."

"I understand perfectly clear, Adriana. It's you who won't listen. He came to LA because of Charlotte. It wasn't a coincidence that he turned up at that gala and professed his undying love for her."

"Well, okay, maybe back then—"

"And then he started following her, and, I swear on my life, he has entered our house."

"Lex, you're crazy, you know that? Okay, so maybe he followed her, but to break and enter? And for what reason?"

"Things started going missing. Things that belonged to Charlotte."

Has my brother had a lobotomy? The lengths he will go to break us up is absurd.

"Is this some kind of sick joke? Julian wouldn't stoop that low."

"Think what you want, Adriana. He's not the man you think he is. I bet every cent I have on that."

We're interrupted by Lex pulling out his cell. It's some business emergency, and he motions that he is heading to a quieter area.

Nikki pushes her way through the crowd and asks me to help with the cake. Still worried about Julian, I look around but can't see him anywhere. Nikki drags me toward the makeshift stage where a few waiters push out a cake. It's on wheels, and on closer inspection, isn't a real cake, and my gut feeling is that something is about to pop out and wish Rocky a happy birthday.

The lights surrounding the area dim, and the DJ remixes the birthday tune as Rocky takes to the stage. With a cheesy wide grin, he takes his place in the center as the crowd goes crazy singing. Eric and Tristan are front row, cells out, taking selfies.

My eyes go searching for Julian, and after scanning the area, I see him standing beside Charlie. Unable to peel my eyes off them, the jealousy is growing and seeping into my skin as Julian leans in and whispers something in her ear. She tilts her head back laughing, not looking the least bit worried that Lex will see her, and all hell will break loose. Julian looks jubilant, his eyes dancing while he continues interacting with her.

He doesn't look at me that way. Why is Lex not stopping this?

I'm torn, jealous, and hurt by his lack of consideration for my feelings. The way he smiles at Charlie, it's obvious the way he feels for her, not to mention his mood changed after he started seeing her again.

You're the idiot, Adriana. Everyone warned you he wasn't ready, and you pushed and pushed.

The crowd whistles and roars as a barely-dressed woman pops out of the cake and does a strip dance for Rocky, rubbing her ass against Rocky as he laps up the attention. Nikki is cheering him on, nudging me with her arm, pointing out how happy he looks with the lady. She's way too happy and calm, normally driven by jealousy which leaves me questioning. With a mischievous grin, I know something doesn't add up. Looking at the lady again, I can't help but notice how tall she is, and the way her hair glistens against the moonlight. Much like Penny's wig... *uh oh*. My eyes zoom in on her throat, and there it is, sticking out like a dog's balls. *The Adam's apple*. Rocky is ignorant, enjoying his moment of freedom.

Oh, I can't watch.

Yes, you can, this is hilarious!

But I'm unable to laugh, and with a forced smile, I count down the seconds until I can leave the stage and sort out what is causing the anger to swirl like a red tide, choking any rational thoughts and driving me to the brink of madness. My insecurities and animosity are beyond any point of turning back.

Lex's words play in my head. *"The same stuff he was going through when he was stalking Charlotte? I understand perfectly clear, Adriana. It's you who won't listen. He came to LA because of Charlotte. It wasn't a coincidence that he turned up at that gala and professed his undying love for her... and then he started following her and, I swear on my life, he entered our house."*

My fists are clenched into a ball, my steps are hard and fast. The temperature has risen, and my body is stifling hot, consumed with jealousy and doubt. I walk back to the table and interrupt Charlie and Julian.

"Adriana, how funny was that! Rocky has no idea." Charlie laughs.

I strike, bitter and resentful. "Don't you think you may have had a little too much to drink, Charlie?"

Julian butts in, immediately defending her, "Adriana, she's had the same amount as you."

The blood in my veins starts to viciously swirl. *He's fucking defending her.* All this time I was blind and didn't see what Lex had warned me about. *He still fucking loves Charlie.*

"Charlie, will you excuse us, please?"

Charlie looks dumbfounded but kindly leaves us alone.

"Adriana, what's with you tonight? That was unfair to Charlie."

My voice trembles in anger. "Did you stalk Charlie and break into their house?"

He is taken aback, and I motion for him to follow me to a quieter area where there are fewer people around. "I've already told you this, it's no secret, and I'm ashamed of my behavior back then."

"You haven't answered my question. Did you break into their home?"

"Of course, you'll believe whatever your brother tells you," he shouts.

"Why won't you answer my question?"

"Yes, it's fucking true. All right? I did all those things

that he told you. I was high half the time, and the minute I sobered up, I used Charlie as a reason to stay clean."

"But you..." I can't even think now. "Why were you angry when we left my parents' house? Were you jealous?"

"Jesus Christ! What the hell is this?"

"You tell me? I'm not the one who goes silent after they hear their ex-fiancée was screwed in the bathroom."

"What do you expect from me, huh?" He pulls off his mask, his hair a wild mess and eyes shadowed in dark circles.

"Is it too much for me to ask you not to care?"

"It bugged me, okay? You tell me she's been fucked in the bathroom just to piss me off. How the hell do you want me to react?"

"I don't want you to react! In fact, I didn't tell you to get a reaction, I was just sounding off because I was disgusted. This is what I was always afraid of... you still have feelings for her. What the fuck is it about Charlie? Do you think about her when we have sex?"

"Is that what you think of me?" he chokes, barely able to speak.

"Well, you never deny it, Julian."

"I shouldn't have to. You have seen the hell I've been through, Adriana, and you want to throw that back in my face?"

"Well, it all makes sense now. I'm just a distraction or even some pawn in your sick twisted game. Why else would you stick around for so long?"

"Because I fucking love you, all right! But what good is that when *you* can't get over *your* insecurities. Elijah didn't abandon you by choice. He was dying, you need to stop being selfish and realize it's not all about you."

I remain quiet, not realizing everyone is gawking around us. Tristan stands close to Julian, waiting with caution.

"We'll talk about this later," I mutter.

"What's the point, Adriana? You've obviously painted quite a pretty picture of me. I can't escape my mistakes, and even when I try, you're pushing me to make friends and attend parties like I'm invincible."

Lex moves quickly to my side. "Do not talk to my sister like that."

"Stay the fuck out of this, will you? You've finally got what you wanted." Julian stands in front of Lex toe to toe, both of them glowering and on the verge of all hell breaking loose.

Lex lowers his voice, "And that's how it will stay."

In a swift move, Julian punches Lex in the face causing a hive of activity and Rocky to step in between them. It's a blur, and the sounds are drowned out, the yelling and screaming as I stand still completely numb for seconds on end. The moment I snap out of it, I see Lex being held back by Rocky, his bloody face mixed with the white face paint is distorted by anger and pure hatred. Julian fares no better. There's blood all over his face and a cut above his eye, Tristan and Eric trying to calm him down as he bites back at Lex, both of them fueled by rage and jealousy.

"Stay the fuck away from my wife," Lex lashes out.

"Always about you, Edwards," Julian spits back.

"You're damn right. My wife, and that's how it'll always stay."

"Can't erase the past, Edwards. I'm not the one bringing it up all the time."

"I don't give a shit. She chose me, you got it?"

I intervene, pushing onto Julian's chest. "Don't do this," I beg of him.

Julian pushes my hands away from his chest, creating a distance between us. "You always push me, asking me about Charlie... am I thinking about her, do I love her? It's all in your imagination, Adriana." He releases a drunken laugh. "So, no, it's always been about you, but now that you're bringing it up, I did love Charlie, I wanted to marry her a long time ago, and wait for it, Edwards, this one's for you. I stopped thinking about how much Charlie loved to be fucked, but always nice to take a walk down memory lane since that's what you supposedly want."

Both Rocky and an onlooker try to hold back Lex all the while as I stand there gobsmacked at Julian's hurtful words. Julian turns to face me, out of breath, eyes wild with rage and hurt as he says the words I've dreaded all along. "I'm done. I can't do this, Adriana, it's too hard." He shakes his head, defeated. "I love you, but you'll always choose your brother over me, and I refuse to go on always being someone's second place. Even I know I don't deserve that."

My voice croaks, and I try to speak to no avail.

With a second attempt, I finally sync my mind and voice. "Julian, don't do this. Please, I didn't mean the things I said."

His eyes have settled, and his brown pupils stare deep into mine, piercing my soul with pain, knowing that the damage is done, and I'm losing the one person who means more to me than anyone else.

The man I love.

Tell him you love him... now.

I want to tell him, but he beats me to the punch. "You doubted me, and I never thought you would do that. It's over, okay?"

Crushed, he walks away, Tristan running after him.

Dazed and confused, arms wrap around me in comfort,

and the moment I realize they belong to Charlie, I stiffen. "Don't touch me," I warn her.

"Adriana, but I—"

I turn to look at her, and with mixed emotions, I lash out as the force of humility hits me so hard I'm seeing nothing but darkness.

"It's always about you, Charlie. He was moving on, but you come here dressed like a *slut,* and what do you do? Drive my boyfriend away from me."

Lex moves toward me. "Apologize for calling her that."

"I won't apologize for anything," I scream back at all of them.

I leave, running as fast as I can through the gardens and onto the driveway. My heart is beating erratically, and my breaths are far and few between. In the complete still of darkness, I'm finally alone but stumble on the stone driveway. I fall to the ground amongst the gravel, my hand scraping along the jagged edges.

There is pain.

But I am numb.

The only pain I feel is that Julian walked away.

He has given up on us.

Again, someone has given up on *me.*

TWENTY-ONE

There's something to be said about a broken heart—it's not only your heart that breaks, it's all of you. Mind, body, and soul.

Alone, I fall into the trap of darkness, silenced by the pain which feels oh so familiar. My heart may have been broken and scarred, but now, the wounds are open, and I'm bleeding.

I see nothing.

I want nothing.

It's cold and lonely, with no warmth or light to guide me.

It doesn't matter how many times I've experienced it, time does not give me the wisdom or strength to handle the situation any better. I should be a pro at this. I've experienced more pain than I ever thought imaginable. Yet, here I am, desolate, weak, and I can barely breathe.

Somehow, I ended up at Eric's, rugged up in a heavy woolen blanket wearing one of his white cotton shirts. Instead of allowing me to sleep, which seems like an impossible task, Tristan and Eric form the pity party by my side, trying to reassure me everything will work out, and that Julian was having a rough night.

Rough night or rough life?

I don't see sense, and every decision I've made since the moment I walked into that support group haunts me. Should I have seen this coming? Am I that gullible? But even after I ask myself those questions, there's one thing which stands out more than anything—he said he loved me.

My eyes eventually start to droop, suspecting Eric slipped something into the Chinese tea he forced me to drink, and sleep's calling me.

Sleep—either my friend or my foe.

Tonight, it's my friend.

I open my eyes to be greeted by a bright light shining throughout the perfectly furnished room. The sun is basking me with all its glory, reminding me it's a new day and a new start to life. Tell me this is a nightmare? My hope is shattered as I see my costume beside me along with my heart, which lays helplessly on the floor smashed into a million pieces.

The apartment is silent, no voices are heard. My cell beside me reads seven, and sadly, no texts or calls wait on the screen, forcing my body to fall back into the cushions. My eyes are sore, closing them momentarily for relief, but the second my sight is blank, Julian's face haunts me.

And the knife twists deeper inside me.

Eric and Tristan come through the front door, dressed in gym gear carrying a white paper bag. They both give me a sympathetic smile, but I have nothing to give in return.

Tristan takes a seat at the edge of the sofa, pulling out a bagel, handing it to me.

I shake my head, refusing.

"Adriana, you can't do this to yourself. You're already a stick," Eric begs me.

I stare blankly at him.

Tristan moves the bagel toward my mouth and pleads with his eyes to take a bite. All I see is Julian—his hair, his jaw, and the way his eyes wrinkle when he smiles. I take a bite, but only one.

"Now let me tell you about my Aunt Patty," Eric says. "Married for twenty years and husband left her for his dental assistant. Busted him in the chair with the twenty-something-year-old using that sucky dental tool on his wang."

"What?" I exclaim, momentarily pulled out of my funk.

"Eric, how is this helping right now?" Tristan complains.

"Was he hard? No, wait, dumb question, you're talking about that thing they put in your mouth that sucks the saliva?"

Tristan shakes his head. "It's not the dentist you made me go to last month, is it?"

"Of course not. His business is in Florida somewhere. And yes, Adriana, that compressor thing. So, as I was saying, she caught him red-handed. According to Aunt Patty, his dick was so tiny she was surprised it didn't get sucked up and flushed down the drain."

Tristan smirks at both of us. "Again, how is this helping right now?"

"She lost like a hundred pounds and looks fabulous. I'm just trying to point out that sometimes a bad situation can turn into something good."

"I'm still trying to understand where the good in this story is?" Tristan scowls, taking a sip of his juice.

"Oh!" Eric laughs to himself. "I forgot to mention that as payback, she started screwing her husband's best friend, and this new guy was hung like a horse. He'd go at it till the cows came home."

My throat makes an odd gurgle, and I realize it's a laugh trying to escape.

"Eric, what is it with your sexual comparison to barnyard animals?"

"Adriana, you haven't even heard the start of it," Tristan warns.

"Look, you laughed, a little giggle. This will work itself out, okay? Just take care of yourself and Andy," Eric reminds me.

I nod with a small smile, grateful for Eric and Tristan's friendship. Eric moves over to my side and hands me the rest of the bagel. I eat it this time and thank him silently for taking care of me.

I announce I'm going to head home after being asked for the hundredth time if I'm okay. The only thing I need right now more than anything is my son.

Sitting on the sofa, I press play on the DVD as Andy and I snuggle to watch the movie *Toy Story 3*. Mary Jean just left to head back home with the promise of visiting again shortly. With my baby curled into my side, I sniff his hair until he pushes me away. Andy never likes to talk during movies, watching intently with his eyes and laughing on cue. Andy loves *Toy Story* and will jump every time he hears his name and say, "Mama! That's my name!"

I laugh as Ken graces the screen with his over-the-top fashion, something which confuses Andy, of course. It's nice to give my mind a break, but it's short-lived as the movie comes to an end. I start to bawl like a baby at the character, Andy, going to college. What the fuck is wrong with me? It's just a damn movie.

Andy has fallen asleep in my arms. I cradle and carry him up the stairs. Inside his room, I place him on his bed, tucking him in. Tiptoeing away, I make it to my room and just to torture myself, I check my cell. *Nothing*. Climbing into bed, my head falls against the pillow. Sleep seems so good right now, and just when I think it's the answer to my problems, my body shudders unexpectedly, and the sobs build up in my chest.

Tonight, I cry into my pillow.

That's day one over.

Day two, I'm a human-robot.

Going through the motions, switching to mom-mode during the day, busying myself with Andy and with some work at the boutique. I don't stop to think about *him* all day. I'm strong. I need to give myself some credit here. Who needs a man, anyway? Okay, a little overboard and googling *First Wives Clubs* in LA seems a little insane and very 'I am woman hear me roar.' I may be all woman, but I stopped roaring sometime after Andy fell asleep. I feel the familiar spiral come on, and just as I break out the sweatpants, Eric is at my front door dressed in his fancy thousand-dollar pajamas.

"Did you drive here in those?" I ask as he stands on my porch.

"Yes, now let me in because that weird lady across the street is eying me from her house. She looks like Kathy

Bates, don't you think? Is your cell charged in case we need help?"

"Get inside, drama queen."

Eric is carrying a bag. He takes me to my bedroom, and we both climb into bed. He pulls out an ancient-looking Walkman and places it between us. He then pulls out a tape that reads *'The Greatest Love Songs of all Time.'*

"How is listening to sad music going to help?"

"My first ever breakup was with a guy named Bobby Hart. I still remember it like it was yesterday. Anyway, my mom gave me this tape. She said you have to go through the motions and let it all out."

He follows by taking out a zip-lock bag full of miniature bottles of alcohol, then another bag full of chocolate bars. With a headphone placed in one ear, he clicks the button and presses play. I recognize the tune immediately as 'I'm All Out of Love' by Air Supply that blasts through the headphones.

Fuck, it hurts like hell.

I find myself singing along, out of tune, and when the pain strikes hard, the little bottle of gin numbs me, and the pain becomes a little less. But after a high, comes the fall which happens somewhere in Sinead O'Connor's 'Nothing Compares to You.' Even Eric starts crying, and just when our tears seemed unstoppable, we lose ourselves in the chocolate and head on to the scotch. Now, the scotch seems to work wonders, using our gospel voices and over-dramatic hand gestures for 'Hero' by Mariah Carey, but then we hit rock bottom. Whitney Houston starts singing 'I Will Always Love You.'

"Eric, I miss him. He said he loved me," I openly cry.

"I know you do. I miss having him around, too. He does love you, Adriana."

"Why did he leave me?"

Eric opens a bottle of vodka and hands it to me. "He's got things to work through. It got hard. He'll come back."

I down the bottle in one go, letting out a rasp as the burn invades my throat. "You can't promise that."

"I swear on my vintage Chanel messenger bag he will return."

"Eric, you can't swear on that. You love that bag."

"Okay, you're right. I swear on my Armani loafers."

"The crocodile skin ones?"

"Uh-huh."

"You hate those shoes. You said they pinch your toes, and you're worried that you'll end up with a fungal toe, and people will make fun of you on the street."

"Did I say that?"

"You did. Back to swearing on the bag."

It may not have been the man I wanted in my bed tonight but snuggling into Eric's side is second best.

I don't cry tonight.

Instead, the nightmares plague me.

The next couple of days, I went through the motions just like Eric said. A major one was guilt. I may have been upset and drunk, but I had no right to call Charlie what I did.

With five days passing, I feel like shit for not contacting her sooner knowing that an apology is well-deserved. The best way to see her will be in her office, and Eric was quick to inform me that she would be at work tomorrow.

With Andy settled into daycare, I make my way across town to Charlie's office.

I sit in front of her desk and wait for her to enter,

fiddling my thumbs nervously as I cross my legs, ignoring the annoying twitch building up in my knees.

The office is small yet modern and posh. Eric's mother had flown over from New York and decorated it in one day. She has connections across the country, and her style is modern chic. Charlie's office is mainly white with a feature wall covered in Damask fabric with a beautiful pattern. The black stands out amongst the white, and behind Charlie's desk are shelves perfectly aligned with files, books, and pictures of her family. The desk in front of me is spotless, not a single speck of dust nor an item of stationery out of place. Lex and Charlie are both clean freaks. I don't consider myself messy, but I'm not exactly going to have a meltdown if a pen is out of place.

A gust of wind enters the room followed by the click of heels. I turn around, and Charlie is walking toward me. At first, she doesn't notice, busily carrying a laptop and several folders. The second she does, she freezes for a brief moment letting out a gasp almost dropping everything. Composing herself, she walks around and places everything on her desk.

"Hi, Charlie," I greet her softly.

She acknowledges me with a lukewarm smile. I deserve it. Working in silence, she plugs the laptop into the docking station and takes a seat. I can't help but notice her dark gray pantsuit. It fits her like a glove, joined with a crisp white fitted shirt. Charlie is naturally beautiful, and it's blatantly obvious at this moment why my brother worships the ground she walks on. I'm tongue-tied, trying to find the right words.

Geez, I've had days to prepare my apology, and now I go blank.

This is starting off really bad.

"God, I'm so sorry for being the biggest bitch on the

planet. It was so uncalled for and not true. I just... fuck, I can't even think straight and apologize right," I babble.

She remains silent, poised, and calm. Pushing her glasses past the bridge of her nose, she leans back into the chair, crossing her legs appropriately.

"It was uncalled for, mean, and very out of character. It hurt to be called such a disgusting word by someone who I consider my sister."

I nod, almost on the verge of tears.

"Adriana, I don't know where this is coming from. Julian adores you, and yet you threw it all in his face because of your insecurities."

"It's not easy being compared to you."

She laughs momentarily. "Adriana, no one is comparing us except for you. You wanted us to all get along, and I tried my damn hardest to control Lex, but it doesn't help that you keep throwing fuel into the fire."

"Well, it's done and over with." My bleak response is the harsh cold reality of it all.

Charlie lets out a long sigh. "Both of you have a lot of personal struggles. Just like any relationship, there's the peak and the fall. This is your fall. Sometimes there are several falls, but getting up and working toward the peak, that's what love is all about."

She's right. Julian and I have our struggles. It's never going to be a perfect love story.

"You love him, Adriana?"

I nod instantly.

"Then heal yourself before you try to heal your relationship. Use this time apart wisely."

"What if he doesn't want that? What if he finds someone else?" I ask in a panic.

"If he loves you like he confessed that night, he won't

look for anyone else. You need to trust his word, too, Adriana, and allow him time to heal."

It makes sense. Both of us rely heavily on each other to fix the broken past never realizing that some things can never be repaired. Just like Julian once told me, putting a Band-Aid on the problem doesn't make it go away.

"I'm sorry, Charlie."

Charlie walks around the desk motioning for me to stand. Wrapping her arms around me, I allow my head to fall on her shoulder, and lo and behold, the waterworks start again covering her jacket.

"You're forgiven, but next time I want an apology basket full of chocolate, flowers, and your Dylan McKay Barbie doll," she says lightheartedly.

"I forgot about him. And besides, there won't be a next time." I smile apologetically.

She takes a seat back in her chair and tells me about Amelia's tantrum occurring in the grocery store yesterday, even showing me a video. It's YouTube-worthy, and wow, what an outburst over some candy. How Charlie remains calm is beyond me, especially with Ava crying in her carrier.

"It was mortifying. Everyone was judging me, and the only reason I filmed it was I knew Lex wouldn't believe me and would probably buy her a pony to cheer her up. You can imagine how surprised I was when Lex got home and had a word with her. She did her whole daddy-I-love-you bullshit, but he was strong and didn't back down."

"Wow, I can't believe Lex disciplined her. He's finally becoming a man."

"Yeah, I know. She's not allowed to play with her Batmobile for a week, and let me tell you, she cried like it was the end of the world. Lex couldn't believe it."

"Sounds like you had one hell of a week."

"Not as bad as yours, Adriana, but I can use a night out with my besties. You free tonight for a quick drink somewhere? We don't need to make it a whole night out, and Lex can watch Andy."

"Sure, you better call drama queen and let him know."

I go to stand, but my dress gets caught in the handle of the chair, and I fall to the floor scraping my wrist on a loose screw drilled into the table. *Ouch!*

"You okay?" Charlie rushes to my side and gasps as she sees the blood on my arm.

"It's okay. Hand me some tissues, please."

She quickly grabs the box, and I dab my arm. Pulling it away, it doesn't appear too deep, only a surface scratch.

"I'm so clumsy. I'll see you tonight."

Charlie says goodbye, and I wave in return. As I leave the office, a huge weight has been lifted off my shoulders, and I count my blessings Charlie is able to forgive me.

That's the thing about family, no matter how violent the storm, they'll always be there to watch the rainbow with you.

I just pray my rainbow will find a way in his heart to forgive me.

TWENTY-TWO

We settled on a Brazilian bar not too far from the beach.

Eric's already complaining about his day at work and that the dry cleaners couldn't remove an ink stain on the crotch of his new dress pants.

"Why is there an ink stain on your crotch?" Charlie asks him.

"For some stupid reason, I keep my pen in my pocket which I never do for this very reason."

"Oh, that's embarrassing." I cringe.

"You're telling me. This hot waiter kept eyeing my crotch, and I was like 'whoa baby, hold your horses, you haven't even taken my drink order yet' but turns out it was the ink stain."

"Are you forgetting about your beautiful man at home?" Charlie reminds him.

"No, but I'm not completely off the market," he tells us.

I place my drink down fast. "Wait." I lift my hand to stop him talking. "You're telling me that you and Tristan have an open relationship?"

"I wouldn't say open, but you know…"

"Does Tristan know?" Charlie is using her interrogation voice, obviously just as shocked as I am about Eric's relationship status.

"We have an understanding," he says flatly.

Both of us wait for his response, and when the tumbleweed drifts past us, I nudge him along. "And that is…"

"Look, we're both young. Who knows what tomorrow will bring? We both agreed that if either of us doesn't feel the same way, it's time to move on. Besides, he got a second callback for a lead in this big Hollywood flick, and well, you know, fame can change him."

"But don't you think that sometimes you need to work on a relationship? It's not always rosy. Okay, I'm the wrong person to be giving relationship advice right now," I admit with a heavy heart.

"How you been feeling?" Eric asks in a quieter tone.

"Honestly? I feel like this is an out-of-body experience. I don't know what happened to me that night. Jealousy possessed me."

Charlie is nodding her head while sipping on her Long Island iced tea.

"Okay, so very awkward, but here goes…" She takes a deep breath, keeping her gaze on me.

"Is this about comparing technique?" Eric's eyes widened. "I just don't think—"

"Will you shut up and let me continue?" Charlie berates him. "And no… what's wrong with you, E? As I was saying, when I was with him, women were like drooling hounds wherever we went, but you know as well as I do that Julian is so kind natured. He'd never intentionally hurt someone he loves."

She takes a long sip of her drink and continues, "Now,

Lex, on the other hand, is the same in that respect. The women are throwing thongs at his face half the time. The difference is that he is an arrogant ass, and women tend to back off unless you're into that whole alpha male bullshit."

"Oh, yes, I understand." Eric points his index finger at his mouth while thinking. "But don't you think they are alike in many ways?"

"Don't look at me. You're asking me to compare my brother and ex-boyfriend."

"Oh, not you, I mean Charlie, but then again... okay, don't shoot me, but aren't you guys the least bit curious to talk about your um... shared experience?"

"Oh, I'll shoot you, Eric. Sometimes I wonder what planet you came from?" Charlie scolds.

"Uranus, like duh?"

"Okay, Eric, you may ask only three questions to both Charlie and me, then we're never having this conversation again. Locking it in the vault, burying it ten feet under the ground, and throwing the key into the bottom of the Mariana Trench."

"What's the Mariana Trench?" he asks.

"The deepest part of the Pacific Ocean which is the deepest ocean in the world. Question two."

"What? No fair! That wasn't a question!"

"I think it was, Eric," Charlie agrees.

He mumbles under his breath, and then his face lights up like a light bulb went off in his head. "Who's bigger, Lex or Julian?"

I spit out my drink across the table spraying Eric. He immediately tells me off, wiping his suit down with napkins. "Eric, what kind of a question is that? I don't want to hear this."

"On par, the same, maybe just a different color,"

Charlie blurts out. "I'm sorry, Adriana, blame the rum inside this drink."

"OMG, totally a spit-roast fantasy of mine."

I shake my head in disbelief. "The both of you are very lucky that I've had two Long Island iced teas because I'm this close to grabbing that old man sitting over there and getting him to turkey slap the crap out of you two."

Eric ignores me, raising his hand to grab our attention. "I have one more question, and this goes to Adriana."

I let out a drawn-out sigh, waiting for his inappropriate question. "If you saw Julian again, right now, would you tell him you love him?"

Taken aback by his question, Charlie and Eric wait impatiently, their eyes on me making me self-conscious.

"If I had the chance, then yes, I would."

They both remain oddly quiet, then change the subject back onto Tristan.

"So, Tristan's thinking about getting a Prince Albert," Eric says casually.

The conversation does a complete one-eighty. I try to drown out their warped discussion about genitalia piercings and switch my attention to the crowd. The bar is dimly lit with spotlights hanging off the walls pointed at the various artwork. They are gorgeous, and I can't help but be mesmerized by the painting of a man and woman entwined naked in the forest. My mind doesn't need to go there, nor does my lady bits. It's time to refocus on something else, and the bearded lady walking past me seems to throw cold water over me. *Wow, now that was a beard!* I'd hate to think what's growing down below if she can't trim her face.

I inform Charlie and Eric that I'm heading to the bar, bored by their conversation. At the bar, I take a seat and stare at the menu wanting to venture out and order something new. I'm not alone for long as a young, good-looking male slips in beside me. He is cute, and I use the word cute because he looks like he's Eric's age. I'm surprised by his forwardness as he begins chatting away, and so as not to be rude, I listen intently.

His name is River, and he just moved here from Texas. His accent is okay. I hate to admit, it's downright sexy. As is the way he licked his lips every time he mentioned the word *rodeo*. Wait until Eric catches wind of this. He'll be visualizing chaps and naked ass cheeks riding bucking bulls.

Perhaps this is my problem. I jumped straight into a relationship with Julian and never played the field. Maybe I need to date, let loose, and have fun, except I'm not that type of woman. I have a son to think about, plus I'm madly in love with Julian.

Okay, stupid plan.

For a brief moment, my eyes wander and quickly do a double-take. *Is that?* No, Adriana, you just miss him, and it's all in your sad imagination. So, one more time just to be sure, I turn around and look again. It's him standing in the corner dressed in a dark gray suit and black collared shirt. There isn't enough light to see the features of his face, but all that flies out the window when I notice a woman with long ebony hair standing alongside him, chatting animatedly as he laughs and smiles along with her. I wait for him to turn around, and the second he does, my heart is beating crazy and has fallen into the pit of my stomach.

We've only been apart for less than two weeks and already he has moved on. I don't walk over to him, it's pretty obvious he is seeing this woman. Body language is a dead giveaway. I turn back around and re-focus on River, but for the life of me, I can't comprehend what he's saying. The fan that's positioned above the bar blows air into my eyes, and I catch a whiff of his scent. *Fuck, your imagination is going nuts.* River slides me over a drink, and just when I go to grab it, a hand slides between us. I recognize his fingers immediately.

Those fingers. My body has officially gone into meltdown mode. Remember where those fingers have been? Do you remember how you screamed from the top of your lungs when you came all over them? I shake my head trying to drown out my inner dialogue. My head doesn't want to face him, but my body does on its own accord. Just be civil, you're a strong woman and can handle this situation maturely.

"Hey, buddy, how 'bout you keep this drink to yourself?" Julian grits his teeth waiting on a response.

Don't make eye contact.

River is annoyed. "If the lady wants a drink, then who are you to stop her?"

"How about I tell the club owner, Mitch, about how you've just slipped a roofie into this glass?"

What the fuck!

River raises his hands before him, standing up and walking away leaving us alone. Julian's face is dead serious. His nostrils are flaring in rage, his eyes are wild and ready to pounce.

"I wouldn't have drunk it anyway," I mumble.

"Yes, you would have. What were you thinking?"

I turn to face him this time. His eyes have softened, and they reflect back at me. For a moment, I think I see love, but it disappears as his eyes turn back to the lady with the ebony hair.

"I'm not thinking," I tell him honestly. "And maybe you should go back to your *date.*"

It cut like a knife, deep and straight to the base of my

heart. Here is the man I love with another woman at a bar. Everything we had that I fought hard for, means absolutely nothing. I can't fight the pang that's wildly spreading throughout me, and any ounce of strength I've gained in the past week is crumbling at a rapid rate.

"Adriana. It's not a date. I'm sorry if it looks like that."

"It looks like you need to get over me, so you're fucking any slut you can get your hands on," I respond bitterly, maturity out the door while the jealousy dominates and has taken hold. I've had enough of this bullshit, and slide off the chair to escape him, but his firm grip on my arm holds me back.

"Tell me, weren't you doing the same thing a minute ago?"

It's laughable. "So what if I did? I don't belong to you. I can fuck whoever the hell I want to."

I regret my words immediately, but his jealous streak that's blindly obvious makes me feel less regretful. *Good, he's hurting just as much.*

"I need to explain what happened that night at Rocky's party."

I wait for his explanation and frustrated, he runs his hands through his messy hair. The second I look away, he lifts my wrist. *Oh shit.* He's the last person who needs to see this even though it looks worse than what it is.

"What the fuck is this?"

"It's not what you think it is. I fell in Charlie's office."

"Is that the story you're going with?"

"Nothing I say or do will make you believe me. Think what you want, Julian. You ended it with me. What I do is no longer any of your concern. Perhaps you should walk back to your girlfriend over there." I'm on the verge of tears and desperate to escape him. Maybe forever.

"Adriana." He holds back my arm once again.

"Let me go."

Through tears, I find Eric and Charlie. One look at me, and they know it's time to leave.

Outside, we're just about to get into a cab when Julian calls out my name. I ignore him, but he is quick to hold the cab door open. "Adriana, please don't do this to yourself," he pleads.

"The fact that you would think that I'd stoop that low again is what hurts the most. I love you, Julian. Not being with you hurts more than I imagined, but I'm strong, I'll get through this."

"Y-You..." he stutters. "You love me?"

I want to say yes. I want to tell him how much I love him, and I want to *show* him. Those words that are critical to this moment refuse to come out, and no matter how much I try to connect my mind and heart, my lips remain tightly sealed.

"Just stay, why don't we talk?"

"I've nothing left to say."

"She's not who you think she is," he repeats.

"What does it matter anymore? You're not mine, you can be with whoever you please. I need to go home to my son now. Goodbye, Julian."

I shrug my arm out of his grip and close the cab door behind me. With Charlie and Eric by my side, the cab drives off, and the strength which consumed me only moments ago falters, and I'm struggling to compose myself. When the bar is out of sight, I think my sobs will release, but I'm drained, and all cried out.

Life is too hard.

Love is too hard.

People keep telling me love will happen again and will

just fall into place. Well, I'm ready to give up, defeated and dead-tired of the emotional rollercoaster I'm riding.

It's all about my son and me now.

I may have missed him, even loved him with all my heart.

And that's why walking away breaks me harder than when he told me it was over.

TWENTY-THREE

"Here, drink this." Charlie hands me a mug. It's hand-painted with pictures of love hearts. I think it's love hearts, or maybe that's all I can see right now. On closer inspection, Amelia's name is scribbled in paint. I take a sip, and the delicious taste of warm chocolate milk delights my taste buds. Charlie sits on the arm of the couch and places her arm around Lex's shoulder.

"Are you sure you don't want something to eat? I could make your favorite sandwich if you want?"

I decline the offer, sinking into the couch and allowing the cushions to embrace me. So, this is why people use so many cushions on their couch. I need to tell Julian that the next time...

Except there is *no* next time.

Charlie announces she is heading to bed due to an early morning court case. She leans down and kisses Lex before disappearing to their bedroom. The cushions surrounding me move as Lex shifts uncomfortably dressed in his pajama bottoms and a white V-neck tee.

"Andy is asleep in Amelia's room. Why don't you sleep here?"

I nod, agreeing. It's all I can muster up. Silence falls between us, and I wish Lex would leave me alone, so I can cry myself to sleep, but he continues to linger.

"Adriana, please stop doing this to yourself," he orders. "I don't like seeing you like this..." He is quick to avert his eyes. "I can't stand to see you like this again."

He has seen me at my worse, and I mean at the bottom of a hole alone in the dark kind of worse. Sometimes, it feels like I'm a burden on my family, and those are the times I sport that fake smile of mine and reassure everyone I'm great.

This isn't one of those times despite how much he wants us apart.

"It fucking hurts. I hate that it hurts. Why would he be with someone else?" I don't expect an answer. I was asking the question to someone who loathes Julian.

Lex's expression is conflicted, and he lets out a long-winded breath obviously debating whether or not he's the right person for this conversation. "Fuck, this is hard to even talk about. It's the case of two scenarios, Adriana. Either it's not what you think it is, or he is trying to use her to forget you."

"Is it that easy for a guy to do that? I mean, to have sex with a stranger just to forget?"

"Yes."

"But I don't understand. I couldn't even imagine touching someone without having a connection."

"Guys don't care. I don't think Charlotte knows this, but after that day I saw her and Julian in the restaurant for the first time, I was desperate for anything to take my mind off her. I thought I was going insane."

"What did you do?"

"I didn't do anything, the chick did."

"Oh."

"I hate even talking about this, and it proves how much I love you, sister, but I have no doubt that it would've been the same for Charlotte with Julian. I mean, she runs into me, and her life is turned upside down. What's the first thing you do?"

You fuck the brains out of your fiancé to forget that your ex, who left you without an explanation nine years ago, just walked back into your life. I don't know who that hurt the most at this moment, Lex or me. How can I be jealous of something that happened in the past? Where was I three years ago? I was married to a man I had planned to spend the rest of my life with. Julian has a past, and so do I. If I didn't dwell so much on the past, then maybe our future may have had a chance, and I wouldn't be in this predicament.

"You must really love me to admit that. You know, Lex, this was never about hurting you or Charlie."

He tilts his head and cracks his neck. "You have to understand my position here, Adriana. He did things that are unforgivable."

"We all do things that are unforgivable. You aren't exactly *perfect* either. We make mistakes, but they are only mistakes if we don't redeem ourselves and learn from them. I know Julian has his flaws, and I also respect your stance on this, but at the end of the day, I deserve to be loved again, and if it's with him, you need to accept that. The heart wants what the heart wants."

"You don't know what he did to Charlotte—"

"I do know, Lex. You've told me, but who am I to judge? It's like we just sit in this circle of pity and point fingers at each other. Julian has his flaws, but fuck, so do I, and stupidly enough, I let that get between us."

He bites back without resisting. "You think it's easy for me to see him near Charlotte given his past? If I lost her... I just couldn't—"

"You won't fucking lose her. She loves you. You have two children together, and because he made a bad decision, it ended up saving your wife and child's life. I can't understand how you can have what the two of you have and still be so insecure."

"And so, you tell me you love him and yet look at where you are? Did your insecurities not get the better of you?"

Touché. It did get the better of me. It's ugly, a disease that spreads like wildfire and can't be tamed.

"You're right. Look at where I am. I failed. I just couldn't control the jealous side of me. With Elijah, it was easy. It's not like girls didn't look at him, but it was never like this. Everywhere I turn, some woman has their eyes on Julian or even their claws. Who's to say that one of those women will give him what I can't?"

"And if you asked him the same question, he will probably say the same thing. You just deal with it, Adriana. Charlotte is... well, fucking stunning. I don't turn a blind eye to every glance she gets, but I can't exactly dress her in a burlap sack and place garlic around her neck to fight off the dirty fuckers who look at her."

"True, but Charlie will make a burlap sack look hot. You're screwed either way."

Lex's mouth widens into a cheeky grin, his eyes light up as he hopelessly smiles acknowledging the sentiment.

The clock on the wall ticks, it's the only sound that can be heard in the room. Tired and sleepy, I let out a yawn.

Lex appears to be wide awake, ignoring my need for sleep. "Andy asked for him tonight."

"Oh, it was bound to happen. What did you say?"

"He asked if he went to the same place his daddy lives at."

My heart drops into my stomach leaving me nauseous and completely gutted. Andy had a bond with him, and during the shit-storm I started, I forgot about how he'd be affected in all of this. My eyes pool over, and not wanting to cry in front of my brother, I raise my head toward the ceiling and remain wide-eyed because the second I blink, I won't be able to stop the tears.

"I don't know how to make this right," I admit.

"Lord knows I can't change what your heart wants because, trust me, I would if I could. You'll figure it out, but for now, just get better, okay?"

He's right. I need to get better for my son and me.

"Lex, can you take me somewhere tomorrow?"

He places his arm around my shoulder and pulls me into an embrace. Kissing the top of my head, he responds softly, "Anywhere you want to go, sis."

It's dark yet bursting with light.

The candles are flickering as they sit in a row beside the altar. The flame is bright and mesmerizing, igniting the tiny ounce of hope I'm barely clinging onto. I'm surrounded in a place which protects me. It eases my fears and calms my nerves.

The pictures on the wall remind me of suffering, and as I kneel on the pew and pray in silence. I'm not sure what or who I am praying for, just guidance and peace. Lex is sitting in a pew behind me. He stares straight ahead with a barren expression. My knees give a slight crack as I stand, walking behind to where Lex is sitting. In silence, we both sit alongside each other, and just before I tell Lex it's time to go, a warm feeling suddenly rushes over me. It's unfamiliar and follows with a slight breeze. I don't even check to see if the doors are open. Instead, I close my eyes, and his voice echoes all around me. I can't make out the words he is saying, but his tone is calm and at peace.

I jump as Lex grabs my hand to squeeze it tight.

The voice stops, and unknowingly, the tears have fallen silently down my face. I miss Elijah, I'll always miss him, but Julian is here, and I need to make things right. I must, once and for all, show him how much I love him.

I speak to Elijah, barely a whisper, and whether or not he can hear me, I say the words I need to get off my chest. *"I'll never truly understand why you left us. I know you can see Julian. I want to tell you, Elijah, that I love him. It'll never be the same as the love I feel for you, but it's just as valuable. He makes me happy, and he loves Andy. I'm finally moving on, just like you told me to. Forgive me for my mistakes and my anger."*

Lex's grip on my hand is tight, and he continues to be mute.

"I thought about being with you so many times, and if it weren't for my family and Julian, I'd have caused more damage than good. I'll never stop loving you and never stop thinking about you. Every time I see Andy's face, you're looking right back at me."

With my voice trembling, I say my final thoughts. *"I love you, Elijah. May you finally rest in peace knowing we're okay."*

I sob uncontrollably, turning into Lex's arms. My chest

hurts, and my ribs ache with every breath I try to catch. Lex moves his hands to the back of my head and holds me tightly to his chest as I clutch onto his jacket.

How long I remain like this is uncertain. When I finally peel myself off him, he stares into my eyes, and in full confidence, says the one thing that reassures me more than I can ever imagine.

"You're going to be just fine, Adriana," he says, followed by a loving smile.

Does it mean what I think it means? That my happiness is important to him, and Julian will finally be accepted? I search his emerald green eyes for an answer, and as desperate as I am to find one, looking back at me is my big brother. Someone who has been by my side from the moment I came into this world, a man who tries to protect me from all the evil in this world, a man who will forever be my blood.

This is no longer a game of who won, and just maybe, I won't be forced to choose one or the other.

In the car, the mood is quiet, but it's what both of us need. The mellow sounds of Bob Marley play softly over the car stereo. With Lex concentrating on driving, I lean my head against the window and watch the city pass us by.

Twenty minutes later, we pull up into the daycare. Both of us get out of the car and make our way to the gated entrance. I punch in my code to open the main door. Lex tells me he is just going to look through the glass window to watch the kids while I sign Andy out. Amelia is at my mom's today along with baby Ava so that Charlie can work.

With the pen in my hand, I go to the clipboard but notice a signature beside his name. I don't recognize it at all and query the young girl working behind the main desk.

"Jennie, why is there a signature beside Andy's name?"

"Oh, about an hour ago his grandpa picked him up," she says plainly.

"My dad's in San Francisco. You must have got it wrong. I'll just go get him from the room."

"No, Mrs. Evans. The man said he was Andy's grandfather," she responds, but this time her face looks panicked. This girl is fucking hopeless, and if this is a joke, it's beyond ridiculous now.

"Jennie, this isn't a joke," I say sternly. "Where's my son?"

Lex walks back from the room with a concerned face. "Andy isn't here."

The bile in my throat rises, and my body starts to shake manically. Jennie begins to stutter out words I can't comprehend. She leaves and returns within seconds with the manager.

"Andrea, where's Andy?" I beg her for answers.

Andrea's face turns to Jennie, and they speak in code, something passes between them, and Jennie begins to clutch her chest while shaking her head.

"I'm sorry, Mrs. Evans. Jennie is new here. We can watch the footage and see who it was." She rushes back to her office, and I follow, hoping it's Julian who picked him up. With the video footage rewound, I see an older-looking man with his head down as Jennie speaks to him. I don't recognize him at all and look over to Lex as the panic sets in.

This isn't happening.

It's a nightmare—just wake up now!

"Where's my baby?" I demand, sobbing as the scream echoes through the office.

Lex grabs his cell and dials 9-1-1. The sound of his voice drowns out as I struggle to find Julian's number, the screen is blurred as I tremble in fear. Finally, the call connects, and I pray he will answer.

"Adriana?"

I sob into the phone, mumbling, paralyzed with shock.

"Adriana, what's wrong?"

"My baby... someone took my baby."

Julian demands to know where I am, but I can barely speak let alone recite the address of the daycare. The cell slides out of my hand and crashes onto the floor. With hope that this is all a cruel joke, I turn to Lex for reassurance, but his face is red as he howls at the manager, her pleading with him to calm down as she cries uncontrollably.

Helpless and frightened, I slide against the wall and sit on the floor hugging my knees as I rock back and forth.

Moments later, Julian bursts through the front door behind the police. He spots me and rushes over falling to his knees. I look directly into his eyes, and suddenly, my blood drains as the realization that Julian is alone and without Andy. Julian places his hand on my face, the panic reflecting in his eyes confirms what my head refuses to believe every parent's worst nightmare.

Someone has kidnapped my son.

TWENTY-FOUR

LEX

As a parent, we're programmed to protect our children from the moment they lay in their mother's womb. Just like in the wild, our instincts are to nurture, care for our children, and ensure they are never harmed or experience suffering or pain. We guide them, educate them, give them the tools to succeed to become the greatest person they can be. The emotions attached to becoming a parent are ones that nothing in life can prepare you for, but somehow, we get through each day, and if there's one thing I know in my life that I did right, it's creating my beautiful girls with Charlotte.

Andy isn't biologically my son, but he is my blood, and from the moment I rested my eyes on this little boy, the connection between us was a force so strong that it caught me by surprise. He's the beautiful, innocent little baby who, at only one week old, has suffered more pain than I have in my entire lifetime.

He lost his father.

I knew I had to protect him. He may not have called me Dad, but I treated him no different to my own daughters. It isn't fair he had a rough start to life, and it's not fair he'd grow up and not understand what it's like to call a man Daddy.

No kid deserves that.

Adriana was bound to find someone, I just didn't expect it to be so soon, and the giant fucking curveball bigger than planet Jupiter, it was Julian Baker.

How this motherfucker managed to waltz back into our lives without me knowing rang alarm bells. I had Bryce do a background check on him again, and it came back all clear. He'd been in Australia promoting some book bullshit, but that didn't ease my apprehension. I was beyond livid, outraged, and lashing out at everyone around me the moment they revealed their affair. It almost cost me my marriage, jumping to all sorts of conclusions that Charlotte was somewhat aware of the situation. I refused to lose my wife, fucking her into oblivion every spare moment we had. She was mine, and who would've thought that I'd complain about a sore dick. Fuck, even so I still carried on. I was on a mission.

And my sister—I've never felt so much hatred as I did when she told me the truth—to disrespect my brother, Elijah, to bring that low-life scum back into our lives after what he did to Charlotte. Just because he 'saved' Charlotte and Ava that night she crashed the car, didn't mean I owed him a damn thing, let alone be grateful he was fucking my sister.

But throughout all this, I remained one step ahead of him, feeding off his weaknesses and creating the temptation. It isn't a coincidence Charlotte was dressed in that costume. She looked hot, and no man could resist her, especially the one who had stalked her for almost a year. The fight between my sister and him was the highlight of the night.

The moment I'd been waiting for—he had given up and told her it was over.

I didn't expect to feel guilty, but it hit me like a wrecking ball, watching my sister suffer. She was spiraling into a depression similar to losing Elijah, and suddenly, I found myself desperately trying to avoid this at all costs, even if it means that I need to show remorse over the whole sorry episode.

That scum I keep referring to—I was no different, and it was Andy's cries for Julian that was a wake-up call if ever I needed one. It killed me to admit that watching Julian with Andy was what hurt the most. He replaced me. I was no longer the man he asked for, and his face stopped lighting up every time I walked into the room. He may have been just a kid and totally unaware his actions could cut so deep, but nevertheless, my hate for Julian grew to an entirely different level.

I was glad to see the back of him, and making sure Andy and I repaired our relationship was my top priority. What I didn't expect, what no parent ever expects, is to be living this fucking nightmare.

Andy has been taken.

The police are a bunch of fucking idiots, spitting out their bullshit to file a report. I'm furious, yelling at the useless fucks for not helping us find my nephew quicker. Adriana is inconsolable, her body limp as Julian holds onto her. His feeble attempts to calm her down are fruitless as she begins to hyperventilate, vomiting all over the floor.

Charlotte rushes to her side, having just arrived as both of them attend to her aid.

This is all his fucking fault.

I cannot reason.

I cannot think straight.

My Andy is missing.

Charlotte is surrounded by paper towels and a bucket, panicked and in tears. She passes a wet towel to Julian, and taking it, he gently wipes her face. Adriana is pale, ghostly white, her eyes dull and lacking any emotion.

Charlotte stands up and walks over, pulling me aside for more information.

"We don't know who this man is," I mutter.

"Can we see the video again? Maybe I might know him?"

I nod, anything to find out who this fucking low-life is who took Andy. We head back into the office and rewind the footage.

Julian enters the room and watches in silence. "I've seen him before."

I turn abruptly to face Julian. *Talk, fucker!* I glare at him waiting for a response.

"The night that Mary Jean was staying at the house, she went out to meet a friend. It was the same man waiting in the car down the street," he says anxiously.

"How do you know? It could be anyone?" Charlotte asks in desperation.

"Pause the footage... there," he commands. I stop the tape. "He has a mole. It's oval-shaped near his mustache. I recognize it."

I call Adriana in, questioning her about Mary Jean.

"She never mentioned him, but I remember that night, I transferred five thousand dollars to her." Her voice is rattled, Charlotte supporting her physically by holding onto her arms. I motion for Charlotte to take her back outside.

Alone with Julian in the room, I think out loud, not expecting a response from the worthless punk. "They couldn't have gotten far. Mary Jean is behind this, and she's not smart enough to cover her tracks."

His voice follows. "Okay, so say they flew out. LAX will have them on file."

"Or they drove... but which way? *Fuck!*" I slam my fist against the desk, the jolt knocking a coffee cup down spilling its contents all over the keyboard.

The fucker ignores me, pulling out his cell and making a call. He begins to speak to someone, and I have no idea who. Seconds later, he hangs up, and his face no longer looks calm.

"I have to go find Andy," he tells me.

"Where the fuck are you going?"

"I'm not sitting around waiting for the cops to do shit. I'm gonna find Andy." He walks past me, and I follow him outside to the hallway. He drops to the floor and cups Adriana's face. "I'm not coming back without him. I promise you."

She can barely move her head, and he kisses her lips reassuring her. I turn away. *What the fuck is going on here?* I pull Charlotte aside and promise I'll call her as soon as I know what the hell we're doing. She understands, quickly jumping up and hugging me before I race out of the building to follow him.

"Fucking tell me what you're doing!" I shout at him.

"I have someone who can help."

"Well, I'm coming with you," I demand.

"Fuck off, Edwards. You don't want to be involved in my shit."

"If your *shit* will help us find my nephew, then you better believe I'm going to be involved," I seethe. "We're taking my car."

The car is clocking record speed, but I don't give a fuck,

following his directions to a run-down part of town. The streets are lined with dilapidated homes and groups of teens hanging around watching us drive with caution. I pull into the driveway of a brown brick home and turn off the engine. The front porch light is on, and all the windows are dark. A shadow peaks through the curtains. It's times like this I wish I carried a gun. In the distance, the sound of a car backfiring startles us.

Julian looks reluctant at first but quickly exits the car. He leans back into my window, commanding me to stay in the car.

I wait impatiently, giving him a few more minutes before I go after him.

He emerges with his jacket closed, nervously checks his surroundings, then hops back into the car, disturbed with a look of sheer terror in his eyes. It would be proper manners is to ask him if he is okay, but fuck that bullshit, where's my nephew?

"A lady and man accompanied with a young boy have checked into a Motel 6 about three hours north."

"How the fuck did you find that out?"

"Just drive. *Now.*"

I start the engine and reverse out of the driveway, the tires screeching as I slam my foot on the brake and shove the stick into gear. He gives me the directions, and I punch them into my GPS.

"Now, fucking tell me how you found that out?" I yell at him.

He doesn't tell me. He throws a bag carrying white substance into my lap. I lower my head to look.

Is this what I think it is? Fuck, it's a bag of cocaine.

"Why is this shit in my car?"

"Because my dealer has connections, and to use them, I had to buy this."

He grits his teeth, and his knuckles are pale white. *He used to be an addict.* The first rational thought is I need to get rid of this shit. I've been there before, succumbed to the white acid to take away the pain. It's a difficult addiction to overcome, and thank God, I had sense to back away when I knew I was hitting that slippery slope. I am all too familiar with that 'high,' and for the sake of finding my nephew, Julian *cannot* be near this stuff.

We drive down the open freeway without saying a word to each other. An hour into the drive, I pull over along the road in a dark and deserted spot.

"Why are you pulling over?" he asks angrily

"We're dumping this shit now. You can't be near it."

I exit the car and walk outside a few feet from where we're parked and spread the powder amongst the trees. *Done.* No fucking temptation when we are looking for Andy. I drive off, and a few moments later, he begins to talk.

"I wouldn't have used it," he mumbles.

"That's what all addicts say."

"Yeah, well, I fucking mean it. That stuff is deadly. If it weren't for you coming back into Charlie's life, I wouldn't have fucking touched it again."

My blood has risen, steaming like boiled water. The nerve of this fucking idiot. "You're going to blame that on me?"

"You have no idea how hard it is to watch someone die in front of your eyes. Watching as their body incinerates, and you can't do a damn thing to stop it."

He closes his eyes and releases a deep breath. I've no idea, and never want to know what it feels like. I can't think of anything more terrifying.

"Yeah, well, coke isn't the answer."

"You think it was all about Charlie... it wasn't. It was the fucking coke driving me to do things. Until you're under the influence, you have no idea how much it can destroy your life and any rational thinking."

My hands grip tightly on the wheel as I rev the engine, the roar loudly rumbles around us.

"You expect me to forgive you?" I laugh in malice.

"How can I expect you to forgive me when I can't even forgive myself?"

I don't respond instantly. *What the fuck does he want from me?* First, he proposes to my wife. Then, he stalks her, putting her in danger, and now he wants forgiveness so he can steal my nephew and brainwash my sister?

Adriana's words ring in my head. *"We all make mistakes, Lex. We're all guilty of doing things that are unforgivable."*

Yeah, well, Julian's list of 'unforgivable mistakes' is too long in my eyes. He isn't going to get an apology from me, but I'm not that inconsiderate. I recognize he has been to hell. It doesn't excuse anything, and to some extent I understand how easily life can fall apart around you. Nine fucking years of living in hell was enough for me to show a small amount of compassion.

"I've been there. When you wake up and realize every decision you have made in your life has been one big mistake and you've broken the only person who's your reason for living, you run to anything that will numb the fucking pain. I spent six months of my life snorting that shit and taking anything else I could get my hands on. Some nights, I had no idea where I was, who was beside me, and what narcotics had been injected into me."

"Then, you know."

"I do know. Nobody else knows this. They only saw businessman Lex driven by power and money. They didn't know that every night I was surrounded by dealers. Pimping their whores and drugs on to me like it was a big fucking game. I'm not proud of that part of my life, and the moment I saw Charlotte again, I knew *you* wouldn't stand in my way."

"It's done, but just so you know, I love your sister and just like you said, *you* won't stand in my way."

I'm a fucking hypocrite and refuse to admit that openly, so instead, my lips remain tightly sealed as we continue to drive to the motel.

The night has fallen, and only a few lights flicker on the motel sign. I park the car in the almost deserted parking lot, and we both make our way to the front desk. The overweight sleazy man sitting on his fat ass behind the desk doesn't even turn our way when the sound of the bell rings. Dressed in a greasy wife-beater and shorts, he faces our way when Julian clears his throat. I hold up the picture of Andy and ask him if he has seen him. He stares blankly at the picture and shakes his head.

"Are you sure?" Julian remains calm, not showing any sign of frustration.

The man shakes his head again. I take out my wallet and throw a wad of cash at him. I don't even count it, and he appears to be pleased, but he doesn't give any further information, instead, taking the cash and shoving it into his pocket.

I'm losing my cool and am ready to pounce, but Julian places his hand against my chest, holding me back.

"I'm sorry you couldn't help us."

What the fuck is this fucker doing!

I follow him outside making our way back to the car. "Now what, huh? Your damn dealer scammed us."

"Well, tell me what you had in mind, Edwards? Waiting for the cops to do jack all?"

"I don't know. I'd have done better than you," I spit back.

"Yeah, well, you've done nothing but fucking complain so far." He moves toward me, eyes wide and full of rage.

"Back the fuck off. I swear, Baker, don't even fucking think about it," I seethe.

He grabs my shirt with his fists, and with fast reflexes, I'm about to swing a punch when his face changes, and he lets go, frozen on the spot staring intently at the concrete. He starts to walk away, but I pull his shoulder back. He shrugs it off and kneels to the curbside to pick up a toy car.

"This belongs to Andy," he says.

"That could be any kid's car."

"No, the windows have been colored in black marker. Andy does this to all his cars. I still remember when I asked him about it, he said 'Uncle Lex has black windows, and I want to be just like him.'"

Andy said that? I crumple to the ground, defeated as the enormity of this situation consumes me. I can't breathe let alone think of what to do next.

Julian continues to stand towering over me as I sit on the curb. "He's here." Julian motions for us sit in the car, so we can talk in private. "We need to come up with a plan."

"Well, the fat fuck at the front desk doesn't give answers with cash."

"Then, we wait."

We sit quietly, waiting as we watch all the motel rooms hoping for a sign of Andy. I call Charlotte briefly, letting her know where we are, and what is happening. She doesn't ask too many questions, trusting our handle on the situation.

"Adriana's asleep. I slipped a pill into her coffee that your mom gave me from your dad's prescriptions. It won't last long, though. Please be careful," she pleads. "And I love you."

"I love you, too," I whisper into the speaker.

I hang up the cell and tell Julian that Adriana is sleeping. Amidst the conversation, a motel door opens. A man dressed in a caramel-colored velour tracksuit exits the motel room carrying a can of beer. The dirty scum walks over to the vending machine and nervously looks around. It's the same man on the video, the mole blatantly obvious as Julian points out. He walks back to the room and closes the door behind him.

Julian and I give each other a look and get out of the car, quietly walking toward the room. I place my ear on the door and hear the sounds of the television. On the count of three, we lean against the door, then force it open barging into the room, The man panics, scurrying to the bathroom and tripping on a suitcase in the middle of the floor.

Julian follows him and grabs his jacket, slamming him against the wall as he yells for help.

"Tell us where Andy is, or you can kiss this life goodbye," Julian grunts.

"I don't... I don't know," he stammers, shaking his body trying to release himself from Julian's grip.

I lean up against him and place my hand under his neck as Julian holds him against the wall. My grip is tight and choking him to death seems inevitable.

"Tell us now," I spit back, directly into his face.

He coughs, almost blue in the face. "The next town over. They aren't here... I swear!"

Julian drops him to the floor, and his body slams against the dirty tile. I'm just about to kick him in the ribs when Julian beats me to it, the man curling over as he begins to cough up blood.

Serves him right, piece of worthless shit!

He catches his breath enough to explain that it wasn't his idea, that Mary Jean was desperate to take Andy. He only agreed to the plan because she paid him five thousand dollars.

Adriana's five thousand dollars.

Julian takes his belt off and wraps it around the man's wrist. I push him out of the room and shove the scum into my backseat warning him if we don't find Andy, we'll dump him in the desert for the vultures to feed off him.

It's only thirty minutes to the next town, but I make it in fifteen, driving at record speed. The sleepy motel appears over the hill, and we pull into the driveway, the gravel hitting the tires as I slam my foot on the brakes. This time, the front desk is manned by an older lady. She hunches as she walks to the counter, lifting her head to look at the photograph Julian holds of Andy. At first, she is reluctant, and then she nods. We beg her for information, and I hand over another wad of cash. She refuses, pushing it back toward me and writes something on a piece of paper. The number says room thirteen. I smile graciously, and we rush out the door in search for room thirteen.

It's down the very back corner, and as soon as we're there, I close my eyes for a split second and pray to heaven above that Andy is alive and safe. We repeat our actions, barging our way through the door with our bodies. The room is silent, and immediately I'm drawn to Andy, lying on the bed curled into a ball. I rush over to him and check his breathing. He is asleep.

Relief washes over me as I fall to my knees thanking the Lord he has protected my little boy. I take count of his body, making sure his limbs, fingers, toes, and every part of him is intact. Dressed in his favorite superhero pajamas, he continues to sleep quietly and peacefully.

Julian is standing above Mary Jean. He looks at me, tormented and riddled with guilt as his face falls. Careful not to wake Andy yet, I walk to where Julian is standing and notice the empty bottle of pills beside her. Julian feels her pulse and shakes his head at me.

She is gone.

Beside her, there is a note. I pick it up, taking a deep breath before reading it.

Adriana,

Please forgive me for my mistakes and what led me to this moment. They say there is no greater pain than to bear a child, but burying your own son is much greater.

Every time I stare into Andy's eyes, I see my baby boy, Elijah. It hurts me every single day, and I can't escape the grief nor the guilt for still breathing when my son is no longer given the chance.

I know you will take care of my grandson.
You were always meant to be in Elijah's life and Andy's mother.
You are the strength I wish I had instilled in me.

Mary Jean

I walk back over to Andy and gently lift him, not wanting him to see Mary Jean in this state. Julian grabs his cell and makes the necessary calls. A minute later, he walks outside the room and stands beside me, stroking Andy's hair. His eyes start to flutter, and slowly, they open.

"Uncle Lex," he mutters softly.

I smile at him, relieved and grateful to have him in my arms. "Hey, Andy, everything's okay."

He places his thumb into his mouth, but with his eyes wide in fear, he lifts his head and turns to face Julian. Reaching his arms out, he begins to cry, "Jay, I thought you were gone to live with my daddy in heaven."

Julian motions for me to pass Andy over, and I finally let go.

Safely in his arms, he rocks him back and forth soothing him, easing his fears. "I was gone for a little while, but I'm here to stay. Okay?"

"Don't ever go, Jay. Makes Mama sad and me sad."

"I'm not going anywhere, buddy," he reassures him.

He tells me to call Adriana, and instantly, I grab my cell. She picks up immediately and sobs into the phone as I tell her what happened. Begging to speak to Julian and Andy, I place her on speakerphone.

"Pooh-bear, it's Mama," she strains, attempting to control her voice.

"Mama, Grandmama said she misses Daddy. She said she is gone to see him," he informs us innocently.

Adriana cries softly. "She did miss him, baby. I miss you. Uncle Lex and Jay will bring you home now."

"Mama, I was scared Jay was going, too, but he said he will stay with us, Mama."

"Julian, are you there?"

"I'm right here, Adriana."

"I love you."

The second Adriana expresses those three powerful words, I know I have no choice.

Julian's expression is one of complacency, and I'd be an idiot not to see that.

My conscience battles with the good and the bad of it all, and if their love is as forceful as Charlotte's and mine, there's no chance in hell I can stop them, even if I try.

Andy nestles himself into Julian's shoulder, and with ease, he repeats the words back to my sister.

"I love you, too. Time to bring your baby home to you."

"Thank you," she tells him.

It's time to say goodbye as the sounds of the sirens come rushing around the corner, but Adriana quickly stops me. "Lex?"

"Yes?"

"Thank you for everything you do for me. I love you, too. Please come home safely to your family now."

I struggle to end the call, and as I do, the weight which remains heavily on my shoulders is lifting at a snail's pace, and it's triggered by the look that Andy gives Julian.

The same look he gives me.

It's of adoration, respect, and love.

I'm not immune to jealousy, and for once, I am putting my sister and her son before my own selfish needs as hard as it may be.

They deserve to be loved. Everyone deserves to experience love. Whatever it may be—fate, destiny—I no longer care. He will take care of them. I'll make sure of that, and I finally take a step back and allow the universe to do its own thing.

"Listen, Edwards, I owe you. For getting rid of it before it became a problem," Julian mumbles under his breath, careful that the cops can't hear.

"Well, I owe you for saving my wife and baby. Call it even, shall we?"

He nods his head, and that was that.

I look into the sky and stare directly into the stars. "Brother, if you can hear me. I'm leaving it all up to you."

And from that moment, Elijah will forever protect us.

That was his nature, and this is his calling.

TWENTY-FIVE

The room falls quiet, and the only sound to grace us is Andy's tiny snores. The night light is on, not wanting to frighten him with the dark. He is nestled between Julian and me as we struggle to get a grip on how emotionally draining this day has been. Not only is Andy back in my arms, but he's also here between us.

Us.

With the faint glow allowing Julian to caress my face, we talk in whispers allowing Andy to get some much-needed sleep.

"There are so many questions..." I trail off.

"And so many answers," he returns.

"What happened the night of the party? I still don't understand what changed?"

"Plain and simple... those parties are full of crack addicts. My dealer was there."

It all makes sense now. Julian is strong-willed, but we all have our weaknesses, and if I didn't lash out with my jealousy, we could've talked it through.

"I pushed you when I should've listened to you."

"Yes, you did, but the truth is that I'm so in love with you that I can't think rationally. With Lex present, Charlie, and my dealer, the scene was too familiar. It was almost like I was afraid of the past rearing its ugly head. When you came to see me, and I was with Charlie, it was only because my dealer was trying to corner me. I was attempting to look happy and distracted because if he knew I was weak or even thought for a moment I had issues, he'd be all over me so fast, you and I would be back to square one."

"You can't resist it if it's in front of you?"

He stays silent, and I don't want to push him further.

"Your brother saved me today from possibly making that mistake again."

"So, then you're even," I state, not expecting a response.

"I want to make one thing clear. I haven't touched the stuff in over a year, but I'm not as strong as you think I am, and that lady at the bar the other night, she is my rehab counselor."

Wow, how easily I misconstrue things. And how very relieved I am.

"You're in rehab?"

"I'm not staying in a rehab clinic, but I attend weekly meetings with specialized counselors who help me move forward. I want to be a better person for you, Andy, and most importantly, myself," he admits.

With his palm resting on my face, I move his fingers toward my mouth and kiss the tips gently.

For now, the nightmare is over.

A week had passed since that dreadful day when Andy went missing, and Mary Jean took her own life. Out of respect to the woman who brought Elijah into this world, we buried her alongside him as close family and friends paid their final respects. I promised myself I wouldn't carry the guilt of her actions for we were all still suffering the loss of Elijah, and individually, we had chosen different paths as a coping mechanism.

It was the wake-up call we all need—life is frighteningly short. That whole tomorrow-I-could-be- hit-by-a-bus saying can't ring truer. The reality is whether it's a bus or cancer, it strikes when we least expect it, and when we're all guilty of thinking it could never happen to us.

And so, I vow to live this life I've been blessed with, and I can't or don't want to imagine it without Julian. He's everything I need, everything I want, and luckily for me, he feels the exact same way. Finally, we both understand the love we feel for each other is too strong to walk away from, too powerful to give up.

There are so many questions yet to be answered.

Where will we live?

Do we want to get married?

But those are all questions in *my* head.

It isn't abnormal to think about the future, but I consider Julian's feelings and don't want to push too much change too soon.

Turns out, I don't have to. Andy's the pusher. Since the moment he was back in my arms, all he wants is *Julian*.

The first few nights Julian slept over, and Andy was beyond ecstatic. He was extremely clingy to the point he wanted to sleep between us every night. It didn't bother Julian at first, but a few days later, he pointed out the obvious—we hadn't been intimate since before he broke it off with me. Both of us have been so protective over Andy and his well-being, we forgot about us, that combined with family dropping by all day long.

Julian and I try to talk in code, not wanting Andy to hear our conversation. It's our only way of expressing our feelings, even to the point where he sends me dirty text messages which can't be said out loud. It's cute, and I'm ridiculously sexually charged. It's a constant throb down below that with the slightest wink or handsome smirk, sends me into a frenzy which not even naked pictures of the ugliest man on earth can tame.

The problem is that both of us are conflicted over Andy's emotional state and our physical need for each other. Some moments we discuss letting my mom come over, so we can go out and drive to a deserted neck of the woods to screw each other until the cows come home. Damn Eric! But the next moment, Andy disappears to the backyard, and we're fretting because he is out of sight. I recall the moment he did that, and the panic that followed.

"This is really hard," I admit.

"It's only hard because you've had to deal first-hand with every parent's nightmare," Julian says softly, wrapping his arms around my waist as we both watch Andy play with Blaze and Ash through the window.

"I'm scared of the long-term effects that this will have on him."

"I met this mother when I was writing an article in the Middle East. She was widowed with five children, her youngest being six. Her husband was killed in a bomb blast, and her eldest son was left deaf in one ear and blind in one eye. The youngest son was saved but had witnessed the horrific injuries firsthand. She told me that he had no recollection of the actual scene, but every so often loud sounds triggered his memory."

I swallow the large lump which has formed in my throat. "How terrible. The poor woman and those children." I let out a small cry, the lonesome tear escaping as I digest his words.

"She's a remarkable woman and has done well considering her circumstances."

"How do you know that?"

"I keep in touch. She has access to email at her local library, and when she visits every so often, she will send me an email updating me on what's going on."

I turn around, my face in line with his. "You keep in contact with all these people you meet?"

"Yes. You form this unique friendship, and the majority of the time these people are pouring their hearts out to you. It's difficult to walk away, so it's nice to keep in contact."

I'm in awe at how much compassion Julian has. To this day, his intelligence surpasses me, and I find myself captivated in his stories. He always knows how to bring me right down to earth, and this time, I know Andy will be okay. Therefore, Julian and I need to have our moment.

That night we tried to carry the sleepyhead to his room, it worked, and just when Julian climbed into bed ready to jump me, Andy's wail stopped us dead in our tracks. With a guilty conscience, Julian carried him back to our bed.

The mornings always make us laugh—Andy sprawled across the bed with his face in Julian's neck and his feet in my face. I'm pushed so far off to the edge, frequently waking up with an extremely bad backache.

It's a failed experiment, and both of us agree we'll give Andy some time to adjust even if it means we need to put our physical relationship on hold.

I'm confident Andy is doing well emotionally and toy with the idea of him going back to daycare. As a parent, I'm furious with the daycare center even after their numerous attempts to apologize for the incident. Jennie was fired, and with a guilty conscience, I tried to talk the manager out of it, but she insisted that a lesson had to be learned. Hence, why policies and protocols were enforced when employed as a carer of young children.

Andy doesn't talk much about going back, but Amelia is a born nagger. Not only has she been over several times to inform Andy of everything he has been missing, it now extends to video calls showing off all her pretty artwork.

The day before Andy is due to officially go back to daycare, an unexpected knock on the door startles us while we're busy preparing goodie bags for Andy's birthday party this weekend.

"Hello! Where's my Spider-boy Andy?" Eric pretends to go searching in the house as Andy stumbles down the stairs.

"I'm here! I'm here, Ewic!"

Eric catches him on the final step and spins him around before latching onto him in a great big hug.

"What's going on?" I ask casually, biting into my apple.

"We're here to take this little guy out," Tristan tells us.

I know I'm nervous as I try to calm my voice. "Where to?"

"The trampoline place around the corner. Relax, we'll be gone for an hour. I'm sure that's all you need." Eric winks at Julian.

Julian almost chokes on the pear he's eating, Tristan patting him on the back, the perfect opportunity to mock him.

"We're going to have fun, right, Andy? Plus, I can show you my somersault moves." Eric is way too excited about this.

"Every time we go to Trampoline World, Eric reenacts the movie *Bring It On* and does all these cheerleader moves. I'm telling you, you're going to break your neck. You're not that limber anymore," Tristan reminds him.

"That's not what your mom said last night," Eric jokes.

"Hey, don't do the mom jokes," Julian scowls. "That's my sister you're talking about. Can you two go now? Take care of Andy, bring him back in one piece, and just for the record, an hour is *never* enough."

The second their car leaves our driveway, the deadbolts are on, and Julian throws me over his shoulder, slapping me on the ass as I squeal in delight. There's no delay, throwing me onto the bed and jumping over me, smashing his lips against mine. I rip the buttons on his shirt exposing his perfectly toned chest that I have missed so much.

His eyes literally devour me as he lifts off my dress, exposing my bra and panties.

He pushes me back down, and amongst the heavy kisses, he slides his hand down below and brushes it along my clit. I arch my back and moan loudly until he tells me that he is entering me. Shoving my panties aside, he toys with the tip of his cock around my entrance.

"I love you, Adriana, but this is going to be hard and fast. Are you with me?"

I nod in excitement, and just when I think I have it all under control, he rams into me so hard, I lose my breath. I try to wrap my arms around his muscular back, but he pulls them up above my head and forces himself harder. It's painful but so delightfully arousing at the same time. His heavy weight pins me down, and I'm helpless beneath him. With every thrust, he rubs against my clit, and the pressure is building. I am lost within him. His grip on my wrist is tight, and with his teeth, he tugs my bra down displaying my breasts. At a ravenous pace, he licks my nipple with the tip of his tongue, circling it with a slow and pleasurable pain, but then he bites down, hard, and I yelp as the sensation connects with the rest of my body.

"So fucking beautiful," he mumbles to himself.

The face of a man as beautiful as Julian's in the heat of the moment is a picture of pure lust, desire, and hunger. The way his jaw tightens, and his mouth is biting down, expresses the primal side of him possessing my body. The dominance and sexual force take me to places only my imagination explores during my private moments. The reality far exceeds my expectations, knowing he is mine, and this intimate connection between us allows me to push my boundaries and experience acts that are unfamiliar or once a taboo. It's the gleam in his eye, the love and reassurance that stops me from feeling any remorse. What we do behind closed doors feels so right and shouldn't be anything to be ashamed of because he loves me.

And I adore our dirty bubble.

I'm about to tell him that it's all over for me, time to break out the bubbly, do my happy dance, when he stops midway. I can't even talk, breathless and weak in the knees. He is dead silent, his stare boring into me making me slightly self-conscious.

"I can't control my need for you. I need you to understand that." There's a grunt which escapes his throat. It's the tiger ready to attack, the shark circling its prey.

"I understand," I whisper, submissive to his demands.

His lips crash onto mine, catching me off-guard and unable to breathe. I suck in air as his tongue rolls with mine allowing a gasp of air to escape. Pulling back, he resumes his position.

"Hard and fast," he mutters.

"Hard and fast," I repeat. "I can handle that."

He releases an ominous laugh, piquing my curiosity. "Baby, no one is ever going to get in our way, and now, you're going to get taste of what it's like to be mine."

I assume that he is going to make me come now, but you know what they say about assuming—it makes an ass out of you and me.

And I'm clearly that ass right now.

He pulls himself out, and instantly I'm at a loss. Moving toward my chest, he unclips my bra and motions for me to hand him my wrists. I do so, and he carefully uses the straps to tie my wrists together, then he pulls them up and ties the other strap looping it around the iron headboard. With one last tug, I'm strapped tight.

I can handle this.

A little kinky, how very exciting!

Next, he pulls my panties down stopping mid-thigh, with his face down toward my pubic bone, he lowers himself and inhales my arousal. With his eyes closed, I see the turmoil in his expression and the way his jaw locks down. He continues, not stopping until they are completely off. Showing off, he clutches them in his hands like they're a prize and moves them toward his face and inhales once again.

"These are soaking wet... you're soaking wet. Tell me, Adriana, you think you can handle what you're about to experience?"

My face widens with a smirk. "Give it to me, all of it. You'll be surprised what my body will do for you."

He's insatiable and fuck me sideways, backward, every which way, this beautiful man is *all* mine.

"I want you to prove it," he tells me.

"Prove what my body will do for you?"

He nods, and without breaking my gaze, he uses my panties to tie my ankles together. It doesn't click, wondering how he will fuck me if my legs are shut tight, but then he bends them, and my legs fall apart tied at the ankle.

"Hard and fast," he repeats.

With his thumb and forefinger, he spreads my lips exposing my clit, and with a slight rub, he glides down to the entrance. He enters me with two fingers, something I can handle. Thrusting hard, no slowness in his movements, he enters his third finger as my body jerks unexpectedly. Twisting and turning, I'm moaning loudly as the pleasure of his fingers inside builds up the moisture allowing him to glide with ease.

"Are you ready?"

I look at him confused, and with a deep thrust, he slides in another finger.

Holy fuck! From the motions, I can tell his thumb isn't inside, and I'm one finger away from being fisted which frightens me to the core. I clench in nerves, but his hard-and-fast command is not allowing me even to think let alone tell him I don't want to go further.

Just go with the flow, Adriana.

There's a slight pain, but I zone out, focusing on other sensations that are screaming out to me, the way my skin is covered in goosebumps, how my nipples are hard and perky. The aches down below are starting to build again, and with every thrust, my muscles begin to clench and pulling me out of the subliminal state is my overwhelming need to pee.

What the?

The urge is building, and I squirm to get him to stop without having to say the words, but it's almost like he knows, lunging his fingers even deeper which only makes it worse. I'm tied, unable to physically move, begging him with my eyes to stop, yet he seems aroused by my uncomfortable state. Just say it now, say you need to pee in case you turn this into a golden shower.

"Hold it in," he says, licking his lips.

So, he knows I need to pee? Why doesn't he stop? I'm panicking at the sensation, and when it's clear he won't back down, I open my mouth to say something, but he beats me to it.

"Focus *on me*."

How can I focus on him when I'm pretty sure I'm about to pee all over him in just a few moments?

Oh, dear God, how mortifying! Okay, just breathe and focus on him.

Let your body trust him, Adriana.

My eyes wander to his cock, standing hard and proud, the tip oozing with his juiciness. Fuck, is he going to come doing this to me? The temperature in my body rises, and the more I focus on him, the more I ache, and the familiar pressure is back, but I can't stop, and I don't want to stop. The sensation prickles every part of my body, and I squirm as he drives his fingers so hard, and then suddenly, he has consumed all of me. *I explode.* He pulls his fingers out in a wild hurry, and all I can feel is the rush, no, more like gush of liquid squirting out of me as my body contracts. I ride out *the* most intense orgasm of my entire life, panting and moaning loudly as my throat caves struggling to come up for air.

Motherfucking holy shit, that was insane. I want to laugh, cry, and scream from the rooftops.

Afraid to open my eyes, he doesn't hold back and slams into me with his cock, gripping onto my ankles mid-air.

I want to see him come.

I want my beautiful man to explode inside me.

And so, I tell him those exact words.

And he comes undone.

Collapsing on top of me, I still don't say anything. I don't think I peed, but could a woman honestly come that much? Unless... *On my God, did I squirt?*

He unties me, and I'm fairly certain I've gone bright red.

"I um... wow, okay." I'm speechless.

"That, my beautiful woman, is what I'm talking about." The grin on his face is priceless.

"Did I do what I think I did?"

He nods, licking his lips, then leaning in to kiss me gently. "You just did what I've fantasized about for a *very* long time. Did you see what your body did for me?"

I'm shy, but I want to explore this topic.

"It was... *surreal*. I mean, at first I wanted to... but then... it just kept going, and it felt like I would not stop coming," I admit with a small laugh.

"It's the most beautiful thing I've ever seen, hence why I lasted—"

"Like thirty seconds?" I interrupt playfully.

"You're being generous, like fifteen."

"Does that mean I can always do that?"

He lies down beside me and strokes the side of my face. "I'd like to hope so. There are so many things you need to do for me... fuck! I'm getting hard again just thinking about it."

"Slow down, cowboy. My lady door needs a new door handle. Perhaps we'll enter by the back next time?"

He growls on purpose and climbs on top of me wide-eyed. "I love you, now, forever."

"I love you, too," I murmur, moving a strand of his hair away from his beautiful eyes.

We don't have much time, but he continues to kiss me.

We both remain quiet. Something doesn't feel right until Julian blurts it out, "Maybe we should go see how they are doing at the trampoline place."

"You read my mind."

We jump up and place our clothes on, but Julian stops me. He brushes my lip with the tip of his thumb, and inside, I'm having another meltdown.

"I've never been so torn," he says quietly.

"About what?"

"I want you so fucking bad it's killing me, yet all I can think about is rushing to Andy to make sure he is okay."

I smile reassuringly. "It's called being a parent."

"I'm scared I'm doing it all wrong," he admits.

I wrap my arms around his waist. "Andy hasn't left your side since the moment he came home. He begs for you to lie in his bed, mumbles your name when he sleeps, and calls for you when he wakes. He *loves* you, Julian. This is new to him as well. If you're making him smile, you're doing something right."

"Thank you." His eyes widen, followed by a mischievous grin. "Okay, is it just me, or do you want to see Eric do his routine on the trampoline?"

"Twisted minds think alike. Grab my cell over there, something tells me it's YouTube-worthy."

We both laugh and rush down the stairs to head out when the doorbell rings catching us off-guard.

Julian looks at me curiously, and I open the door to be met with a courier. He hands the package to Julian, signing for it and saying thank you. Baffled, he opens the brown box, and underneath the bubble wrap is a plaque.

I read the words, and the moment it sinks in, I turn to look at Julian with the widest smile waiting for his reaction.

His book is officially a number one *New York Times* Best Seller.

The gold writing confirms what I always knew, Julian is talented and is now taking the world by storm.

Almost dropping the plaque, he wraps his arms around my waist as I jump up to hug him tight.

"You did it, baby!" I couldn't have been any prouder than this moment to be in love with this intelligent and kindhearted man.

"We're celebrating tonight. Nothing big, don't want Andy to be too tired for his birthday party tomorrow," he adds.

"You know..." I say with a devilish grin, "... we do have a spare minute to celebrate on our own."

"I only need fifteen seconds." He smirks, lifting and moving me toward the staircase where he places me on all fours and takes me from me behind.

TWENTY-SIX

Planning a child's birthday is one of life's greatest pleasures.

I know that one day Andy will grow up and parties will be a thing of the past, my excuse for lavishing him with ridiculous gifts and over-the-top decorations.

Andy is going through a huge Spiderman phase, so it makes sense to decorate the house with his favorite superhero. Outside on the patio are plenty of red and blue balloons, positioned around the tables decorated with Spiderman plates and cups. Across the roofline hangs cobwebs with tiny black plastic spiders trapped inside them.

Julian is busy dressing Andy, so I can finish the final touches when he races out of the house dressed as Spiderman, of course. His cute tiny face is hidden by the mask, and his excitement is demonstrated by the karate moves he keeps doing. I kneel and ask him for a hug at which he informs me that superheroes *don't* hug their moms.

Great, it's starting already.

That dampens my mood, and Julian picks up on it straight away.

"Hey, Spiderman, I bet your muscles are super strong and that you can squash this lady?"

Andy nods, and he runs back squeezing me really tight. I take advantage of it and hug him so hard before he runs into the backyard chasing Ash and Blaze. Julian comes up from behind and embraces me. I allow myself a moment to rest in his arms. Birthdays are an emotional time—a day that marks my little boy growing up. It feels like only yesterday, he came into the world, and time just continues to fly by.

My parents are the first to arrive, carrying way too many gifts. My mom busies herself in the kitchen, organizing platters and snacks for the guests. I'm not surprised my dad has pulled Julian aside. Much to my surprise, they organized a trip to South America together during a luncheon they both attended the other day. Julian postponed his trip to Morocco with everything that went on with Andy, yet was desperate to visit a small town which has been wiped out by floods a year ago. My dad is equally as keen to provide some medical assistance as their hospital was demolished. Both of them are extremely passionate, and occasionally, I'll sit down to listen to their plans, enthralled in how much is involved and what it does for the town people.

"The flights are booked, so next Thursday, we'll be leaving," my dad tells me.

It's selfish of me to sulk, so instead, I busy myself with my mom who deep-down knows how much I'll struggle. "Only two weeks, Adriana. Just think of how Daddy and Julian are helping those families, okay?"

The squeal of Amelia followed by an unsteady Ava invades the kitchen. Amelia is long gone, jumping like a frog on crack on the bouncing castle outside. Ava is stopped by my mom. I love this little girl so much. She has a calm and quiet nature, flying under the radar largely due to her sister's energetic personality. Charlie enters the room, but her face looks livid, and without saying hello, she dumps a baby bag on the ground and storms off outside.

What was that about?

Lex walks into the kitchen but does not follow Charlie outside. His face looks softer, not at all like Charlie's. These two are worse than Nikki and Rocky at times. I pray Julian and I will *not* end up being that type of couple.

"What going on with Charlie?" I prod.

"She's pissed off at me."

"What's new?" I say flatly.

"I got her pregnant again."

I almost drop the jug I'm holding onto. "Lex? Are you for real?"

He gives me a weak smile, even in his state of shock.

It seems like the perfect opportunity to point out the obvious. "The psychic said—"

"I knew you would say that. Do not, and I repeat, *do not* bring that lady up in front of Charlotte."

I laugh. "Congratulations, bro."

"I can't do this, Adriana. Three kids under four?" I can hear the panic in his voice.

"Of course, you can do this. Besides, you don't really have a choice now. You can't put the mouse back in the hole. I can't believe I'm going to be an aunty again!" I squeal.

"Yeah, if only Charlotte could share your enthusiasm," he mutters, walking off to the backyard.

I watch through the window as he tries to place his hand on her shoulder, but her glare is so icy that he backs off and heads over to where my dad is firing up the grill.

All the guests have finally arrived, including Hazel, Penny, Fred, and Jerry. All four of them are like family to both Julian and me, even though at times, Jerry argues that family is for losers, but to know Jerry is to love him, quirks and all. Around Andy, he changes, becoming a big kid at heart and protects him like a big brother would.

"You've done amazing, Adriana." Hazel smiles beside me.

"You know what?" I say, unable to hide the grin on my face. "I have, haven't I?"

Hazel embraces me, proud of my willingness to admit I've done something right in my life despite my constant need to drag my failures to the surface.

"It's always there, sweetheart. You just need to fall to be able to look up and see the stars."

Mom steps outside, and I quickly introduce her to Hazel. They hug it out. Mom's so grateful to finally meet Hazel and the rest of our friends after I've spoken so much about them the last few weeks.

The guests are chatting amongst themselves as the kids play happily in the bouncing castle. Birthdays are so tiring. Between making sure everyone is fed to entertaining the kids with games, I'm ready to bring out the cake.

My mom carries the cake outside, proud of her creation. It's a three-tiered fondant cake which all the kids gather around, oohing and aahing, not to mention one of Andy's little friends who has jabbed his chubby finger into the cake already.

We all warm up our lungs and commence the traditional birthday salute, singing loudly at the birthday boy.

"Blow out your candles, Andy." I nudge him gently.

Andy stares at the cake, frightened by all the attention he is receiving, and buries his face into Julian's neck. Julian whispers something in his ear convincing him to turn around. He blows out all three candles as our family and friends cheer him on. I clap along with them, posing with Julian and Andy as my mom snaps away with her camera.

My baby is a big boy now.

I grab the knife to cut the cake as a distraction to stop the tears from flowing. Eric stands beside me, his drool almost touching the ground as he eyes off the white chocolate mud cake. Penny is just as bad, biting her nails contemplating whether she indulges in the cake or not.

"I'd be in negative Weight Watchers points if I ate that cake," he announces.

Rocky pulls up beside him. "Dude, that's kinda gay being on Weight Watchers, isn't it?"

"Well, first of all, I am gay, and second, it won't hurt you to look in the mirror once in a while."

"What's that supposed to mean?"

"It means that someone's carrying around a spare tire."

I burst out laughing, not the best thing to do with a knife in hand. Rocky has put on a few pounds, but I wouldn't call him fat.

"It's sympathy weight," he tells us.

"Excuse me?" Nikki yells. "Are you trying to say *I'm* the fat one now?"

"No, babe, all I'm saying is that maybe you should lay off the hormones, you know, estrogen makes you hungry."

Charlie has joined us at the table and has caught wind of the conversation. We both whistle at the same time, shaking our heads at Rocky. He's in deep shit now.

"Keep digging, Romano, 'cause you're about ten feet under, and I guarantee you, you ain't getting any conjugal visits from me," Nikki warns him.

Eric, the cause of this petty fight, slaps his knees as he cackles uncontrollably. Sometimes, Eric just has no idea when to stop.

"Nikki, if it makes you feel any better, Eric split his pants at Starbucks the other day. He went to pick up a quarter, and a little girl pointed it out to everyone." Tristan laughs.

Penny shakes her head while pursing her lips. "Oh, honey, with an ass like yours, you would've been the talk of the town."

"Why would you tell everyone that? I died of embarrassment. I can never go back there again."

Tristan nods. "He was the talk of the town, especially because he wore his leopard print thong."

Our collective loud gasps are enough for Eric to bury his head into his hands. Penny is clutching her chest but quickly nods her head as if agreeing with his choice to wear leopard print thongs.

"It was laundry day, okay?" Eric barrels, frustrated. "Quit judging me... I had nothing else to wear."

"Hmm... actually, that does make me feel better." Nikki smirks.

Charlie takes a slice of cake, shoving it into her mouth with enjoyment. She licks her lips, but then her face changes, almost looking nauseous. She mumbles under her breath, and all I can hear is, "Fucking jerk can't wear a goddamn condom."

I place my arm around her, coercing her to smile. She gives in a little and takes another slice of cake, this time a much bigger piece.

"Well, I'll be sporting cankles soon, thanks to that jerk over there." She points her finger at Lex.

Eric and Tristan are the first to react, sandwiching Charlie in a group hug. Rocky looks over to Nikki, and her face drops immediately. I know they are trying for another baby, and perhaps this isn't the best thing to hear right now. She walks off to a secluded part of the patio and takes a seat, watching her son, Will, play ball with Andy. I rest my hand on Rocky's forearm, informing him that I'll go talk to her. He's concerned, and it's obvious how much this is taking a toll on both of them.

"You wanna talk about it?" I ask, sitting beside her.

She smiles at me, but underneath, I can see the pain she's in. Trying for a baby when everyone around you is falling pregnant is a difficult emotion to get a grip on.

"I know it's hard to hear someone else is pregnant when you're trying," I tell her, straight from my own experience. "When Elijah finally agreed to IVF, we only had one chance. Five eggs, and only one made it to become an embryo. Now that little embryo is trying to kick Rocky in the nuts."

Rocky is playing with the kids, but as Andy gets him straight between the legs, Rocky winces. Oh well, he brought it on himself by saying he was invincible.

Nikki isn't like Charlie or Kate, even though she's a strong-willed woman. She is very reserved at times and keeps her life private. Rocky's the woman in the relationship, always gasbagging about one thing or another.

"Just don't understand why it's so hard," she admits.

"Uh-huh, or why sixteen-year-old girls have sex once and get pregnant?"

"Yes! I blame that jealousy on Rocky for always watching MTV while we're in bed." This time, she loosens up.

I place my hand on hers, extending the friendship. "It *will* happen when the time's right. Whether it be naturally or with IVF, and when it does, this feeling will be a thing of the past."

"Thank you, Adriana." She smiles, relaxing her shoulders. "So, what about you and Julian? Babies on the cards?"

"We have our plate full with Andy, and to be honest, I want to enjoy him. I want to enjoy us for now."

"Oh, I hear you. Your kitty must be as high as a kite right now," she teases.

I laugh and realize if there's anyone who can give me sex advice, it's Nikki since Charlie is officially off duty.

"Can I ask you a question?"

"Sure."

"Squirting... have you done it?"

"No. Well, not naturally. Rocky is obsessed with it, so I spent some time researching how to do it, and well, I'm not blessed that way."

"I don't get it, so then what do you do?"

"Well, I kinda squirt water up there, and when I come, the contractions just squirt it out." She laughs.

"Wow! I didn't realize it's this huge thing..."

"Totally. Guys are like obsessed with it," she says casually, and due to my silence, puts two and two together followed by a loud gasp. "Oh, Adriana, please tell me you're one of these people who can? Let me live vicariously through you."

My face reddens. "Yes, but Nikki, I don't know whether to be mortified or grateful."

"*Grateful*... a squirter is always grateful," she reassures me.

We both burst out laughing loud enough that Charlie makes her way over to us. She asks to talk to Nikki in private, so I leave them to it and make my way over to the other parents. Doing my duty as party host, I immerse myself in the conversations as we talk about our kids and compare parenting tips.

Both Nikki and Charlie return, the two of them looking much happier. I'm glad they had a moment to talk things out but made a mental note to check in with Nikki in a few days to make sure she is okay.

"So, go tell Adriana the great news?" Nikki nudges her with a grin.

"There's great news?"

Charlie rolls her eyes at Nikki the same time Eric has caught wind of the conversation. When it came to so-called news or gossip, Eric is always front row and center with popcorn in hand.

"It's not great news, just news," Charlie clarifies. "My cousin, Noah, is coming to stay with us for a bit next month."

Eric's eyes widen while his hand clasps his chest as if you've just told him he's won an Oscar.

"Noah, your hot, *'spank me sideways because I want a piece of those man buns'* cousin?"

I raise my hand toward my mouth, covering the small laugh which escapes me. Charlie's cousin Noah is hot, and yes, thanks to Eric I have seen his Instagram page. Charlie never speaks about him much except for him being a few years younger than her. The guy can pull off a suit, that's for sure. And okay, the shirtless gym pictures are damn sexy. I blame Eric—his online stalking is borderline creepy.

"Can you not?" Charlie scowls, shaking her head. "He's my baby cousin. Go back to saying inappropriate things about my husband. That's less disturbing."

"Baby cousin? Oh, honey, have you seen him in a suit? Let's just say when you zoom in, his rooster is saying cock-a-doodle-doo."

"This conversation is over. It's like me talking about Lex in front of Adriana."

I let out a huff. "Um, which you have s*everal* times. You know what? This is great payback. Go on Eric, tell Charlie about the gym shorts picture where you swore you saw his balls."

Charlie opens her mouth wide, shocked I'd even gone there. Serves her right, like I want to hear about my brother and his insatiable dick.

With a devious smirk plastered on Eric's face, Charlie walks off and leaves us behind.

"So, I'm thinking massive welcome party and we hook him up with Kate?" Eric suggests, waiting for my response.

"Oh, nice plan. You think she'd be into him?"

"Honey..." Eric places his hand on my shoulder. "Do you think this is my first rodeo? You leave this to me and focus on your gorgeous boyfriend."

"If I wasn't married, I'd so be tapping Noah's man buns," Nikki says as we all watch Rocky show the kids how he can eat two hot dogs in one sitting.

"I want to say you're a lucky woman, but I'm torn between the thought and wondering how Rocky can fit so much in his mouth?" Eric questions.

Nikki shakes her head with a look of disgust. "Maybe Noah can be my toy boy on the side?"

Both Eric and I laugh at the same time.

Rocky is unaffected by our curious stares, enjoying the children's demands as they challenge him to fit more hot dogs in his mouth. This could go two ways real fast.

"Poor Noah, he hasn't step foot in L.A. and already he is a hot commodity," I mention quietly, feeling sorry for the guy if Eric makes it his mission to interfere in his love life.

"Well... that's what happens when you're blessed with good genes," Eric is quick to point out. "I'll be gentle on him, I promise."

The party is slowly winding down as my neighbors and some parents attempt to go with screaming children, probably high on sugar and refusing to leave. Andy grabs a few goodie bags and hands them out, settling them almost instantly. Nikki and Rocky call it a day with a late flight back to New York due to Will's baseball game tomorrow. They say their goodbyes, and an emotional Charlie hugs Will for a long time. He is close to her height, almost a teen, having shot up obviously taking after Rocky. He's a gorgeous kid, and with that gene pool, he's going to break hearts all over the world.

"You're growing up way too fast," Charlie cries softly.

"It's only because you don't see me every day, Charlie," he reminds her.

"You used to call me Cha Cha." She laughs through her tears.

"I also used to wear diapers," he jokes. "I'll be back next summer."

Charlie hugs him again, making him promise to call her each week. They have a special bond, and it's touching to see how motherly she is with Will. Sometimes, I can't believe that Lex and Charlie could've also had a child that age. Fate works in mysterious ways.

With everyone gone, Eric and Tristan stay back along with Charlie and Lex. Tristan, my savior, walks around with a garbage bag collecting trash. Eric moans as Tristan forces him to do the same. They work in tandem silence, and just when Eric says something about floating cake in a kid's cup, Tristan leans in and kisses him lovingly. As they pull away from each other, Eric's face is of pure contentment, smiling back at Tristan as they both take a moment to appreciate each other.

"So, tomorrow's the big day?" Julian asks, patting Tristan on the shoulder.

Tristan has been cast as a lead in a Hollywood blockbuster being filmed in Dubai. The fame is already starting with hordes of girls begging for selfies wherever they see him. According to Eric, he will be gone for three months, and this will be the test as to how strong their relationship is.

Charlie is quick to inform me that Eric already has leave booked in, and although he hates to admit it, he loves Tristan and can't imagine being apart from him.

"Yep, tomorrow I'm off," Tristan says.

"I'll miss you, kid, but I'm stopping over next month, so we'll catch up then," Julian adds before they man-hug it out.

Charlie is sitting on the steps with Lex. They both sit in silence as Lex is careful to keep a small distance between them. I take a seat beside Charlie, my feet throbbing from walking around for hours. Julian steps through the back door and sits on the other side of me. I lean my head on his shoulder as he kisses the top of my head. Taking a moment to let it all sink in, I relax knowing it's all over, and everyone enjoyed themselves without any drama.

For the better part, that search to find Andy did wonders for Lex and Julian. Neither one of them will ever admit it, but ever since they came home, there seems to be some unspoken understanding between them. They aren't the best of friends, and probably will never be. I don't care as long as I have both these men in my life, the rest will just fall where it may.

Amelia and Andy are still running in circles chasing Blaze and Ash around the backyard. Ava attempts to follow them, her tiny feet walking unsteady, barely able to catch up. She tumbles over but is quick to stand without shedding a single tear. We watch as they continue to play, silenced by their overactive imaginations.

"Andy, Batman has to marry Robin. Ewic said they're gay like him and Tristan," Amelia informs him.

Andy has no clue what that means, shrugging his shoulders at her.

"Batman and Robin will have superhero babies," Amelia explodes.

"Now that I have a daddy, Mama can have babies, too."

"Is Jay your daddy?" Amelia asks innocently.

"Yes, because he loves Mama."

"But you call him Jay?"

The question stumps Andy for a moment.

He runs over to Julian, followed by Amelia.

"Jay, can I call you, Daddy?"

Julian glances at me seeking approval, and I smile reassuring him. I couldn't have thought of a more perfect present for Andy.

Julian's face answers before his mouth opens. "I will be honored to be called that."

Andy throws himself at Julian and hugs him tight. Julian buries his head into Andy's hair, not letting go. I move in closer to them and kiss Julian on the cheek, then Andy on his head.

Charlie's hormones are seriously out of control as she wipes away her tears. Lex tries to comfort her, and finally she leans her head into him and murmurs, "I love you," and Lex follows, "Love you, too, baby mama."

Andy pulls away enough so he can ask Julian a question. "Daddy, can you take me to school tomorrow, so I can show everyone you're my daddy?"

Julian nods and grips my hand tightly, overwhelmed by emotions.

Eric walks over and takes out his cell. "Let me get a photo of you guys."

I scooch over a little toward Charlie and rest my arm on Julian's knee as he leans into my side.

"On the count of three, say crabs!"

The four of us groan at Eric, then laugh in unison, and we all say, "Crabs!"

Eric walks over and shows us the screen of his phone. The four of us are smiling at the camera, and I know by looking at this photograph, this is meant to be. It doesn't matter how we got here or what happened, we're here. Somehow, we have come together.

It's far from conventional, you could even say it's fucked up, but we're all right where we belong.

We are one family.

And, as I look one more time at the picture, I see two orbs, one between Lex and Charlie—it's small, but it's there, right beside them. The other is just off to the side of my shoulder. There's no question in my mind, and I don't care about the light in the sky, the dust in the air, or the glare off the windows or whatever the skeptics might say, I believe it to be only one thing.

Elijah.

He will always be with us, inside my heart and in the eyes of our son.

I may have been a warrior, but he has been my protector. I was dying, and the darkness that surrounded me was my demon.

Today, I'm alive, and I have a purpose.

To be the best mother I can be to my son.

To love unconditionally.

And most importantly, to finally feel free to follow my heart and love the man who brought me back to life. *Julian.*

I may have fallen more times than I allowed myself to stand, but finally, I understand that the world isn't an evil place. There is love, there is compassion, and we all have our battles, but we somehow draw strength when everything seems impossible. To conquer these battles is worth a celebration.

And I've no doubt my angel is finally dancing.

He's proud, and I can now rest knowing that finally, I've let go of the anger and am able to happily follow his wishes.

I have learned to love.

Again.

EPILOGUE

Life changes in ways we don't expect.

It's always been my dream to open my own boutique and showcase my designs, but with Julian in my life, I found a greater purpose. His publisher signed him to a four-book deal, and it means he will continue to travel and write his stories. He initially declined the *New York Times* job, but they wanted him, offering him more money and flexibility to do video meetings rather than fly to New York.

After accompanying him on a few trips, there's one thing I'm certain of—it isn't the glam celebrities who need my clothing, but the countless women I've met abroad. They can barely cover their bodies due to low socio-economic environments, not to mention have several children who need basic necessities such as food and water. In turn, this leaves them open to the men of their villages who ravage them, and once again, they will end up with another mouth to feed.

Lex accompanied us on that trip along with my dad. It was an eye-opener for both of us. Julian is comfortable being in a third-world country and spending time with the families as is my dad, who will medically assist, but Lex and I, we're sheltered.

Lex has the wealth, I have the creativity, and we came together to put our knowledge and wealth to use. Lex was able to negotiate fabric at a low cost, and I'm able to provide jobs to women who need work to provide for their families. It's a win-win situation spending countless hours with these women in their homes, which brings me so much pleasure. I spend time showing them my creations, and together we create modest garments for ladies in the villages and school uniforms for the local children.

This trip, however, is different.

My palms are sweating profusely, but Julian doesn't let go. The room is dim, the worn-out curtains are barely shutting out the light. With every inch, every step closer, my heart is beating louder. I want to drop to my knees, my heart aching as I take in how dilapidated the room is. The air is thick and humid, and my breathing is out of sync.

This is not fair.

The world is not fair.

Life is not fair.

The bed is small made of rusted steel pillars. Dirty stained sheets are all I can see lying on top of the bed, but then, like the flick of a switch, my world and heart are turned upside-down in one split second.

I'm floating toward the bed, and Julian is squeezing my hand for dear life. My eyes can't fathom what I see, the beauty and life which belongs to us.

My dad stands beside the bed with his bag open wide. He takes out the necessary instruments and does what he's medically trained to do. Julian and I watch intently, every move, every reflex down to the expressions on my dad's face.

Is it concern? Is it worry? My stomach churns nervously as we wait for his conclusion.

It happens an hour later, the smile which brightens up the room, the hope and prayers that have been answered.

My voice is hoarse, and with a nervous tremble, I ask, "Is everything okay, Dad?"

He doesn't say a word, carefully placing his instruments in his bag. Once zipped, he focuses his attention back on the bed and carefully, he lifts and cradles her in his arms. "There are just a few little things, but nothing that concerns me too much. You have my full consent to take my granddaughter home." He smiles, carefully rocking her in his arms.

I stare at her tiny face—*she is perfect*.

I turn to look at Julian, his wide smile reassures me that we've made the right decision.

She belongs in our family.

The moment I've been waiting for over the last twelve weeks has finally arrived, and without a thought, she is placed in my arms. The emotions finally take over, and the happy tears flow freely as I lean down and kiss her face. She is exceedingly small for her age, but I try not to focus on the negative because the overwhelming feeling of peace finally settles over me. Julian places his arms around me and bends down to kiss her hair. Even Julian struggles to hold back his own tears, and with that sight alone, I hand him *our* daughter.

There are no words for how content I feel as I watch him cradle our child for the first time. Without any hesitation, his love and acceptance make me more complete than I have ever felt, and for the first time in my life, I'll admit that. I will not compare nor will I allow myself to feel guilty.

The day Julian came home from that South American

trip with my dad, I knew something was terribly wrong. He was withdrawn, and when he explained the terrible situations he found himself in, I understood why he was traumatized and unable to get the image of this baby girl out of his head.

That night when Andy went to sleep, he showed me the videos, and my heart wept along with his. She'd been found beside the decomposing garbage in a worn-out part of town in the middle of the night under the pale moonlight.

A local had handed her over to the nuns, and without the proper care, she'd have only lived a few days. My dad just happened to be in the right place at the right time. He treated her injuries and illness giving her a chance to grow up to live a normal life. All she needed was a family to love her and treat her as their own. The moment I saw the man I love weep openly about this little girl, I knew that both our hearts were entirely in sync, and this was *our* daughter.

And today, she officially became a part of our family.

Julian whispers softly, careful not to wake her, "She's perfect."

"I know," I respond with a smile, stroking her soft curls and running the tips of my fingers along her precious skin careful to memorize every groove, every bump, finally landing a delicate kiss to the tip of her nose. Everything feels so familiar like she is a part of me that I've been missing. My affection toward her surpasses my expectations, and my motherly instincts instantly kick in. Is she hungry? Is she wet?

"She is perfect, Julian, and I think it's time to take her home."

The paperwork is done, and with my dad's medical approval, we thank the nuns at the orphanage. Just before we exit the building, the nun who took care of her reaches out and gestures the sign of the cross on her forehead, blessing her before we leave. I thank her kindly and head outside to get into the car.

It's a three-hour drive back to the capital city and being organized, I have all the necessary items to feed and dress her. In the car, I continue to stare at her face, mesmerized and unable to turn away. She is beautiful with slightly tanned skin, dark brown hair, and her long luscious eyelashes flutter on her cheeks as she sleeps. Her features are small, but that's to be expected at her age. We hit a bump in the road which causes her to stir. Both of us wait in anticipation as her eyes begin to open. My heart is racing as I wait for the moment when her eyes connect with ours, and the second they do, all my walls break down, and I'm an emotional mess.

Julian tries to comfort me, using his spare arm to pull me into his side. "Hey, she's with us now."

My sobs are loud, but my dad reassures me everything is going to be fine.

"You promise me they can't take her?"

Through streaming tears, I stare into her eyes. She seems to be able to see me, moving her pupils when my smile becomes a joyous laugh.

"Adriana, everything is done, signed, and sealed. We're taking her home. I promise you with all my life that no one can take her."

We arrive at the hotel and enter the suite where Lex and my mother are waiting. My mom is crying, carrying a yellow blanket covered in colorful stripes. "This belonged to you, Adriana, and now it belongs to your daughter."

I embrace her for a long time, not wanting to let go. I'm not going to cry anymore because this is a moment worth celebrating. Lex is standing beside my mom, reserved and unusually quiet. Slowly, his face widens into a smile, and I encourage him to take a look. He peeks in the blanket, and the moment he does, his face melts, and he asks to hold her. Julian passes our little girl to him with ease, and I watch my brother cradle our daughter.

"Hey, beautiful girl, I'm your Uncle Lex," he coos.

She makes a tiny sound, a baby gurgle.

"Look, Lex, she smiled at you."

Proudly, he asks, "What's her name?"

Julian and I glance at each other, and he motions for me to announce it.

"Luna Emily Baker." I'm honored to be the first to tell everyone her name. "Because under the moon, on that dark night, she somehow defeated all odds until she was found."

Lex repeats her name softly, gazing into her eyes. "This calls for a celebration."

He passes her to my mom who's desperately waiting to hold her and moves his hands toward the pocket of his shirt. I can see three cigars sitting in the pocket, and he pulls them out handing one to Julian and my dad. He follows with a lighter and clears his throat. "Congratulations, Julian. She's beautiful."

My dad puts his arm around Julian as the three of them laugh in the other room. I'm not quite sure what's funny but seeing the three of them smile and be merry with one another melts me beyond belief. It's a sight I never thought I'd see.

"You see that in there, Luna? That's your crazy family," I say to her.

Luna's eyes follow my movement, and I smile hopelessly at our daughter. It's time to take her home, back to the States, so she can finally meet Andy. My mom starts to pack her things, and as we all gather our belongings to leave the hotel, Julian politely holds the door open for me as we're the last ones in the room.

"Ready to go home, Luna, to meet your brother?" Julian murmurs.

"Ready to go home, Daddy?" I reply with a smile.

Julian tilts his head and plants a soft kiss on my lips. "I love you."

I giggle into his mouth, careful not to squash Luna between us. "Love you, too. But wait, I just have one more question..."

He rolls his eyes at me but follows through with a smirk. "Yes, Miss Know-It-All, what's your question now?"

"When are you going to ask me to marry you?" I blurt out.

Unable to control the smile which lights up his entire face, he leans into baby Luna and whispers, "Finally, I've been waiting a lifetime for this question. Hopefully, Mommy says, yes?"

"Yes!" I shout, placing my arm around his neck as I stand on my tiptoes and kiss my future husband deeply.

Finally, we are a complete family.

BONUS SCENE
CHARLIE

The morning after Lex finds out about Julian.

The key sits inside the lock, unmoved while I stand still battling with my thoughts as to what lies inside our home.

I lift my phone to see my inbox blown up with messages.

Lex: *Answer my fucking calls Charlotte!*

Lex: *If you don't answer me, he is going to be wishing he is dead.*

Lex: *Why does it always have to be between me and him? This was supposed to be fucking over. You are my wife so why are we back here again?*

Eric: *HOLY FUCKBALLS! Call me NOW.*

Nikki: *Charlie...I heard what happened. Shock would be an understatement, but it all makes sense. Lex must be livid. Call me when you've tamed your beast.*

Kate: *What the hell happened?? Lex is blowing up my phone and accusing me of covering for you? CALL ME ASAP.*

Eric: *Just so you know... your husband has blacklisted me. Beautiful asshole.*

There is a heaviness all over my body. It tightens my chest, slumps my shoulders, causes my knees to weaken from the simplest task of simply standing. A shooting pain soars across my temple, a mild headache on the verge of something greater from the sheer stress of this situation.

My bond with Adriana started way before Lex. Something, or perhaps the universe, drew us together at such a young age. Yes, we had our nine years apart, but things slowly went back to normal between us until Elijah passed away.

I felt helpless, unworthy in her presence of trying to be the pillar of strength she needed, when I struggled myself with losing Elijah, and almost my marriage. The overall impact his death had on everyone who knew him was something we never imagined we would have to experience.

And then there was Andy.

Life's unfair, he didn't deserve to grow up without a father.

Yet somewhere over the last six months, I knew something had changed with Adriana. It slowly began to eat away at me—her resistance to share her private life.

Both Lex and I spoke about it, and he too saw a change. We both assumed she was struggling with the guilt, which is why we didn't push her too much.

What we didn't expect was *Julian*.

Last night's revelations caused a swirl of emotions, even my normally controlled self could not handle. It all made sense—the secrecy and refusing to share with me. Though, I knew Eric was aware of what, or who was happening, it still didn't make any sense.

My first reaction was of shock, assuming she did this to hurt Lex and me. And to add to that maybe Julian wanted back in my life somehow.

It was a selfish presumption.

When Adriana finally opened up and explained how this all unfolded, it began to make sense. And the more she poured her heart out, the more I realized how real this was for both of them.

Nothing could change the way her eyes sparkled when she spoke about him, or her remorseful expression when she told me she'd been cutting herself to deal with the pain.

I felt sick to the stomach and incredibly apologetic for not realizing the extent and damage of losing Elijah had done to her, wishing I had made more of an effort.

But again, the universe had other plans, and it happened to involve my ex-fiancé.

Yet, perhaps the biggest hurdle, roadblock, hindrance, and complicated matter in this love affair is my husband.

Lex Edwards.

Unfortunately, I've been privy to Lex's rage on more than one occasion. Jealousy is an ugly trait and one he can't seem to rid himself of, no matter how hard he tries.

After Julian saved Ava and me, I had managed to calm

him down enough to be able to see the so-called bigger picture.

Without Julian—we wouldn't have survived.

But last night, Lex's ego took a hit of epic proportions, and his jealousy is a force to be reckoned with. He said things, uncalled for, and disrespectful about my loyalty. My temper sparked, anger shot through me like hot lava. Only when we were at Adriana's house, did it all begin to sink in. The hard reality is that I didn't blame him for acting this way despite my warning for him to back the hell away and stay home. This was never going to go down well, and frankly, we're dealing with the one man who will forever be Lex's weakness. I know that Lex knew that, yet Adriana didn't know the extent of Lex's insecurities when it comes to Julian.

Behind this door are the ramifications of last night.

I take a deep breath, turning the key slowly, cautious of what lies inside. As the door opens, the grand entrance is in view.

Everything is in-tact, nothing out of the ordinary.

The silence creeps across the house, not a single sound is heard. I take small steps toward the kitchen, instantly noticing the medicine cabinet open and various contents scattered across the countertop. Letting out the breath I've been holding, I place my purse down and decide to clean it later, my immediate thought to find Lex assuming he's passed out in our bed.

Our bedroom remains the same—bed perfectly made and unslept in.

The kids are at Emily's, so their rooms remain empty.

Making my way back down the staircase, I walk the long hallway toward his office.

The door is shut.

I place my ear against it—silence again.

Opening it slowly, darkness consumes me. The drapes are shut, the small lamp on his large desk is illuminating the empty bottle of whiskey and his phone. Slowly, my eyes move up until I see his face. Lex is staring at the empty glass held in his hand. His other hand is bandaged, explaining the mess in the kitchen.

I take a step in closing the door behind me, watching him not even move at the sound of my presence. With a pained stare, his eyes look withdrawn and tired from no sleep and too much liquor. I'm torn between my anger and need to reassure him everything will work out.

But I know my husband all too well—he's hurting and needs time to process.

My words twist around my tongue, trying to come out without a heated exchange. "I'm going to talk," I tell him, clearing my throat and keeping my distance. "I'm going to say what I need to say, then walk out of this room if you don't want to talk."

He continues to sit still, not even a flinch.

"I had no idea this was going on. But I understand now why she didn't tell me. I wouldn't have been able to hide their relationship from you. Adriana may be like family, but you are my husband. I made vows to you, and I've always been honest with you throughout our marriage."

Lex's eyes wander across to me, yet unable to meet my gaze. Instead, they linger where I stand, vacant, and wordless.

"I'm hurt at the names you called me, insinuating I could be romantically or sexually linked to Julian in any form. I respect your position here and understand your hurt and anger. But this is Adriana's life and not mine," I say, my arms folded across my chest as if I'm trying to shield myself from what he's about to unleash. "This is not my choice, and yes, if I had some control over the universe, he probably wouldn't have been the person I would choose for her. But she cares deeply for him, and given what she's gone through, I *will* respect her decision and do not want to be caught in the crossfire because I shouldn't even be a part of *their* equation."

His gaze shifts back toward the glass, probably wishing he had more alcohol.

Exhausted from last night, I let out a sigh knowing all this is fruitless. "I'm tired, Lex. All I ask from you is to please sober up before the girls come home tonight."

With a heavy heart, I turn my back as he calls my name. Spinning back, my eyes lay upon him, and finally, he meets my gaze.

"I'm sorry."

I nod, unsure of what to say besides what's in my heart. "I know. Still hurts, just so you know." So, I close the door behind me and leave him be, knowing he needs to be alone, and nothing I say or do will change that. My feet drag up the stairs, barely able to make it to the top. I must have only had three hours of sleep at best. Removing the clothes I borrowed from Adriana, I throw a tank and pair of bed shorts on then climb into bed.

The pillow sinks beneath my face, the comfortable doona and sheets wrapping my body with warmth. My eyes close and I begin to doze off. They're heavy and tired, unable to stay open a moment longer.

I let out a moan, the bed shuffling beside me. The weight of my eyes too heavy, I can't open them until gentle arms wrap around my body, and the fresh smell of body wash invades my senses. Lips are buried in my neck, but they are slow and sensual, not the usual frenzied panic I've grown accustomed to every time Lex gets his hands on me.

"Charlotte," he whispers in my ear. "Please turn around."

My heart is fluttering, ready to meet my destiny of the enchanting emerald eyes. I turn around, shuffling until I'm on my side. I see the anguish in his expression, and despite it all, I know he needs me more than anything to reassure him, it will be okay.

My fingers reach out, caressing his cheek. "It's always been you... and will *always* be you. Please stop torturing yourself."

"I can't lose you."

"It's not possible," I murmur, tracing his lips as he lets out a soft moan. "But you must control yourself, Lex. For the sake of the girls and me, especially if he's going to stick around."

Lex doesn't say a word, perhaps the reality is finally sinking in. With a sigh, he buries his head into my chest, and I hold onto him. His vulnerability is laid out, no holding back, as I stroke his hair to calm his racing heart, which beats against my stomach as we lay side-by-side.

I don't know how long we're like this for, but we both manage to fall asleep in each other's arms. It's exactly what we both need.

At least, that's what I thought until I'm woken with my tank top pulled down and his mouth on my breasts.

I let out a long-winded moan, arching my back, quickly glimpsing at the time to make sure the girls aren't coming home anytime soon. We have two hours, exactly.

Lex catches me looking at the time. "You're so predictable. How long do we have?"

"Two hours."

With his eyes piercing mine and his tongue running against his bottom lip, I watch as a devious smirk finally graces his lips, and I know I'm in trouble.

"You know what's about to happen?" he asks, demanding my attention with his tone.

I nod, unable to hide my smile.

"We are going to fuck," he tells me. "And we are going to fuck hard for two whole hours. And I'm going bareback because I need to feel you completely. You understand?"

I open my mouth to say something, but he covers it with his hand, trapping my words.

"Don't even think about what that witch said about you getting pregnant. I'm not wearing a condom. Full stop! But if it eases your stress levels, I'll pull out, and you can suck me off. Deal?"

I shake my head with a small laugh, punching him gently in the chest. "You're a selfish jerk. You know that?"

Lex places his mouth on mine, sucking my bottom lip, leaving me breathless before pulling away. "I never hear you complaining."

I hate that he's right. Why would I complain? But I am not going to back down so easily, I have what he so desperately wants.

"I'll have to think about your offer."

This time, he shakes his head, unable to hide his grin. He doesn't say anything, moving on top of me and sliding himself in without any warning. I gasp, closing my eyes as desire spreads throughout me like wildfire.

"You still thinking?" he groans, thrusting in me as I watch all his muscles tighten while hovering above me.

I place my hands on his face, begging him to stop for

just a moment. Our eyes meet, the intense stare crumbling all the walls within me.

I need him, maybe more than ever.

As I gaze into the emerald green orbs, I feel complete once again.

"Show me what you got... baby."

CHASING FATE

Chasing Fate
An Enemies to Lovers Romance
The Dark Love Series Book 5

BLURB

I screwed up my perfect bachelor life in one single night. After that, I end up crashing at my cousin Charlie's house with her family, which means kids.

It gets worse...
Charlie doesn't care for my single life.
She has it in her head I am a heartless playboy—Noah Mason will never commit to a woman.

My only saving grace is Kate, Charlie's best friend.
Kate is everything I need in my life right now—she's sexy, intelligent, and willing to have unadulterated fun.
And we're having the time of our lives.
That is until Kate dares me to commit to only one woman.

My so-called victim—a Hollywood movie star.
But I have to get past a roadblock first—her personal assistant.

Commitment is one thing, falling in love is another.
And I refuse to lose the bet.
There's only one small problem....
Am I chasing the wrong woman?

ALSO BY KAT T. MASEN

The Dark Love Series

Featuring Lex & Charlie

Chasing Love: A Billionaire Love Triangle

Chasing Us: A Second Chance Love Triangle

Chasing Her: A Stalker Romance

Chasing Him: A Forbidden Second Chance Romance

Chasing Fate: An Enemies-to-Lovers Romance

Chasing Heartbreak: A Friends-to-Lovers Romance

The Forbidden Love Series

(Dark Love Series Second Generation)

Featuring Amelia Edwards

The Trouble With Love: An Age Gap Romance

The Trouble With Us: A Second Chance Love Triangle

The Trouble With Him: A Secret Pregnancy Romance

The Trouble With Her: A Friends-to-Lovers Romance

The Trouble With Fate: An Enemies-to-Lovers Romance

Also by Kat T. Masen

The Office Rival: An Enemies-to-Lovers Romance

The Marriage Rival: An Office Romance

Bad Boy Player: A Brother's Best Friend Romance

Roomie Wars Box Set (Books 1 to 3): Friends-to-Lovers Series

ABOUT THE AUTHOR

Born and bred in Sydney, Australia, **Kat T. Masen** is a mother to four crazy boys and wife to one sane husband. Growing up in a generation where social media and fancy gadgets didn't exist, she enjoyed reading from an early age and found herself immersed in these stories. After meeting friends on Twitter who loved to read as much as she did, her passion for writing began, and the friendships continued on despite the distance.

"I'm known to be crazy and humorous. Show me the most random picture of a dog in a wig, and I'll be laughing for days."

Download free bonus content, purchase signed paperbacks & bookish merchandise.
Visit: **www.kattmasen.com**

Made in the USA
Coppell, TX
11 July 2024